*The Naqab Bedouins*

# THE NAQAB BEDOUINS

## A Century of Politics and Resistance

MANSOUR NASASRA

COLUMBIA UNIVERSITY PRESS *NEW YORK*

Columbia University Press
*Publishers Since 1893*
New York   Chichester, West Sussex
cup.columbia.edu

Paperback edition, 2022


Library of Congress Cataloging-in-Publication Data
Names: Nasasra, Mansour, author.
Title: The Naqab bedouins : a century of politics and resistance /
Mansour Nasasra.
Description: New York : Columbia University Press, [2017] |
Includes bibliographical references and index.
Identifiers: LCCN 2016041869 (print) | LCCN 2016042993 (ebook) |
ISBN 9780231175302 (cloth) | ISBN 9780231175319 (pbk.) | ISBN 9780231543873 (e-book)
Subjects: LCSH: Bedouins—Israel—Negev. | Bedouins—Israel—Negev—History.
Classification: LCC DS113.7 .N35 2017 (print) | LCC DS113.7 (ebook) |
DDC 305.892/72056949—dc23
LC record available at https://lccn.loc.gov/2016041869

Cover design: Milenda Nan Ok Lee

Cover image: United Kingdom Public Records Office,
Foreign Office Papers, 195/2106.

# Contents

# Illustrations and Tables

## Illustrations



## Tables

# Note on Transliteration

THE SYSTEM OF ARABIC transliteration used in this book is that of *The International Journal of Middle East Studies*, including some modifications:

| | |
|---|---|
| ب = b | ص = s |
| ت = t | ض = dd |
| ث = th | ط = t |
| ج = j | ظ = z |
| ح = h | ع = ʿ |
| خ = kh | غ = gh |
| د = d | ف = f |
| ذ = dh | ق = g |
| ر = r | ك = k |
| ز = z | ل = l |
| س = s | م = m |
| ش = sh | ن = n |
| ه = h | و = w |
| و = y | ء = ʾ |

# Acknowledgments

THIS BOOK WOULD NOT have been possible without the support of many people throughout my postgraduate research in the UK in Oxford starting in 2005 and Exeter starting in 2007. My research journey was made possible through a number of institutions and funding possibilities. After surviving the first two years in Exeter without funding, continuing my research was made possible by the great generosity of Dr. Sultan Bin Mohammed Al Qassimi, whose sponsorship over two years enabled me to complete my work and to whom I owe my most sincere thanks. Professor Tim Niblock of the Institute of Arab and Islamic Studies at Exeter is also thanked warmly for his help in this respect.

I have been privileged to work with Professor Bruce Stanley, whom I first met in Jerusalem in 2006. He encouraged me to start this research project. From the beginning he has offered warm support and encouragement. Bruce's supervision and guidance throughout the research and writing process has made the research a challenging, exciting, and rewarding experience. I am profoundly grateful to him for all he has done for me. During the writing of this book, I have developed an engaged relationship with a number of academics who were generous in sharing their knowledge and sources with me. I thank them all for their input and for facilitating my research in various ways: Mick Dumper, Daniel Neep, Gerd Nonneman, Nadje al Ali, Oren Yiftachel, Ahmad Amara, Neve Gordon, Mandy Turner, Yoav Alon, Relli Shechter, and Larbi Sadiki, who have contributed both academically and intellectually to my work. Special thanks to Professor Lila Abu-Lughod, Columbia University, for her great support and insights while finishing this project. Thanks to Professor Yezid Sayigh and Professor Ilan Pappe for their great support and valuable feedback on this project.

Likewise, the support and encouragement of friends and colleagues at Exeter and beyond has also been of great help to me: Helen Hawari, Aida Essaid, Amneh Badran, Khalid al-Mezaini, Suad George, Adham Saouli, Ghada Aqeel, Suliman al-Sanne (Abu Khaldon), Mohammad Sakhnini, Maha Samman, Dimah Mahmoud, Heba Ali, Lucy Semaan, Richard Radcliffe, Sophie Richer Devroe, James Koranyi, Omar al-Nasasrah, Amal al-Sanne, Alice Wilson, Fiona McKay, Amira Muftah, and Mark and Hilary Clemoes. Thank you for making my journey into an experience that has been both memorable and rich. I am especially grateful to individuals and interviewees in the Naqab, Biʾr al-Sabaʿ, Jordan, Israel, and the UK who shared their time, their knowledge, and their stories with me. It is good to hear their voices. My thanks also to the staff at the various archive collections in the UK and Israel who helpfully provided me with documentary sources, and special thanks to Lord Oxford (Julian Asquith) and his family, Raymond and Claire Asquith, for giving me the chance to look at his valuable source materials. Thanks also to Beatrice Curty Golay (Meylan-Geneva) and R. H. Arnow (NY) for their support during the beginning of my research project in Exeter. My special thanks to Lindy Ayubi for her professional editing and her kind support during the final touches of this project.

Last but not least, and with the deepest gratitude, I acknowledge the contribution of my family. My lovely parents (Mohammad and Sabha), sisters, and brother have helped me in so many ways. Without their patience, understanding, and support over the last seven years, it would have been impossible to achieve this work. This book is dedicated to my lovely father, Mohammad Mustafa al-Nasasra, who struggled against cancer and passed away when he was fifty-six years old, before seeing this book.

# Abbreviations

| | |
|---|---|
| BDA | Bedouin Development Authority |
| BEA | Bedouin Education Authority |
| CO | Colonial Office |
| CZA | Central Zionist Archive |
| FO | Foreign Office |
| IDFA | Archives of Israel Defense Forces |
| IDP | Internally Displaced Peoples |
| ILA | Israel Land Administration |
| ISA | Israel State Archive |
| JAFI | Jewish Agency for Israel |
| JNF | Jewish National Fund |
| KCLMA | Kings College London Military Archive |
| KKL | Kereen Kayement Le Yisrael |
| KLA | Kibbutz Lahav Archive |
| LCHMA | Liddell Hart Centre for Military Archives |
| MECA | Middle East Centre Archives |
| MK | Member of Knesset |
| PEF | Palestine Exploration Fund |
| PRO | Public Records Office |
| UNGA | United Nations General Assembly |
| UNRWA | United Nations Relief and Works Agency |
| UNGA | United Nations General Assembly |
| UN | United Nations |
| UNTSO | United Nations Truce Supervision Organization |
| WO | War Office |
| WZO | World Zionist Organization |

*The Naqab Bedouins*

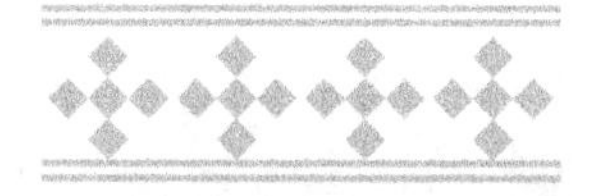

# Introduction

DURING THE LAST FEW DECADES, there has been growing scholarly debate about subaltern politics, the politics of Bedouin tribes in the Middle East, and the politics of indigenous peoples. In contributing to these ongoing debates this book provides a comprehensive and informed account of the Bedouin in southern Palestine during Ottoman and British colonial rule. This book focuses mainly on the Bedouin in the Naqab/Biʾr al-Sabaʿ from the creation of Israel and the Nakba in 1948 up to the present.[1]

No significant effort has been made to keep a record of the Bedouin struggle since the historical documentation of Bedouin history during the British Mandate by Aref al-Aref. At this critical juncture in Middle Eastern affairs, this book represents one of the first attempts to chronicle Bedouin history and politics of the last century. This book also documents the broader relevance of Bedouin history and politics to understanding minorities' and indigenous peoples' relations in the region and beyond. The existing literature on the Bedouin is quite limited and reveals some striking gaps. In the available sources a significant component, mainly, writing the history of the Bedouin, has met with certain constraints. This leads one to conclude that their history and politics were never considered significant. This limitation (extending from the late decades of the Ottoman Empire through the British Mandate period and into the present era under the state of Israel) can be identified whenever the Bedouin case is discussed since most scholarly works covering these periods lack critical and in-depth analysis.

Using archival data from Britain and Israel and extensive fieldwork in the Naqab, the United Kingdom, and Jordan, this text aims to do something not previously done: to undertake a critical examination of the indigenous Palestinian Bedouin and their way of surviving under strict state policies since the late Ottoman era. If one looks at a significant part of the existing literature on the Bedouin, their experience is presented as passive and their agency is denied. This has not been my own experience, however, and I wanted, therefore, to understand the early evolution of Ottoman and British policies toward the Bedouin in order to have a better understanding of how we interpret the contemporary situation and politics. To understand what is unique in the case of the Bedouin in the Naqab I will also bring into play some other Bedouin communities and indigenous peoples throughout the region and their experiences in relation to the states in which they find themselves.

In order to understand more clearly the overall situation of the Bedouin in southern Israel between 1948 and today, it is necessary to see how they responded to the power used by the new Israeli state. I wish to deepen the understanding of the Bedouin as an organic part of the Palestinian indigenous minority in Israel by bringing an original view to fill the gap in the literature left by many other scholars.

Although conventional scholarship has viewed the Naqab Bedouin as victims or passive recipients, it is important to reconceptualize them as agents who, in defending their community and identity, have both failed and succeeded in manipulating attempts to subjugate and control their indigenous life. The book challenges the customary notion of Bedouin docility under military rule. They have greater abilities than might have been anticipated. The thesis to be investigated is that despite conventional wisdom, the Bedouin were more powerful than expected and played a role in shaping their own destiny. There is limited research on Bedouin politics and history in the Naqab, particularly under the military government from 1948 to 1967. This ignorance about the actual events and dynamics of Bedouin-state relations during the period can be found among those implementing the state's policies as well as in the subsequent academic literature.

The aim of this book is not just to present the history and politics of the Bedouin of the Naqab and Biʾr al-Sabaʿ but to show that in every historical period they were not passive subjects of domination, whether by the Ottomans, by the British, or, since 1948, the Israeli state. Instead, they have resisted this domination in a multitude of forms and actions. The book aims to contribute to scholarly debates in relation to the Bedouin in four main circles. First, it contributes to the debates on the Bedouin communities in southern Palestine during the late Ottoman era by addressing the nature of the relationship between the Bedouin and the Ottoman government in Istanbul. The interaction of the Ottomans with the Bedouin from 1900 to 1917 is the key focus of the first part of the book. Second, the book proposes a new understanding of British colonial rule in southern Palestine and their relations with the Bedouin through examining the perceptions of the colonial authorities toward their communities. By looking at the dynamics between the colonial state and the Bedouin communities in the frontier areas such as Transjordan, Sinai, and Beersheba and comparing this to how the Bedouin were perceived by other communities in Palestine, the book sheds new light on the nature of colonial power relations.

Third, the most significant part of the book supports a broader understating of Bedouin- Israeli state relations during the period of military rule from 1948 to 1967 and up to the present. This part also examines the ongoing debates about Bedouin indigenous rights and land ownership. By linking the Bedouin case to the theoretical debates on resistance and indigeniety, the book also contributes to the ongoing development of the field of indigenous peoples' politics and investigates whether that discipline can assist in understanding the situation of the Bedouin in the Naqab. By looking at the nonviolent resistance adopted by the Bedouin communities in the Naqab, the study draws attention to the different strategies used by the Bedouin to resist the oppressive regime of the military rule.

Fourth, the book continues the debate on the ongoing Bedouin struggle for recognition since the Oslo peace agreements. This section focuses on Bedouin politics since the 1990s and current Israeli plans (known as the Prawer plan) to relocate around 40,000 Bedouin away from their historical villages and land. In this regard it provides an essential source for the history and progress of the indigenous Bedouin of the Naqab in their struggle with the Israeli state system.

The text first establishes a theoretical foundation and defines the key concepts used throughout. Chapter 1 introduces concepts of power relations between minorities and states that will help explain the paradox of power. This approach identifies examples of resistance among other minorities and indigenous peoples in order to see which have been applied by the Naqab Bedouin in their particular struggle. This chapter undertakes a critical examination of the notions of indigeneity and Bedouin identity and their applicability. The aim is to expand the debate on indigeneity and the Bedouin case by asking the question, "How useful is it to consider the Bedouin as indigenous peoples or natives in the Naqab?" Identifying the Naqab Bedouin as an indigenous people opens up the broader question of how one defines the rest of the Palestinian community in Israel since there is no settled consensus over terms and definitions. I maintain that the use of "indigenous" approaches remains controversial and did not grant rights to the Bedouin until today. This definition has been labeled as inapplicable to the Naqab Bedouin, and there are invisible politics behind labeling the definition this way. My aim is not to present the Bedouin as indigenous and the rest of the Palestinians as not indigenous but rather to contribute to this growing field of scholarship and address the rights of indigenous peoples from the perspective of international law. All Palestinians are considered indigenous to the land, so despite taking this approach the most marginalized Bedouin communities may benefit only according to international law once the matter of their rights becomes a question of the rights of an indigenous people.

Chapter 2 provides a brief overview of the Bedouin in the Middle East and then focuses on the history of Ottoman rule in southern Palestine during the nineteenth and early twentieth centuries. It examines Ottoman relations with the indigenous Bedouin in southern Palestine, focusing in particular on the methods of rule used by the Ottomans to control them. I highlight Bedouin clashes with and resistance to oppressive Ottoman policies. The building of Beersheba as a symbol of Ottoman rule in the desert is central to this chapter.

Chapter 3 examines British colonial relations with the Bedouin of southern Palestine and compares this situation with those of other Bedouin communities in the region, mainly Transjordan and Sinai. It pays special attention to the debate over how the colonial state dealt with Bedouin land ownership and addresses the interterritorial tribunal among Transjordan, Sinai, and Beersheba. The Palestine Police and the Bedouin Palestine Police are central to this chapter, which also highlights how the Bedouin were active members of Palestinian organizations in Jerusalem and Gaza and were not disconnected from the rest of the Palestinian communities in Palestine.

Chapter 4 presents an in-depth historical narrative of the Zionist movement's interest in southern Palestine and the Naqab region. Chapter 5 addresses the creation of military rule between 1948 and 1950 as a system for controlling the Palestinian Arab minority. With its emphasis on the Bedouin case, the chapter uncovers Israel's complex relationship with the indigenous and native population during the initial years of its existence. I examine the early days of military rule, along with a range of early Israeli policies for dealing with the remnant native tribes.

Chapter 6 addresses the mechanisms by which Israel sought to reshape the structure and future of these native tribes. The military rule tried to govern the Bedouin by framing them within a new tribal order and using multiple legal tricks to oppress them. The chapter argues that the main policies applied to the Bedouin in the early 1950s after they had been concentrated in the enclosed military zone (the Arabic term is "*siyaj*") included separating the Bedouin tribes from the rest of the Palestinians in Israel and retaining the loyal ones; expelling Bedouin tribes from the western Naqab into the *siyaj*; appointing new tribal shaikhs; and expropriating Bedouin land by enacting various land laws and registration policies. Archival reports from the United Nations, for example, highlight the rights of the Bedouin as native people and as refugees.

Chapter 7 assesses the survival (*sumud*) of the Bedouin under military rule and the patron-client relationship that emerged between Bedouin shaikhs and Israeli officials. It also highlights Israel's policies for co-opting shaikhs by examining the leased land policy and its role in providing travel permits for tribal members. I examine the methods used by Bedouin shaikhs to resist the military government through noncooperation. Another important theme is the Bedouin survival mechanism of cross-border relations.

Chapter 8 addresses the second phase of military rule from 1956 to 1963. It investigates the modified policies offered by military rule after 1956 and discusses the key themes of this period. Here the debate on Bedouin land claims is significant. The chapter argues that Bedouin voices were both consistent and persistent in claiming their land and in calling for the right of return to their indigenous land and historical villages.

Chapter 9 explains Israeli plans for modernizing and for settling the Bedouin in urban centers and examines how the Bedouin resisted these plans. This chapter also reviews the final stages of military rule and its formal abolition. Another important issue is unplanned building by the Bedouin to prove ownership of their land (an aspect of *sumud*) and the escalation of their land campaign. The chapter argues that despite the formal announcement on November 6, 1966, of the end of military rule, its dynamic continued for a number of years afterward and its functions were replaced by other state agencies that effectively represented a new form of military control. I argue that the military regulations were finally abolished only in 1967 after the war, not in 1966.

Chapter 10 addresses the post-military-government era and examines the new structures and governance bodies for encouraging Bedouin urbanization. It discusses current dynamics between the Israeli authorities and the Bedouin, specifically the Prawer plan and the Bedouin reaction to it. It argues that the internationalization of the Bedouin struggle, alongside the support of the entire Palestinian community in Israel, has halted the plans for relocation of the Bedouin. This chapter also addresses the Bedouin situation since the Oslo agreements and the most recent years of the Bedouin struggle for recognition.

The book concludes by looking at the nonviolent actions and resistance of the Bedouin to military rule, which represents a contribution to the field of subaltern agency and indigenous resistance. The last point of chapter 11 addresses the contemporary situation of the Bedouin and sheds light on the ongoing denial of the Bedouin land ownership cases in the Israeli court system. It also demonstrates how the constant denial of Bedouin rights supports the notion that the Israeli government will not bring about justice for the Bedouin cause through a judicial system that continues to ignore Bedouin demands and their historical rights.

ONE

# Understanding the State Project

## *Power, Resistance, and Indigeneity*

THE EXISTING LITERATURE clarifies a wide spectrum of state-society relations and deepens our perception of state actions, roles, and behavior (Barkey and Parikh 1991, 532). Joel Migdal (1988) highlights the way that society plays a crucial role in shaping the state and identifies the importance of the state in influencing the society. It is difficult to realize the separation of state-society relations since states need society for their developmental aims (Migdal 1988, 181; see also Ayubi 1995).

It remains difficult to define the concept of the "state" in a perfect manner (Mitchell 1991, 77). Until recently, the notion of the state was of little interest to social scientists and ignored in the academic literature from the late 1950s until the mid-1970s; only in the 1970s and 1980s did a sudden upsurge of interest in the study of the state begin to appear in academic debates.[1] Until then scholars had written about government, leadership, voting, and political development, among other political matters, but the "state" concept was not in use (Krasner et al. 1984, 234). However, in the study of political science the state is a core institution and is widely discussed by scholars. It is also critically important in the international arena and in world politics. States have sovereignty over a population in a certain territory and exercise power within a society (Ayubi 1995, 30).

Max Weber's classic definition of the modern state and how it works is helpful in this respect: it is "a compulsory political association with continuous organization [whose] administrative staff successfully uphold a claim to the monopoly of legitimate use of force in the enforcement of its order . . . within a given territorial area" (Weber 1947, 154). He provides certain indicators that can be used to qualify the state, including the need for a bureaucratic structure, legal extractive power, a coercive organization (i.e., monopoly that legitimizes the use of physical violence), and a financial and tax system; he also addresses the uncontested area of rational legal authority in a given demarcated territory. There are numerous states that fit Weber's classic definition, especially in the Middle East. My focus is more on settler, ethnocratic, and colonial states in relation to minorities in the Middle East.

Migdal (1988, 19) introduced another important definition of the state (which applies to some Middle Eastern countries), describing it as

> an organization, composed of numerous agencies led and coordinated by the state's leadership (executive authority) that has the ability or authority to make and implement the binding rules for all the people as well as the parameters of rule-making for other social organizations in a given territory, using force, if necessary, to have its way.

According to Migdal (1988, 6), the state is a necessary institution that exercises its sovereignty over people and territory by employing rules and the use of power, and it may behave with two different faces, being repressive for some groups and supportive of others. Other scholars treat the state as a body that works to formulate its aims and strategies according to its economic, political, and social goals. However, state goals do not necessarily reflect society's needs. Power is necessarily imposed by the state to enable it to accomplish its will on society (Barkey and Parikh 1991). The numerous goals of the state as an autonomous unit include its strategies for using internal resources, affecting social processes, and shaping ethnic identity (Gurr 1993, 3). Colonial and settler states face problems in dominating native and indigenous groups that inhabited their territory before any state was established. This can be true of the Ottoman regime in southern Palestine, the British Mandate, and Israeli military rule.

The literature provides various examples of nation-states including the British state and the French state (Barkey and Parikh 1991), as well as Middle East states, settler states, ethnocratic states, and colonial states (Ayubi 1995; Yiftachel 2003, 2012). Axtmann (2004) discusses the emergence of states such as those of the Middle East established after the Second World War following a prolonged struggle with colonialist states. Charles Tilly, examining the case of European countries, famously argued that "war makes the state, and the state makes the war." He noted that this could be applied to many cases in Europe where states were established as a result of coercive exploitation or organized crime (Tilly 1985, 169–70).

New states set out to build the state through actions and goals that together constitute a state building project. These projects require the effective use of state authority and the adoption of coercive power to achieve their aims and plans. As James Scott notes, "Many state activities aim at transforming the population, space, and nature under their jurisdiction into . . . closed systems that offer no surprises and that can best be observed and controlled" (Scott 1998, 82). States aim to establish a stable system by imposing rules and regulations to dominate their societies. They seek predominance over their territory and population through enforcing power and exercising coercive tactics and rules to prevent disobedience and rebellion. The state is also an alien external organization that seeks to penetrate a hostile society. Thus, its capacity to transform the population is restricted: "The ability of the state to impose its schemes on society [is] limited by [its] modest ambitions and its limited capacity" (Scott 1998, 88). Similarly, a state's ability to ensure stability and achieve its goals might clash with powerful groups within its territory.[2] It is obvious that by seeking control over people and territory the final aim of states is autonomy.

When discussing state power, Michael Mann (1984) differentiates between two aspects: despotic power and infrastructural power. Despotic power concerns the "power of the state elite, the range of actions which the elite is empowered to undertake without routine, [and] institutionalized negotiation with civil society groups," and infrastructural power is "the capacity of the state actually to penetrate civil society, and to implement logistically political decisions throughout the realm" (Mann 1984, 113). The state uses power to infiltrate everyday life in society through various means: taxing wealth, accumulating extensive data and information about its citizens, imposing its will on the population, influencing the economy, and controlling subsistence through jobs. In turn, through its functional relationship with its citizens the state should provide internal order and security, military defense, a communications infrastructure, and economic redistribution. Thus, by penetrating social life and making itself essential, the state reinforces its infrastructural power, which in turn strengthens its political power (Mann 1984, 114). Mann considers the territorial centrality of the state the most important component of a state's power (1984, 122–23).

Modern states strive to build nations and produce national identities, which may override ethnic groups that have similar aims. As a result, a state's goals can—and generally do—go against those of other groups on their territory, such as ethnic groups and religious organizations (Migdal 1988, 30). States also use power as an instrument to achieve their aims; however, as power can be resisted, this is not always successful.

The rise of most settler states has resulted in conflicts with ethnic and indigenous groups that continue as the state project is imposed on them. Gurr (1993) provides extensive case studies of conflicts between minority groups and nation-states. In many instances the minorities were mobilized in reaction to oppressive methods and strategies used by the state to achieve its goals. Ultimately, many such groups were assimilated or integrated into state life. States also use repressive and coercive methods, such as censorship and multiple restrictions, to reduce or avoid any domestic threat to their authority (Davenport 1995). By using such methods they aim to impose order and authority to ensure the safety of their own citizens.

The way that new settler and ethnocratic states deal with the minorities and indigenous peoples that fall within their newly constructed boundaries is of considerable interest, especially when the struggle of indigenous people is studied through a focus on the state project drive and the particular ideology of the new state. This will help toward understanding the supposed power deficit that such people appear to have in relation to the developing state. To maintain their rights, achieve a kind of cultural freedom, and retain their indigenous way of life on their historical territory, indigenous people must struggle politically against new, settler, and ethnocratic states.

The scope and goals of a new state's building projects are in direct opposition to the claims of indigenous people since both make claims over land and territory. As Tully (2000) notes, indigenous peoples present demands, from the right of self-determination to shared jurisdiction over resources, mainly land. Indigenous peoples look for justice in order to achieve their claims; however, because of their insistence in claiming their land and other rights, they may well clash with settler societies, to whom they pose a threat. Settler states tend not to agree to, or even accept, the claims of indigenous and native peoples since this challenges their legitimacy to impose their own will on the rest. James Anaya (2004) also points out that most nation-states do not recognize indigenous peoples. Because they pose a direct challenge to the project of the new state, indigenous and minority peoples are targeted for early and sustained attack. The strategies vary, but all are extreme, focused, and committed to removing the challenge to sovereignty that they represent. Indigenous peoples in white settler societies were sometimes subject to segregation and discrimination and generally threatened in their very physical survival to an extent quite incomparable to anything experienced by most stateless nations.

In addition to aggressive attack, settler-colonial states also ignore indigenous peoples' rights. Yiftachel notes that leaving indigenous people out of its plans by controlling their lands and resources is "the nature of the settler state" as it seeks territorial expansion (Yiftachel 2003, 23). The Naqab Bedouin, who confounded the state by using the land of their ancestors for purposes different from those conceived in the "state project," were treated as "invaders" by Israel (Yiftachel 1998). Ted Gurr and Barbara Harff also agree that states use a range of techniques, such as manipulating indigenous land, discriminating against indigenous people on a daily basis, and exploiting their resources in order to subsume them into the state project (Gurr and Harff 2004, 25).

A particularly useful notion for understanding the asymmetrical relationship between a state and its indigenous people is "internal colonialism." The term was defined by Williams (1977, 273) as "the domination by a racially and culturally different foreign conquering group, imposed in the name of dogmatically asserted racial, ethnic or cultural superiority, on a materially inferior indigenous population." Noting its use in relation to various global cases, Hind explains that the internal colonialism model was developed historically for the peripheries of European states and describes an ongoing debate about its uses (Hind 1984, 543).

Settler states developed internal colonialism as a system or package of actions, policies, and regulations to control indigenous peoples; they imposed this system on indigenous communities (such as Australia, New Zealand, the United States, Canada, and Israel) who struggled and resisted settler states in order to gain self-government in their land (Tully 2000; Yiftachel 2003). In this regard, Scott remarks that "modern statecraft is largely a project of internal colonization" (1998, 82). The debate on colonialism can, in fact, fit in with Scott's account of state expansion, where the state is always an alien, external organization that seeks to penetrate a hostile society (Scott 1998).

The concept of internal colonialism as developed by Elia Zureik (1979) proves useful in Palestine/Israel, where Israel practices a system of political domination toward its Palestinian Arab minority, which is culturally distinct and is subject to different political controls. The Arabs are not only excluded from particular sociopolitical positions but also face various discriminatory policies (Zureik 1979). As Yiftachel (2013, 292–95) confirms, the Bedouin in the Naqab also faced internal colonial policies and practices.

In the case of Israeli-Palestinian minority relations, internal colonialism is a threat to indigenous minorities such as the Naqab Bedouins because of the "power deficit"—i.e., the domination by Israel; the Israeli exploitation of Palestinians' resources, such as land; and the discrimination the Palestinians experience on many levels. One can argue that the Israeli authorities during the period of military rule used internal colonialism toward the Bedouin by exploiting their resources and made attempts to control them through planned sedentarization and urbanization. As a result of internal colonialism practices, the Bedouin lost part of their culture, were forced to live in urban villages against their will, lost almost all their land, were separated from the other Palestinian communities, and were forced to work as cheap labor.

## Indigenous Peoples vis-à-vis Settler Societies

Scholarly use of the concept of "indigenous peoples" appeared during the 1970s (cf. Kingsbury 1998, 414; Smith 1999, 7). Smith remarks that the term "indigenous" is "problematic" as well as unclear since there are many other terms that have a similar and overlapping meaning: e.g., "first peoples," "First Nations," "people of the land," "Aboriginals," and "Fourth World peoples" (Smith 1999, 6). These are often used in referring to indigenous communities in New Zealand, Australia, Mexico, and Brazil. Similarly, the concept of "Bedouin" is used to refer to the indigenous Arabs in southern Palestine/Israel. According to scholars of international law, the "indigenous-native" concept was neither fashionable nor even applied before the Second World War but has emerged in international law over the last thirty or so years as a means of classifying a wide range of indigenous communities, including those noted above (Brownlie 1992, 55–57; Tully 2000, 37).

The term indigenous people, according to Kingsbury, "was once a vague rhetorical device that distinguished the original inhabitants of a region from the colonial conquerors" (quoted in Worden 1998, 122), but much has been written about the concept within the United Nations, the International Labor Organization (ILO), and the World Bank. Although there are no collectively agreed definitions of indigenous people and their rights, the explanation proposed in 1986 by the UN special rapporteur Jose Martinez Cobo was adopted: it describes numerous aspects that apply specifically to indigenous peoples:

> Indigenous communities, peoples and nations are those which, having a historical continuity with pre-invasion and pre-colonial societies that developed on their territories, consider themselves distinct from other sectors of the societies now prevailing in those territories, or parts of them. They form at present non-dominant sectors of society and are determined to preserve, develop and transmit to future generations their ancestral territories, and their ethnic identity, as the basis of their continued existence as peoples, in accordance with their own cultural patterns, social institutions and legal systems. (COBO 1986)

According to Cobo's definition, indigenous people constitute a nation that has lived for generations in a territory invaded and controlled by a settler society. Members of an indigenous people have some important common traits, such as language, culture, land, identity, and historical continuity, and their role in the current society is marginal.

Brownlie (1988) in particular moved the debate forward in his work on the rights of peoples in modern international law. Aware that use of the concept indigenous people and recognition of indigenous claims might be sensitive matters, he preferred to use the term "minority" (Brownlie, 16). He identified claims as a core element of indigenous peoples' rights, and, noting the importance of sensitivity to "indigenous peoples' claims," he developed three characteristic examples: the claim for positive action to maintain the cultural and linguistic identity of communities; the claim for adequate protection of land rights in traditional territories; and the claim for the political and legal principle of self-determination (1988, 3–4).

Brownlie prefers the concept of "minority," rather than "indigenous peoples" since the claims of the latter include being separated and treated differently from minorities, especially regarding self-determination.

However, in his work on the rights of people (particularly indigenous peoples), Richard Falk (1988) recognized the indigenous claim. His analysis supports the use of the term "indigenous people"; furthermore, he acknowledges the legitimacy of their claims, noting that these represent a significant challenge to state authority. He also agrees that "indigenous people's claims" should be recognized and taken seriously by international law for full self-determination:

> It is not surprising that indigenous peoples are victimized by traditional procedure and frameworks. For one thing, indigenous peoples, to the extent that they centre their grievances around encroachments upon their collective identity, represent a competing nationalism within the boundaries of the state. Such claims, posited in a variety of forms, challenge two fundamental statist notions—that of territorial sovereignty, and that of a unified "nationality" juridically administered by government organs.
> (FALK 1988, 18)

Falk is thus very supportive of the claims of indigenous peoples, including the possibility of their exercising their identity and even some sort of autonomy. Recognition of indigenous claims and self-government should be treated differently in international law, even if they clash with a state's project and interest. Falk is particularly strong on the notion that an indigenous people should challenge sovereignty and unified nationality, since new states in particular regard indigenous rights and claims as unacceptable. At its most basic, the state project is about establishing a new sovereignty and a unified nationality through which to empower the state's actions; indigenous peoples stand against these core aspects of the state project.

Benedict Kingsbury has also played a vital role in this discourse, arguing that despite protracted discussions on the definition of "indigenous people," there is still no total agreement (Kingsbury 2001, 106). He suggests that the fundamental claims raised by indigenous people include five particular categories: human rights and nondiscrimination, minorities, self-determination claims, historic sovereignty, and claims to be recognized as indigenous peoples (Kingsbury 2001, 69). He concludes that "indigenous people as a global concept is unworkable and dangerously incoherent, but has some adherents. But it is a concept of great normative power for many relatively powerless groups that have suffered grievous abuses" (1998, 415). I agree with Kingsbury on this point since use of the "indigenous peoples" concept can empower the status of specific groups and grant them certain rights under international law, even though the concept might not work if it is used in aggressive ways. In the Naqab context, use of the indigenous concept empowers the Bedouin and serves as a legal and international tool to grant them land rights and protection. In opposition to the new states' projects, indigenous people have developed various techniques to achieve their aims: i.e., to protect what has survived of their traditional land, culture, and resources (Gurr and Harff 2004, 165).

Tully (2000) identifies two forms of resistance to colonialism that have emerged among indigenous peoples: struggling against the structure of domination and attempting to modify governmental systems of control. Tactics include using words and deeds in day-to-day activities, exercising their own authority in their territory, and appealing to international law (e.g., in the form of what became the UN Declaration on the Rights of Indigenous People). Canada's indigenous people practiced the art of using words and deeds to resist colonialism. Tully describes how they also carried out everyday acts of protecting, recovering, and gathering together, as well as keeping, reviving, teaching, and adapting their indigenous life in order to prevent it from being destroyed. Such "self-conscious traditionalism" has also included traditional medicine, healing, and child-rearing practices, as well as the revitalization of justice circles, indigenous languages, and political structures (Tully 2000, 58–59). It is important in this work to test the diverse forms of resistance that Tully identifies.

The aboriginals in Australia,[3] who resisted in order to have their land rights recognized, constitute a similar case. For the Australian Aborigines, struggle over land rights was critical. Linda Smith (1999) argues that while indigenous people's resistance could be traced back to before the Second World War, the 1960s "saw the taking of direct action across several different states and the Northern Territories. Challenges were made by Aborigine groups for title to lands which were consistently refused by the courts and the state governments" (109). Their struggle also included "direct action, petitions, a tent embassy in 1972 (a tent embassy was established also by

Maori in New Zealand), silent protests, [and] challenges both through the courts and state government" (109).

One might argue that the "tent embassy" adopted by the Australian Aboriginals in 1972 was the most effective form of resistance. According to Andrew Schaap, its establishment in front of Parliament House in Canberra in 1972 was the strongest political demonstration in the history of Australia, and a form of political agency that put the Australian state under political threat (Schaap 2009, 210–211). Indigenous people have, in fact, achieved some success in their struggle, as shown by the more recent case of the New Zealand Maoris who succeeded in winning the right to self-determination (Armstrong 2010).

Champagne (2003) stresses the importance of indigenous peoples writing their history from their own perspective. Since history has often marginalized their voices, they should take a more decisive role in rewriting it. Globally such communities "will be highly motivated to preserve their core institutions and values and will resist change that threatens to disturb materially those institutions without an acceptable rationale" (Champagne 2003, xx, xxvi, xxxi). It is, however, extremely difficult for colonial and ethnocratic states to recognize such claims by indigenous people (Champagne 2003, xxv). Ethnocratic and colonial states come to fear indigenous peoples who do not hide their desire to protect their historical land and resources. Indigenous Bedouin claims for formal territorial recognition still represent an important phenomenon, as in the case of the Maʿza Bedouin in Egypt and amongst Bedouin under the Baʿth regime in Syria (Hobbs 2014; Chatty 2014).

## *Controversial Indigeneity and Bedouin Identity*

Identifying the Naqab Bedouin as an indigenous people opens up the broader question of how one defines the rest of the Palestinian minority in Israel. The position taken in this book is that all the Palestinians, including the Bedouin, should be considered as indigenous to the land (cf. Nasasra 2012). The present chapter does not propose that the Bedouin are indigenous and the rest of the Palestinians are not indigenous; rather, it aims to tie the Bedouin struggle to the global indigeneity movement by seeking to secure their rights according to international regulations and norms. I use indigeneity as a legal tool only. In the current context, international law is one of the only avenues through which to ensure Bedouin land and indigenous rights, thereby contributing to the empowerment of this most fragile Palestinian community.

The use of indigenous approaches in this context remains controversial: Israel does not recognize the Bedouin as indigenous or native to the land, even though they were acknowledged as such during Ottoman and British rules. The fact that both Ottomans and the British recognized Bedouin customary laws and tribunals is significant proof of their status as indigenous to the land (Nasasra 2011a, 2011b), so that applying that status to them offers insight into multiple indigenous rights, as well as providing a useful analytical framework.

The use of indigenous approaches, most prominently by Abu Saad (Champagne and Abu Saad 2003), but also by Yiftachel (2003; 2008) and Kedar (2004), has a surprisingly controversial politics despite its factual applicability; it remains both controversial and debatable (cf. Kark and Frantzman 2012). For instance, at a simple level it implies Bedouin presence before the arrival of new settlers in the Naqab region and also contradicts the Israeli authorities' approach of presenting the Bedouin as "invaders" of state land who lack any historical attachment to Biʾr al-Sabaʿ. As a result, use of the term "indigenous" has been contested as inapplicable to the Naqab Bedouin by Israeli scholars (Kark and Frantzman 2012). It is also contested by scholars for whom the indigenous concept has associations with certain preurban attributes that no longer apply to the Bedouin society in the Naqab (Law-Yone 2003, 183). It is also challenged by nationalist Palestinian scholars, such as Salman Abu-Sitta, because its use implies a potential separation of the Bedouin from the rest of the Palestinian people (cf. Nasasra et al. 2014).

Interestingly, local elders never use the term "indigenous people." Rather, they refer to themselves as "*ʾurban al-sabaʿ*," the "Arabs of Beersheba," although the term is slipping out of use and is restricted to Bedouin from the Nakba generation. Scholars such as Abu-Sitta also critique the use of "Naqab" as an inauthentic term to define the Bedouin, arguing that "Palestinian Bedouin of Beersheba" should be used. For example, pre-1917 maps do not use the term "Naqab," though the British archives refer to "Negeb" and "Beersheba junction" or "Southern Country." The authentic and indigenous name for the people is "*ʾurban al-sabaʿ*," but even that does not predate the twentieth century and the founding of Biʾr al-Sabaʿ. It is also increasingly controversial to separate out the Bedouin as an ethnic community. This is seen as an attempt to further their fragmentation, though in its various perspectives this controversy contains the ghosts of many simultaneous but different battles.

In defining the Naqab Bedouin as an indigenous people, Kedar, a leading law scholar, discusses their status from an international legal perspective and as an internally displaced people, and agrees that the notion of indigeneity applies (Kedar 2004). Other organizations, such as the Negev Coexistence Forum (NCF) and the Regional Council of Unrecognized Villages (RCUV), have considered the Bedouin to be indigenous peoples, though many other Arab activists and academics in Israel choose to use the term "national minority" instead. However, despite the controversial use of the concept, the Naqab Bedouin meet the criteria of indigenous people as presented by Cobo and others. Within the past few years (since 2007), the Naqab Bedouin have joined the Permanent Forum on Indigenous Issues at the United Nations. The decision to accept them as a member of the organization was made after a group of Bedouin lawyers, NGOs, and activists decided to join the UN as indigenous people and sent delegates to represent them at UN meetings. This group is active in the UN, and a representative tries to go annually to the UN to attend the indigenous peoples' meeting. Women from Bedouin organizations also play a significant role in attending UN meetings and campaigning for Bedouin rights internationally. Some scholars, such as Ann-Elise Lewallen (2003), linked indigenous women's activism to the global indigenous women's movement for indigenous rights. However, in the Naqab context, I argue that joining the UN as indigenous peoples was not a shared community decision, and a number of local Bedouin leaders and community activists contested this identification, with some even arguing that identifying the Bedouin as indigenous peoples further increases their fragmentation from the Palestinian minority in Israel.

Even so, without taking the debate on indigeneity into consideration, ordinary Bedouins identify themselves as natives by referring to themselves as "*ahl al-ard*" or "*al-bilad*," the owners of the land. Bedouin history, identity, and land ownership are connected despite life in a modern state. A similar context is also evident in northern Syria, where tribal identity and genealogy continue to be an important component of Bedouin identity (Lange 2014). The Bedouin today are the descendants of the main tribal clans who lived in the Naqab and southern Palestine before the creation of the state of Israel. They preserve their affinity to their land and have followed pastoralism and agriculture. This is not unique to them, as similar habits can be found among

Bedouin tribes in northern Arabia (cf. Hobbs 2014). Like other Bedouin communities in the Middle East, such as the northern *badiya* in Jordan, where Bedouin still preserve their Bedouin identity and practice their traditional songs, poetry, and wedding festivals (cf. Hood and al-Oun 2014), the Naqab Bedouin maintain their identity through various traditional daily performances. Discussing the *badiya* of Syria and Lebanon and the rapid changes the Bedouin have faced under the modern state, Chatty (2014, 29) argues that "regardless of their multiple occupations and residence patterns, they remain Bedouin culturally as long as they maintain close social ties with pastoral kin and retain the local linguistic and cultural markers that identify them as Bedouin."

Historically, the Bedouin in the Naqab used wells as a source of water and maintained traditional agriculture and indigenous traditional knowledge. They have also protected their cemeteries and the villages that existed before 1948. They use their own Bedouin dialect, laws, and customs. They preserve beliefs that are based on those of their Islamic communities. They have a sense of belonging to migratory tribes and preserve their traditional economy and customary laws. In addition, they still identify themselves according to tribal lines, with a strong sense of oral history, kinship, marriage norms, intermarriage relations, and hospitality aspects and a special attachment to historical territory, as well as to a Bedouin desert dialect that is still well supported. In this context of upholding their Bedouin and tribal identities, the Bedouin in the Naqab share similarities with other Bedouin communities in the Middle East, such as those in Lebanon and Syria (cf. Chatty 2014), although the Bedoon (Bedouin) in gulf countries such as Kuwait are not granted citizenship by the state (cf. Herb 2009).

Finally, in their efforts to gain their rights as native people, the Bedouin have shifted during the past two decades toward using the Israeli political and juridical system for recognition of their land ownership according to their traditional tribal and customary laws (recent instances are the Israeli court debates around al-ʿAraqib, ʿAtir Um al-Hiran, and al-Sira, among others). For example, the indigeneity of the Bedouin in the Naqab can be recognized by their use of indigenous tribunal courts. Their mechanisms for conflict resolution existed and were recognized by the Ottomans and under the British Mandate and persist to the present, reinforcing their indigenous customary status.

Culturally, language and dialect represent another way of protecting indigenous life. The Bedouin Arabic dialect in the Naqab (the desert dialect) is retained, as are Bedouin customs and norms, despite the local population's having had to confront plans for forced sedentarization and modernization. Israel's policies of Bedouin assimilation have failed since half of the community rejected the idea of moving to urban areas. Even those who were forced to move and now live in towns still follow their cultural traditions. They are not integrated into the Israeli population and in various ways still behave as indigenous people, protecting their tribal space and identity by inhabiting their own neighborhoods and at times refusing to mix with other tribes in the same locality.

However, there are those who identify the Bedouin as an "ethnic group," rather than as indigenous or a minority. The official Israeli narrative (including Israel's media sources) treats the Bedouin as a separate group and tries to frame them as ethnic and to dissociate them from the rest of the country's Palestinian minority. To further the fragmentation of the Palestinian Arab minority, the state of Israel has, since its creation, treated the Bedouin as a separate ethnic group by referring to them as "good Arabs" or "our Bedouin" or by using terms such as the "Bedouin sector" or "Bedouin area." Even in the army, Bedouin, like the Druze, were placed in separate military units as a form of ethnic organization (Kanaaneh 2009, 51–52).

In fact, separate state agencies, e.g., the Bedouin Development Authority (BDA) and the Bedouin Education Authority (BEA), were created especially to deal with the "Bedouin problem" and Bedouin "encroachment," as an ethnic group, on state land. The Israeli authorities clearly deal with the Bedouin as a separate group needing special attention, even when it comes to intermarriage and demographic threats, which Rhoda Kanaaneh equates to the situation of other Palestinians in Israel (Kanaaneh 2002).

Meanwhile, for some scholars, e.g., Jakubowska (1992), Cohen (2010), and Law-Yone (2003), there is no such thing as Bedouin identity in the Naqab; the state is trying to frame the Bedouin as an "ethnic group" to disconnect them from the rest of the Palestinians in Israel. Jakubowska (1992) maintains that Israel has created an ethnic identity for the Bedouin to separate them from the main Palestinian Arab population. He believes that the government's policy is to treat them as a separate ethnic group in order to impose its hegemony on them, a view supported by Maddrell (1990, 20). Yet the Bedouin cannot be treated as an ethnic group on the basis of having a different religion—they are Palestinian Arabs and Muslims, and Ibn Khaldun, the fourteenth-century Arab historian and sociologist called them "true Arabs" (Ibn Khaldun 1969). Treating them as an ethnic group undoubtedly serves the state's vision of co-opting and ruling the Bedouin, analogous with the British and French colonial treatment of Bedouin communities in Jordan, Syria, Lebanon, and other Middle Eastern countries. The Israeli objective of framing a distinct Bedouin identity for the Naqab Bedouin has failed because the Bedouin have become increasingly aware of the deep dichotomy of Israel's policy of fragmentation.

Not only in the Naqab and Biʾr al-Sabaʿ but across the region (the Levant, Egypt, north Arabia, and Jordan), Bedouin tribes have preserved their identity and strong kinship relations despite the emergence of new states and citizenship. Regarding the formation of the state system, as Chatty (2014) argues in the context of Bedouin of Bilad al-Sham,

> despite the formal annulling of the Bedouin tribes' legal status in Syrian law in 1958 and the unwillingness of the Lebanese state to recognize Bedouin as citizens, tribal identity and the authority attached to tribal leaders continued to exist and were played out in different ways in both countries, reflecting the different approaches to authority of each state.
> (16)

Bedouin communities in contemporary Syria and Lebanon have maintained their tribal identity although they face certain challenges (Chatty 2014, 30), whereas the Bedouin in the Naqab, despite different state laws and regulations, preserve their tribal identity in all matters of conflict resolution and continue to deal with their internal issues according to their customary laws, which function as a significant component of their identity.

Law-Yone (2003) goes even further from the "indigenous peoples" concept, arguing that because "almost all the true nomadic populations in Israel have become sedentarized, it is technically incorrect to call them Bedouin" (Law-Yone 2003, 183). This shows that he is in fact trapped in modernization theory. Israel's policy of forcing the Bedouin to live as a sedentarized community is a component of the state's goal of modernizing them. Yet Bedouin identity is preserved despite all the changes they have faced during the last decades. Bogumila Hall argues that "despite the state's ongoing policies aimed at transforming the rural Bedouins into an 'urban proletariat', the community's sense of identity and attachment to their lifestyle have not dissolved" (Hall 2014, 160).

But even if, like other Bedouin communities in the Middle East, they do live in planned towns, the Naqab Bedouin still practice their culture and all meaningful aspects of indigenous Bedouin life. They have not marginalized their past by creating Bedouin towns and urban communities. Bedouin in the northern *badiya* of Jordan also faced settlement plans (Abu Jaber, Gharaibeh, and Hill 1987), and their Bedouin identity remains a key component of their life today.

Applying this controversial concept of indigeneity to the peoples of the Naqab has sparked much debate in Israeli academia (cf. Yahel, Kark, and Frantzman 2012). Palestinian scholars have also criticized its use as having the potential to split the Bedouin from other Palestinians. Such use also implies a legal and international rather than a political solution to the Palestinian question, as well as acceptance of the state's policies in return for recognition of indigenous rights. I have, however, partly adopted the legal concept, believing that it strengthens the status of the Bedouin under international law and that because Bedouin land rights were recognized according to their customary laws (under the Ottomans and the British in southern Palestine), the Bedouin today might be given more rights under international law.

The concept of an indigenous people has been chosen as a natural and historical form of Bedouin identity and power that can be used to articulate the voices of the community and enable them to be heard and discussed by international legal entities. This becomes a way of opposing the identification of the Bedouin as an ethnic group since the Bedouin were historically regarded by the Ottoman and British Mandate rulers as indigenous to the land and were organic part of the Palestinian body politic and official institutions in both Jerusalem and Gaza. An article on "Settlement in the Negev" written in 1940 by Sir G. E. Kirk, an expert on the Middle East, confirmed that the mandatory authorities recognized this factor:

> I do not deny that some settlement in the northern and western Negeb is possible. It is vitally important, however, in that case that the Arab cultivator-herdsmen, who now inhabit the district to the number of several thousands, should be adequately protected. Like all primitive people they are attached to their tribal lands . . . the Empire that regards the rights of the aborigines of Australia and New Guinea must consider the fate of these simple people of south Palestine.
>
> (*DAILY TELEGRAPH*, MARCH 15, 1940)

Accepting this indigenous status immediately opens up the study of various types of resistance carried out by other indigenous peoples worldwide for preserving their culture and indigenous practices. Indeed, I think that simply using the concept is a form of power since it challenges the victimization of the Bedouin. Adopting the term also serves the purpose of cultural "resistance" and even implies a new set of power relations. Certainly, all this is highly relevant to the case of the Naqab Bedouin, despite arguments to the contrary, particularly among those who regard the Bedouin as an ethnic group and not as indigenous to the land. Nevertheless, even if the indigenous paradigms are adopted in the case of the Bedouin, it is hard to see any automatic improvement in their situation since the society suffers from extreme and pressing issues that need long-term planning by government and local municipalities. Using international legal tools would speed up the process of addressing the core concerns of the Bedouin.

### *Shift in Identity from Indigeneity to Wataniyya?*

Despite referring to the Bedouin as indigenous peoples, both historically and from an international law perspective, one can argue that, in the pressurized political context and the struggle with Israel over land ownership, a new paradigm has recently been developed within the community. This suggests that a shift is taking place from an indigenous Bedouin definition to a nationalist or *watani* paradigm. A similar process happened with other Bedouin communities in the Middle East when they became part of the modern state: they preserved their tribal identity and were also integrated into the state system. The best example of this is Jordan, where Bedouin work in official government institution and politics. Lyne (1989, 24) notes that in Jordan "Bedouin tribes have come to symbolize Jordan's national identity."

In the Naqab, the politicization of the community since the Oslo Accords and the emergence of indigenous political parties in the Naqab have contributed significantly to the rise of a national ideology led by political coalitions such as the Joint List (including Balad, the Communist Party, and the Islamic Movement). This debate pushes aside indigeneity approaches and connects the Bedouin struggle for recognition to the wider situation of being Palestinian in Israel. Today the Naqab Bedouin struggle is much like that of other Bedouin communities such as the Palestinian Bedouin of Area C and their call for the right to be accepted. There is a growing link between the Bedouin cause, the situation of East Jerusalem, and Arab villages in Israel such as Dahmash (Lydda). These communities face similar struggles for rights and recognition.

In the past decade or so, the Naqab Bedouin have become a potent symbol of the Palestinian minority's struggle for their land rights. One of the main reasons is the role of the Islamic movement in the Naqab, where religiosity among the Naqab Bedouin has increased. The state of Israel's marginalization of the Bedouin and the vacuum it has left have facilitated the growing role played by the Islamic movement, and the movement's popularity has increased with the rebuilding of demolished Bedouin houses and provision of basic services to poor families.

Another significant factor arising from the escalation of Israeli policies has been the recognition among researchers of a shift in the way this community is identified, from "Naqab Bedouin" or "indigenous Bedouin" to "Palestinian Bedouin." Similarly, for all its work as a signifier of the current nationalist struggle and the contesting of colonial boxes, the newly predominant terminology of the Naqab has an elusive authenticity and is the subject of keen disputes (cf. Nasasra et al. 2014). A more recent element has been the growth of the Balad and the Islamic movement parties and their role in local politics among the Bedouin (see chapter 10). Voting levels for Arab parties have increased, and there is clearly a sense of greater identification with being Palestinian in Israel (see chapters 10 and 11). In the most recent elections in Israel, for the first time for decades al-Tajamuʿa party (Balad) won hundreds of thousands of votes from the Bedouin villages and towns. Its growing power throughout the Naqab, as well as the rise of local Tajamuʿa leaders among the Bedouin, has contributed to an increasing sense of Palestinian identity.

Within civil society, the growing numbers of women's organizations in the Naqab and their interaction with other Arab women's organizations in the Galilee, the north, and Jerusalem have contributed to a greater awareness of women's rights among the Bedouin. Adalah, the legal center for the Arab minority, has started to play a stronger role in Naqab land ownership cases in the Israeli courts. A branch of Adalah in which women lawyers play an active part was launched in the Naqab and has contributed to reinforcing the relationship with the Galilee and the north. Female academics from the

Naqab have also begun to research and write extensively about the impact of the Nakba among women and children in the Naqab. Their identifying of the Bedouin as Palestinians has also been notable (Aburabia 2014).

This new nationalist paradigm has tended to reposition the Bedouin and to link them to wider trajectories in Israel/Palestine and to the rest of the Palestinian society, an approach that reflects the political fading away of the idea of the Bedouin as "good Arabs" within Israel. New research is revising Naqab Bedouin discreteness by exploring (through comparative studies with minorities elsewhere or studies of cross-border relations and indigenous peoples globally) the connected nature of Bedouin society with Palestinians throughout Israel/Palestine and emphasizing the commonalities rather than the particularities of state imposition. There have also been attempts to situate Bedouin history within the history of the Palestinian people rather than positioning it on a discrete trajectory from nomadism to modernity (cf. Nasasra et al. 2014).

Yet while these linkages are contemporaneous with the political dynamics noted above and are related to rethinking Bedouin identity, reaffirming their Palestinian-ness, and attributing a nationalist awakening to changing voting habits, political rhetoric, and military affiliations, the dynamics are also ambiguous. This Palestinian-ism, at least in its current articulation, is predominantly a minority politics within Israel. The Naqab is a nationalist symbol primarily for the Palestinians inside, as part of a Palestinian minority consolidating itself as a political community. As such, what unites the Naqab Bedouin and the wider indigenous population of historical Palestine is not their inherent Palestinian-ness but their contemporary political predicaments and subjectivities.

The shift from indigenous to *watani* can be clearly seen in current instances of village demolitions in the Naqab. The plight of the villages of al-ʿAraqib (2010) and the ongoing court struggle on the future of ʿAtir Um al-Hiran (2015) suddenly came to symbolize the land struggle between the Naqab Bedouin and the authorities, while the demolitions unified the cause of the Palestinian Arab minority within Israel, and for the first time brought other Palestinian solidarity groups to the Naqab. For example, demonstrations against the razing of the village of al-ʿAraqib were organized in almost every Arab town in the Galilee and the Triangle and even in Shaikh Jarrah in East Jerusalem and the village of Dahmash, and the local indigenous people were mobilized in weekly demonstrations within the Naqab. To support the Bedouin cause of al-ʿAraqib and ʿAtir Um al-Hiran, and in opposition to policies that relocate the Bedouin, the High Follow Up Committee for the Palestinian Arab Minority in Israel declared one day strikes on a number of occasions. More recently (2013), the committee called for major demonstrations in Beersheba to support recognition of al-ʿAraqib and Um al-Hiran and also organized a meeting in the village. Ikrima Sabri, the mufti of Jerusalem, was among the leaders who showed solidarity by coming south to the Naqab. Both the Islamic movement and other Arab parties and local grassroots organizations played a significant role in the recognition campaign, which continues to this day.

The developing shift from an indigenous identity to one that embraces *watani* and Palestinian-ism opens a new debate as to how analysts can best understand the current struggle of the Bedouin population. Rejecting identification as an ethnic group, the Bedouin can be categorized both as a native and as an organic component of the Palestinian Arab minority in Israel.

## *The Paradox of Power and the Use of Power as a Relationship*

The literature offers three different understandings of power—as capacity, thing, or relationship. The traditional view suggests that power is a thing rather than a relationship and further defines power as a state's military capability—i.e., possessing tanks and aircraft and using them for various aims (Hindess 1996). Yet, in the ongoing debate about power, many scholars concur that it is better to treat power as a relationship. David Baldwin states that there is "agreement that power should be treated (more) as a relationship between two or more people than as a property of any one of them" (Baldwin 1989, 3). In my view, power as a relationship is most suitable for understanding the dynamics between Israel and its indigenous Bedouin citizens. Power as a capacity does not apply because it takes an accounting of the Bedouins' resources and material possessions and then assumes that they are powerless.

A number of authors approach power as a relationship rather than as a thing and also introduce the concept of paradoxes of power. Foucault, for example, suggests a conception of power as a relationship because it is everywhere; in almost every interaction we can identify an exercise of power.

We influence others and are influenced by others. As Hindess (1996, 150) notes, "Foucault insists both that power is ubiquitous and that there can be no personalities that are formed independently of its effects."

Frederick Frey focuses on the problems of measuring power: "Let us define power as a relationship such that the behavior of one actor (individual or collective) alters the behavior of another actor" (Frey 1971, 1,089). For him, power is a causal relationship among actors. The reaction of an individual to the use of power might not be anticipated. The powerful actor is the one who influences the behavior of others at a particular time and place, but may, in turn, be influenced by their behavior at a later time. In the case of the Bedouin, since power is a relationship, an Israeli exercise of power may have some effect, but the same power exercise at a different time may not have the same effect. Each exercise of power is contextualized by issue and time.

David Baldwin discusses the concept of power as a relationship and the inconsistencies that arise from it, arguing that in many cases we misunderstand power, especially the "paradoxes of power" (1989, 1–2) and that weak and powerless classes do influence the behavior even of powerful figures and states. There are many cases where the supposedly powerful do not get what they want from the supposedly weak; this, he maintains, constitutes the paradox of power. Does this mean that the weak are really powerful in ways that our analysis has simply missed? Or might it be that by focusing on power as a "thing" (the military capabilities and money and resources of power), our analysis is wrong? Instead of calculating who has the military capabilities, can we, by looking at issue- and time-specific power attempts to judge the relationships of power, actually improve our analysis?

The Naqab Bedouin can be viewed through the lens of the paradox of power since we can never guarantee who influences whom. Did the Bedouin influence the state (under both the Ottomans and the British and, later, the Israeli authorities), or does the state influence the Bedouin? Because power has changed over time, as has the degree and intention of resistance, I argue that there are, in fact, too many paradoxes of power between the Bedouin and the state. Therefore, we must apply a different conceptualization of power because of the impossibility of predicting what will ultimately happen between the Israeli authorities and the Bedouin in the struggle over land ownership. In this regard, Baldwin's understanding of power as paradoxical is useful; he highlights many examples where the weak were able to influence the strong and sometimes managed to win.

Power must therefore be viewed as more nuanced and relational. The Bedouin have resisted and struggled, initially during the periods of Ottoman and British rule and increasingly under Israeli rule since the Israeli authorities failed to understand Bedouin culture and, indeed, aimed to destroy their culture, control them as an ethnic group, and dissociate them from the rest of the Palestinians. However, the Bedouin have succeeded in surviving for more than sixty years in the Naqab, and although Israel demolished their houses, confiscated their lands and fragmented them as a distinct people, Israeli power was less than efficient against them. Quite simply, the Bedouin are not passive; they produce different kinds of activism in order to survive. This is grassroots resistance, albeit of a low resource kind.

Applying the concept of power as a relationship should help clarify the situation between the Bedouin and the Israeli authorities. The Israeli authorities use various policies to remove the Bedouin from their land, but the Bedouin react and rebuild their demolished houses, which shows the relational nature of the power dynamic. It has been assumed that the Bedouin did not have power and were passive and weak in relation to the Ottoman Empire, the British Mandate, and the Israeli military authorities. In the existing scholarship that examines the period covered by this book, the Bedouin are seen as passive, defeated, and unresponsive to state policies, nor is there any evaluation of the ebb and flow of power relationships in which the Bedouin and the state are engaged, which form a complicated pattern of mutual power attempts and resistance. If power is taken as a thing, analysis of the Bedouin will always make them the losers.

Since resistance is central to this research, I apply two useful methods with regard to the Naqab Bedouin. The first is to understand power as a relationship that exists between two or more actors. In the case of the Naqab, it is between the Bedouin and the Ottomans, the British, and Israel. The second is to look for paradoxes in power relations. A paradox of power exists in the relationship between the state and the Bedouin because we do not know who influences whom and because there seem to be cases where the Bedouin might be expected to lose and they do not; paradoxically, we cannot predict who will win each exchange since power changes over time.

## The Resistance Debate

In order to put this study into a broader context, it is also necessary to understand the notion of "resistance" as propounded by various scholars. Barbalet (1985, 531) argues that "the concept of 'resistance' is necessary for understanding power relations and irreducible to the concept of 'power.'" Recently, the topic of resistance has attracted more attention, but despite being tackled from various angles, there is no scholarly agreement about how to define and conceptualize it because of the diversity of actions that have been suggested as types or forms of resistance. As Jeffrey Rubin claims, "There are confusions and disagreements about the meaning of resistance and about the significance of those acts that are labelled as resistance" (Rubin 1996, 238), and Rose Weitz argues that "to date, the term resistance remains loosely defined, allowing some scholars to see it almost everywhere and others almost nowhere" (Weitz 2001, 669). Hollander and Einwohner note that "although there is virtual consensus that resistance involves oppositional action of some kind, there is considerable disagreement about whether resistance must be intended by actors and whether it must be recognised by targets and/or observers" (Hollander and Einwohner 2004, 544).

In the case of Bedouin actions and resistance against Ottoman, British, and Israeli military rule, I look for resistance that is made with intention, but I do not always expect that this resistance will be recognized by the target. I aim to look at intention toward and recognition of Bedouin resistance. The problem is partly with the issue of intent and meaning. In this regard Asef Bayat (2000) notes that "many authors in the resistance paradigm have simply abandoned intent and meaning, focusing instead eclectically on both intended and unintended practices as the manifestation of 'resistance'"; he also asks, "Does resistance mean defending an already achieved gain or making fresh demands?" (Bayat 2000, 543).

How do we deal with these concerns? Rubin suggests an important possibility: "One could limit the term resistance to actions that have some degree of consciousness and collectivity about them, as well as some explicit attention to a broad structure of domination, and choose a different word for other sorts of actions that oppose power" (Rubin 1996, 239). In his definition, consciousness, intentionality, challenge of power, and collective action are components of resistance. Thus, we are taken back to the close relationship between power attempts (by a new state) and the challenge to power that is the core of resistance (the Bedouin). Recognizing the importance of understanding the connection between resistance and power, I wish to analyze resistance since it will help in determining the power of the Bedouin as natives. In such circumstances, people have power over the state, as I discuss later in this book.

Scott (1985) seems to be clear about the identification of resistance:

> I might claim that class resistance includes *any* act(s) by member(s) of a subordinate class that is or are *intended* either to mitigate or deny claims (for example, landlords, large farmers, the state) or to advance its own claims (for example, work, land, charity, respect) vis-à-vis those superordinate classes. (290)

Scott is relaxed about adopting this approach toward resistance because "it does have several advantages [and it] focuses on intentions rather than consequences, recognizing that many acts of resistance may fail to achieve their intended results" (290). He also agrees on distinctions between different kinds of resistance: "Real resistance, it is argued, is (a) organized, systematic, and cooperative, (b) principled or selfless, (c) has revolutionary consequences, and/or (d) embodies ideas or intentions that negate the basis of domination itself" (292). This is a strong definition and implies a high degree of organization and scale.

Hollander and Einwohner loosen the definition somewhat by suggesting that the scale of resistance, individual or collective, must be taken into consideration: "An act of resistance may be individual or collective, widespread or locally confined. Related to scale is *the level of coordination* among the resisters, that is, the extent to which they purposefully act together" (2004, 536).

Thus, I consider that resistance includes a level of awareness, not fully intended, and that it can be collective and individual. I accept part of what Hollander and Einwohner are arguing since it helps in testing the case of the Naqab Bedouin under Ottoman, British, and Israeli military rule; I also take their point that resistance involves active forms of verbal, cognitive, and physical behavior. Therefore, under military rule in the Naqab (1948–1967), resistance included any nonviolent action taken to marginalize the government's methods of control or achieve the immediate goal of enhancing indigenous Bedouin life and strengthening Bedouin survival mechanisms (see chapter 11).

### *Nonviolent and Everyday Resistance*

There is a considerable body of scholarly work that suggests a potentially useful range of forms of resistance. Much is focused on violent resistance, with less available on nonviolent resistance; interestingly, most of the research into nonviolent resistance addresses strategies of defense, such as the famous case of Gandhi. However, the work of Gene Sharp helps to correct the balance. Sharp (1973), a leading scholar on nonviolent action, demonstrates a wide range of peaceful forms of action with wide relevance for my analysis. He identifies 198 methods of nonviolent action and divides them into various categories, offering a wide spectrum of activities and actions that might be available to those engaged in resisting states.

Sharp's broad definition of nonviolent action is very helpful in understanding the struggle of the Naqab Bedouin. Sharp defines nonviolent action as

> a generic term covering dozens of specific methods of protest, noncooperation and intervention, in all of which the actionist conducts the conflict by doing—or refusing to do—certain things without using physical violence. As a consequence, therefore nonviolent action is not passive. It is not inaction. It is action that is nonviolent.
>
> (SHARP 1973, 64)

Accordingly, nonviolent actions are classified as disobedient activity toward the powerful, e.g., the state. As recorded by Sharp, this may include as many as 200 tactics of nonviolent action, including symbolic protest, social noncooperation, economic boycott, labor strikes, political noncooperation, and nonviolent intervention (Sharp 1990, 1–2).

Nonviolence is an alternative or adjunct to violent resistance and aims to promote change in relationships of power. In particular, as Sharp argues, a key goal of nonviolent action is also to modify the points of view of those with whom the actors compete, changing their beliefs and attitudes. Nonviolent actions may also attempt to change policies and opinions for the actors' benefit, as nonpassive action (Sharp 1973, 68). The Bedouin may have used many of the forms of nonviolent action suggested by Sharp; they also appear to have used many other methods.

One of the most popular activists to have raised the banner of nonviolent action was Mohandas Gandhi of India: "Passive resistance has been conceived and is regarded as a weapon of the weak. Whilst it avoids violence, not being open to the weak, it does not exclude its use if, in the opinion of a passive resister, the occasion demands it" (Gandhi 1951, 3). Gandhi's aim was to free his nation. He adopted various nonviolent tactics as the most effective way to make the British leave his country, and his call for civil disobedience included resistance to payment of taxes, mass meetings, huge parades, seditious speeches, a boycott of foreign textile imports, and so on. Sharp (1973, 84–86) identified three main methods of nonviolence—protest, noncooperation, and intervention—and argues that disobedience or noncooperation, a key tool for Gandhi, represented one of the most powerful forms of nonviolent resistance.

Sharp's schema of nonviolent actions is extraordinarily useful for examining the Naqab Bedouin struggle against Israeli military rule, as well as for understanding Bedouin actions in relation to Ottoman oppression and British colonial policies (Sharp 1990, 13). He includes as nonviolent protest such objects as "records, radio and television" (Sharp 1973, 129), and other relevant forms include "expressing moral condemnation," "group lobbying," "political non-cooperation," "refusal to recognize a particular regime," and "popular non-obedience" (304). I refer throughout this book to various nonviolent actions and cultural resistance and other forms used by the Bedouin that could fit into this category.

Another important set of ideas about peaceful resistance by indigenous peoples derives from the work of Oren Yiftachel, who approaches new nations and settler states in relation to the resistance of indigenous peoples, particularly the Naqab Bedouin. He also highlights settler-state projects, for example, in the United States, Canada, Australia, Israel, South Africa, and New Zealand. His analysis of Naqab Bedouin resistance is especially informative. The Bedouin struggled against Israeli policies that sought to expropriate their land, relocated them to the *siyaj* area (the enclosed zone in which they were concentrated under military rule), and endeavored to urbanize them. He notes how they resisted policies that involved concentrating them into new townships to reduce their land, Judaizing the Naqab, and encouraging Jewish settlements. The Bedouin duly developed a counter-ideology and, by managing to remain partly on their land, showed a useful resistance to the state's numerous policies (Yiftachel 2003). This counter-ideology began to develop in the Naqab toward the end of the military-government period and recently has been escalating.

Yiftachel introduces Israel as an ethnocratic state whose aims in the Naqab have to contend with Bedouin actions and specific forms of resistance. Although he does not deal with the time period in which I am interested, his categories of present-day resistance can inform my analysis of the earlier period. In particular I draw on his discussion of these forms of Bedouin resistance: *sumud*; resisting Judaization and modernization; living in urbanized townships; legal struggles; and the development of a counter-ideology to survive on their land.

Similarly, I learned much from James Scott's theory of resistance (1977, 1987, 1990, 1985) while trying to adapt it for the Naqab Bedouin case. His 1985 study was based on fieldwork in Malaysia, where he explored the range of tactics adopted by Malaysian villagers in their daily lives to overthrow the power elite and reject their claims. The peasants challenged the hegemony of their oppressors in order to gain a chance for justice and for a better life by using "everyday forms of resistance," which Scott divides into symbolic resistance, cultural resistance, anonymity of resistance, and ideological underpinnings.[4] They adopted these forms of resistance instead of engaging in open revolution that ultimately might have achieved nothing (Scott 1985). Scott focuses less on direct forms of resistance and more on indirect weapons of the weak. His argument for doing so is telling:

> For all these reasons it occurred to me that the emphasis on peasant rebellion was misplaced. Instead, it seemed far more important to understand what we might call everyday forms of peasant resistance—the prosaic but constant struggle between peasantry and those who seek to extract labor, food, taxes, rents, and interest from them. Most of the forms this struggle takes stop well short of collective outright defiance. Here I have in mind the ordinary weapons of relatively powerless groups: foot dragging, dissimulation, false compliance, pilfering, feigned ignorance, slander, arson, sabotage, and so forth.
> (SCOTT 1985, 29)

Scott adopts the terms "the weapons of the weak" and "everyday forms of resistance" to refer to the various forms of resistance used by the peasantry to defend their interests in preference to open revolt that might threaten their security. Rather than riots, demonstrations, arson, organized social banditry, or open violence, the villagers used forms of resistance that included daily struggle for survival to gain their rights and better status. He called this "primitive" or "everyday" resistance (Scott 1985, 273), noting that because the powerless rarely have the resources to resist their superordinates in public, "everyday acts of resistance make no headlines" (Scott 1985, xvi–xvii).

Scott's argument that everyday forms of peasant resistance still qualify as resistance, to the extent that they "deny or mitigate claims from appropriating classes" (1985, 302), remains convincing. Of course, everyday forms of resistance are not necessarily accepted by the dominant class as resistance. The term "everyday" resistance can apply to everyday Bedouin resistance toward Ottoman, British, Israeli military rule, and modern resistance. Scott looks particularly at what he calls "symbolic or ideological resistance," where resistance is not just collective action or social movements, since peasants also avoid any "direct confrontation" with authority (1987, 419–20). The everyday forms of peasant resistance are neither "formally organized" nor employed "self-consciously" (1987, 421). For Scott, "the goal . . . of the great bulk of peasant resistance is not to overthrow or transform a system of domination but rather to survive—today, this week, this season—within it" (1987, 424).

Two of Scott's most interesting case studies of everyday resistance are peasant resistance to the Islamic *zakat* (tithes) in Kedah, Malaysia, and the resistance by the French peasantry to the tithe in France. In Malaysia, resistance to paying *zakat* was not a public protest by the peasants; they simply "evaded" and "defied" it, for instance, by farmers refusing to register their cultivated land and avoiding and evading declarations about the size of their fields and harvests (1987, 426). Thus, "by steady stubborn resistance" peasants reduced the amount of tax they paid, along with "silent struggle" and useful "techniques of evasion" (431). For Scott, the goal of everyday resistance was "immediate and personal gains in a fashion that minimizes the risks of open confrontation" (449).

In another informative study, Scott (1990) expands his theory to apply to all rural and urban subordinate groups, identifying "low profile forms of resistance that dare not speak in their own name" (1990, 19). In discussing relations between dominant classes and powerless groups he makes a clear distinction between two concepts by identifying two main relationships of power: "public transcript," where the interaction is open and public, and "hidden transcript" and "infra-politics," where the discourse is off-stage and informal (1990, 2–4). Powerless and indigenous groups choose hidden transcript for their own safety, avoiding public transcript, which is too risky.

Scott speaks of "hidden resistance" against a dominant figure as the safe expression of aggression that serves as a substitute, albeit second-best, for the real thing, i.e., direct aggression. Amongst the peasantry, resistance was found "less in the open protests, petitions, riots, and revolts that did occasionally erupt but rather in a quiet but massive pattern of evasion" (1990, 195). He also emphasizes that spontaneous action is impossible without anonymity.

Scott rounds off his concept of declared and disguised resistance as opposing the exercise of material status and ideological domination by offering numerous examples of resistance that he identifies as hidden or public transcript against the dominant structure. The "forms of disguised low profile, undisclosed resistance—"infrapolitics"—included such aspects as everyday forms of resistance, anger, aggression, gossip, carnival symbolism, autonomous social space, millennial religions, class heroes, development of dissident subcultures, and so on (1990, 198). He refers to infrapolitics as "essentially the strategic form of resistance [that] subjects must assume under conditions of great peril," in which no "public claims are made"; it is "real politics" (1990, 199–200).[5]

There are some who criticize Scott for choosing to write about hidden or covert forms of resistance. Matthew Gutmann, among others, argues that "far from needing to narrow our understanding of which forms of resistance are worthwhile to study, we must study both overt and covert forms and the relations between them" (Gutmann 1993, 76). His criticism is helpful since it is essential to study the relationship between hidden and public transcript. In my analysis of everyday forms of Bedouin resistance, I adopt Scott's definition of peasant resistance:

> Peasants resistance is any act by a peasant (or peasants) that is intended either to mitigate or deny claims (e.g., rents, taxes, corvée, deference) made on that class by superordinate classes (e.g., landlords, the state, moneylenders) or to advance peasant claims (e.g., to land, work, charity, respect) vis-à-vis these superordinate classes.
>
> (SCOTT 1987, 419)

In his theory of everyday resistance and the weapons of the weak, Scott notes that peasant resistance is effective: "The generalized, persistent practice of everyday forms of resistance underwritten by a subculture of complicity can achieve many, if not all, of the results aimed at by the social movement" (1987, 422). In this case, one might fault him for preferring covert forms of resistance and diminishing the role of social movement and direct action, and one must certainly question what benefits accrue to the peasants from their everyday hidden resistance and whether it changes their lives. One must also remember to look for intention and agency. But the concepts of intentional resistance and consciousness can usefully be applied in examining the Naqab Bedouin under Ottoman, British, and Israeli military rule.

Timothy Mitchell (1990) disagrees with Scott's model of resistance: "The argument that choosing petty resistance rather than direct confrontation is the result of a rational decision depends not only on an evaluation of the situation . . . but on a general historical estimate of where peasants lie" (Mitchell 1990, 555). I agree with Mitchell, but the case in the Naqab is different since for their own safety the Bedouin habitually avoided direct confrontation with the state; they needed to be hidden, otherwise they would easily lose the battle. Asef Bayat (2000) also addresses this issue of lower-class resistance:

> The fact that people are able to help themselves and extend their networks surely shows their daily activism and struggles. However, by doing so the actors may hardly win any space from the state (or other sources of power, like capital and patriarchy)—they are not necessarily challenging domination. (545)

Here Bayat suggests that lower-class struggle is unlikely to achieve success by directly challenging state domination. I take his point that groups such as those in the Naqab challenge states for survival. Importantly, this fits with an attempt to understand the state-Bedouin power relationship in ways that are both issue- and time-specific. To the casual observer, the Bedouin may appear to be passive and accepting of state power, if one is looking only for large-scale direct confrontations of state hegemony. However, an adjustment of viewpoint enables one to see a wide range of resistance, and some successes, occurring across time and issues.

In fact, Scott could also be criticized for his comments in the works cited above about what can be achieved by peasant and poor communities using hidden transcript and everyday forms of resistance. He may, in fact, be overstating the ability of hidden transcript to effect change, and one needs to be careful not to overstate the Bedouin ability to alter their situation. However, it appears that Scott's hidden transcript should work very well for the Naqab case; he writes that "direct assertion of opposition was ordinarily very dangerous" (Scott 1990, 189), which is true for the Bedouin. I believe it will be useful to examine how the Bedouin employed hidden transcript and avoided a direct confrontation with the states. It is important to remember, both for me as an analyst and for the states concerned, that, as Scott says, it is difficult to monitor the hidden transcript since "the dominant can rarely monitor fully the hidden transcript" (1990, 191). Many authors have criticized Scott's work and his understanding of resistance, but his position can be defended. In the long run, his model of resistance can be useful, and powerless and marginalized groups such as the Bedouin can benefit from it.

TWO

# Ruling the Desert

## *Ottoman Policies Toward the Frontiers*

### The Middle East Bedouin Tribes and the State

FOR CENTURIES BEDOUIN TRIBES have inhabited parts of the Middle East and North Africa. The word "Bedouin," derived from the Arabic terms "*badawi*," or "*badu*," is commonly used to describe seminomadic pastoral people who inhabit the desert, the "*badiya*," as a way of life. The word conjures up many images. One of the earliest scholars to have written on the Bedouin was Ibn Khaldun, the renowned fourteenth century Arab historian, sociologist, and philosopher. Perceiving them as "savage" but "real Arabs" who had existed prior to sedentary populations, he explained the Bedouin by stressing notions of "*ʿasabiyya*" and intertribal relations, describing how loyalty, kinship, family, and blood ties were important in understanding tribal order and structure (Ibn Khaldun 1969).

Since the late eighteenth century, there have been many accounts of Bedouin culture and history that have portrayed them as backward living in harsh desert conditions (Musil 1928; Lawrence [1926] 1997; Glubb 1976; Deringil 2003). Some have painted a more romanticized image, depicting the Bedouin as noble.

The Bedouin have provoked scholarly debates regarding Bedouin livelihood, pastoral nomadism, and migration, as well as their ability to adapt to the ecological environment of the desert, to seasonal availability of pasture and water, and to socioeconomic and sociopolitical changes. There has also been a focus on the efforts of new states to make the Bedouin settle down (al-Aref 1999; Abu Rabia 1994, 2001; Eickelman 1989; Chatty 1986). Other debates have concentrated on Bedouin social organization and internal tribal order. These debates have included Bedouin tribes and have discussed tribal structure, hierarchy, solidarity, honor, political organization, oral history, and tribal leadership roles (Chatty 1986; Eickelman 1989; Marx 1967; Muhsam 1966; Shryock 1977; Shuqayr 1991; al-Aref 1999; Abu-Lughod 1986).

Other scholars have discussed the interaction between Bedouin tribes and external authorities, a relationship that has taken different forms such as alliances with states or with other tribes to achieve a common purpose. The shaikh, as the tribe's leader, manages these interactions (Eickelman 1989; Khoury and Kostiner 1991) Meanwhile, the group's honor (*sharaf*) is important for creating internal solidarity among the members of each individual tribe (Abu-Lughod 1986, 40; al-Aref 1999).

Bedouin interaction with modern states has been significant. This includes attempts by states to "modernize" and sedentarize the Bedouin or even to incorporate them into the machinery of the state. The modern state faced great difficulties in dealing with Bedouin control over the desert and trade routes. As a result, sedentarization projects were implemented to reduce the Bedouin threat to the central power of modern and nation-states. Incorporating the Bedouin into a central administrative center constituted a significant attempt to rule them.

Eugene Rogan (1999) notes that the Tanzimat of the Ottoman Empire represented the first significant step toward incorporating the Bedouin into a central administrative center. In trying to settle intertribal disputes, the Ottomans were the first to initiate sedentarization plans, especially by introducing land laws. In 1858, as part of the Tanzimat, the Ottoman authorities decided to undertake a large-scale land reform including Palestine (Rogan 1999). The Ottoman Tanzimat and land codes affected the Bedouin in the Middle East, including the Naqab Bedouin since the Ottoman land codes defined most of the land as belonging to the state.

Following the Ottoman Empire's unsuccessful sedentarization plans (Nasasra 2011b), other countries in the Middle East initiated similar plans. Saudi Arabia is an example of a centralized settlement project initiated by a Middle Eastern state. The Saudi attempt to consolidate authority in the hands of a ruling dynasty is an obvious example of sedentarization plans. Since the foundation of the Saudi state in 1932, official policy for controlling the Bedouin has shifted from religious reasons toward the financial co-option of Bedouin tribal leaders in order to secure their loyalty (Fabietti 2000). The intention behind Ibn Saud's plans for settling the Bedouin tribes was to reduce tribal raids and strengthen his centralized authority. His policy involved bringing the pastoral tribes under his control by inducing them to give up raiding and nomadism (Hourani 1991; Musil 1928). Fearing his control, the Bedouin rebelled against Ibn Saud and continued their cross-border relations.

The Bedouin tribes faced different policies in different countries. One can argue that in some cases, the Bedouin played a critical role in state-formation processes. In Syria, for example, the Bedouin were contained by a French system of divide and rule. They were not challenged by the French to settle down but were given the opportunity to set up their own state (Chatty 2010). Following the departure of the French from Syria, and similar to the situation in Saudi Arabia, the Bedouin in Syria faced settlement plans. The Bedouin in the newly independent Syria were perceived as a state within a state that challenged the central government (Rae 2000, 4). As a result, the Bedouin were regarded as a threat to the settled population and to the state's central authority.

As discussed by Chatty (2010, 36), the Syrian government wanted the Bedouin to move toward settlement and to follow the laws of the state. It therefore adopted a policy of settling the Bedouin as a key strategy for incorporating them into the state's administrative system. Chatty describes these new Syrian policies aimed at the Bedouin as "deeply offensive" to this population (37). Transforming the Bedouin into "good citizens" and making them "liable" to Syrian law was official policy and included in the constitution, where one article states that "the government shall undertake to settle the nomads" (36).

Unlike Syria, one can argue that Jordan represents the best case of Bedouin tribes having been integrated into the machinery of the state. After the formation of the Jordanian state under the British Mandate, the Bedouin tribes were the backbone of the Jordanian regime. To this day, the tribes maintain special relations with the monarchy (Alon 2005, 213). Beginning in 1917, the Bedouin of Jordan were allowed to continue their semi-settled way of life. According to Alon (2005, 213), the British sought to implement their rule by increasing the tribal shaikhs' administrative duties and responsibilities, a system of control (divide and rule) similar to that used by other colonial states in the region.

The Jordanian case shows clearly how the Mandatory government administered through divide and rule. In 1929, the Bedouin under the

Mandatory government were incorporated into the state system, especially when they became a significant part of the special army unit known as the Desert Patrol (Glubb 1976). The Jordanian government also made efforts to incorporate the tribes into the state. According to Kostiner (2000, 92), Sharif ʿAbdallah's significant achievement was "the pacification, incorporation, and co-optation of the tribes into the machinery of the state." Unlike other governments in the region, the government in Transjordan did not try to destroy tribalism but worked to enhance tribal practices and politics and even to revive their identity (Alon 2005, 214).

If we look at modern states, such as Jordan, Egypt, Syria, and Lebanon, we can observe different approaches in dealing with the Bedouin tribes. In Saudi Arabia, according to Kostiner (2000), the tribes were at the heart of both military and political power and expanded the state's territories. However, tribal power under the Saudi state was severely restricted. In other cases, such as Jordan, tribes were integrated into the state. In Egypt, the tribes have always been in a fragile position in relation to the state. The Bedouin in Sinai faced both Israeli and Egyptian rule (Lavie 1990).

The case of the Bedouin in Jordan is a good example of how the Bedouin were treated as part of and integrated into a new nation-state. As Kostiner (2000, 89) notes, after 1921 the Bedouin tribes in Transjordan constituted half of the population. Bedouin tribes were an important component of the Jordanian army and the Arab Legion, and Glubb Pasha established a special Desert Patrol consisting entirely of Bedouin soldiers (Glubb 1976). The Bedouin tribes continued to play a major role in the Kingdom of Jordan.

If we look at the situation of Bedouin across the Middle East in general, we can see that during the nineteenth and the twentieth centuries they were increasingly incorporated into centralized state systems. Transforming the Bedouin into good citizens and making them liable to state laws was the most common policy adopted by the Middle East states toward the Bedouin communities.

## The Southern Palestine Bedouin and Ottoman Rule

For almost 400 years Palestine was controlled by the Ottoman Empire (1516–1917), and from 1516 the Naqab and Biʾr al-Sabaʿ (Bilad Ghaza) region was ruled from either Gaza or Jerusalem (al-Aref 1999, 31–32). The Ottoman era in Palestine was the longest in Bedouin history, and the Biʾr al-Sabaʿ Bedouin remember it as a tough and oppressive experience that left them antagonistic toward the empire. Ottoman policy toward the tribes of southern Palestine became apparent following the establishment of a new administrative center in Biʾr al-Sabaʿ in 1900 from which the power of the state would emanate.

As with their policies in Transjordan, Ottoman attempts to pacify the tribes in southern Palestine were ineffectual. As a result of marginalizing the frontier areas, the Ottomans were unable to achieve any significant level of control over the Bedouin tribes. This marginalization, combined with their oppressive policies toward the Bedouin, led to significant resistance from the local tribes.

Bedouin tribes populated several parts of Palestine, including the Naqab and Biʾr al-Sabaʿ in the south and parts of the Galilee in northern Palestine. The Ottoman authorities created the subdistrict of Biʾr al-Sabaʿ as a separate *kaza*, or jurisdiction, in 1901 (PRO, FO 195/2106). Until then, the Arabs of Biʾr al-Sabaʿ were called "*ʿurban Ghaza*" (*Al-ʿArab* newspaper, Jerusalem, 28 April 1934). Southern Palestine had been inhabited for centuries by Bedouin tribes, mainly seminomadic pastoralists. British archival reports from 1933 note that "the Negev [Biʾr al-Sabaʿ], as this Southern part of Palestine is called, is inhabited almost entirely by Bedouin tribes" (GB99, KCLMA O'Connor 3/14/53).

Under Ottoman rule, Bedouin tribes accounted in 1914 for 55,000 people. The British census undertaken in 1922 estimated their number at 71,115. Muhsam (1966, 9–24) estimates that by 1946, Bedouin numbers were between 65,000 and 90,000. Under Ottoman and British rule, the nine main tribal confederations were the Tayaha, Tarabin, ʿAzazma, ʿHanajreh, Jabarat, Saʾidiyeen, Aheiwat, and Jahalin (al-Aref 1999; Marx 1967; Nasasra 2011b). Other Bedouin tribes that had inhabited the Biʾr al-Sabaʿ region for centuries included the Maʿaniya Bedouin, along with other small tribes that relied mainly on agriculture for their livelihood.

The Ottomans controlled Palestine since 1519, and until 1900 Ottoman-Bedouin relations had been dominated by Bedouin clashes with the policies of the Ottoman state (Bailey 1980, 35–80; Maʾoz, 1968). Despite ongoing disputes among Bedouin tribes, Ottoman attempts to stabilize the Biʾr al-Sabaʿ had been ineffective (Abu Saad and Creamer 2012), and only after

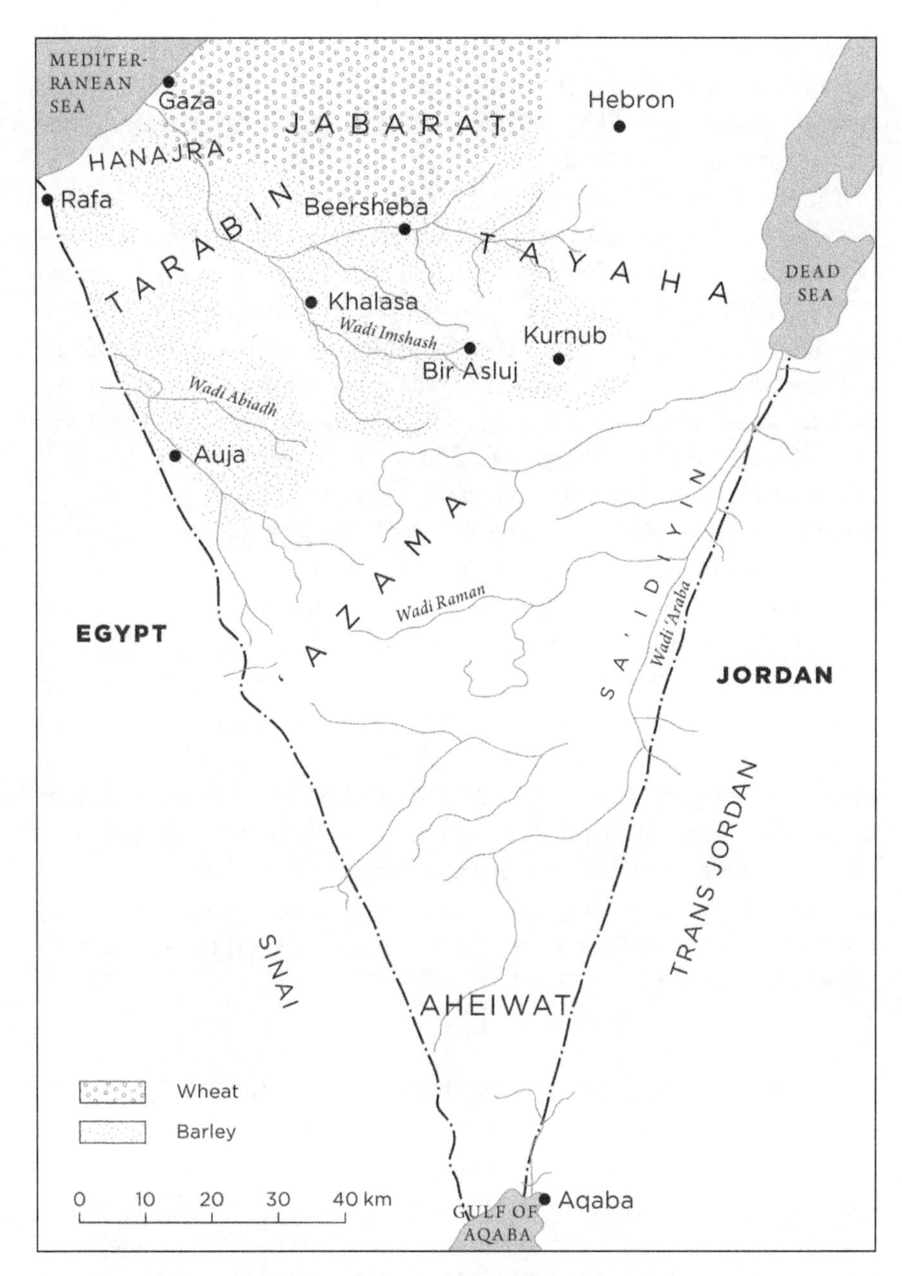


FIGURE 2.1 Tribal map of southern Palestine Bedouins. *Source*: Author.

Beersheba was established as a new administrative center in 1900 did Ottoman officials begin to pay closer attention to the region. Despite local resistance, such tactics also included efforts to undertake censuses of the nomadic populations (Deringil 2003, 321).

The Beersheba Bedouin, who often refer to themselves as the Arabs of Biʾr al-Sabaʿ (*ʿurban al-sabaʾ* and sometimes *ʿurban Ghaza*), dominated one of the most strategic regions in the Middle East, including its historical and archaeological sites. In writing about the region in the 1930s, Major C. S. Jarvis, the governor of Sinai, noted: "the principal importance of the Negeb in Byzantine times was its value as a trade route. Situated . . . between the Mediterranean and the Red Sea, and by land between Palestine, Egypt and Syria, it was the key to three or four of the most important trade routes of the Middle East" (PRO, FO 371/20885; also Levin, Kark and Galilee 2010, 1–18). Jarvis also spoke of a number of historical (e.g., Byzantine) towns that confirmed the Naqab's historical past: Khalasa, Reheibe, al-ʿAuja, Sbeite, Wadi al-Shalala, Tal Jamah, Tal al-Faraaʾ, Tal Al-Hissy, Tal al-Malah, ʿAbda, and Qurnub (PRO, FO 371/61868). Further detailed knowledge on the distribution of Bedouin tribes was provided by the Palestine Exploration Fund (PEF) in 1881. As a result of touring Palestine, the fund's team produced twenty-six maps, including several that recorded the distribution of the Bedouin of southern Palestine, titled "Negeb or South Country" and other maps titled "Beersheba Junction" (Julian Asquith [Lord Oxford] private archive, Somerset). The PEF maps, particularly the one relating to the Bedouin of Biʾr al-Sabaʿ, are regarded as some of the earliest maps to cover the distribution of the Bedouin in detail while also dividing them according to territory and regions.

## Military Instability in Southern Palestine During the Late Ottoman Era

Under Ottoman rule, Palestine was divided into the Northern District, Jerusalem, and the Southern District (that includes Beersheba, Jaffa, and Gaza) (Esco Foundation for Palestine 1947, 297–301). In 1901, the Ottomans created the subdistrict of Biʾr al-Sabaʿ as a separate jurisdiction or *kaza* (PRO, FO 195/2106).

An autonomous Egypt under Muhammad ʿAli was becoming aggressive by the early nineteenth century. In 1831 Ibrahim Pasha's army captured the

Biʾr al-Sabaʿ from the Ottomans (Maʾoz 1968, 130), only to withdraw in 1840 after a relatively brief period of rule over Syria and Palestine (al-Aref 1999, 243).The Biʾr al-Sabaʿ Bedouin, being strongly opposed to Egyptian invasion of their land and antagonistic toward the conquerors, had rebelled in 1834 against Ibrahim Pasha (Maʾoz 1968, 14) who, because of tribal power and independence in southern Palestine and Transjordan, had struggled to dominate them (Bailey 1980, 38,60–61). Following Egypt's withdrawal from southern Palestine, the British extended their influence over the whole area, formally taking control over Egypt in 1882 (Shuqayr 1991, 727). Lord Cromer, appointed as governor to stabilize the situation (588–589), made attempts from 1892 onward to demarcate the borders between the Sinai Peninsula and southern Palestine.

Given the British presence in Egypt after 1882, Ottoman control of the southern border of the Jerusalem district and southern Palestine became important for security (Avci 2009, 973). Avci notes that until the end of the nineteenth century the Ottomans had shown no interest in the Beersheba area and did not attempt to develop it administratively. Only by recreating Beersheba as a new administrative center in 1900 was a direct connection established between the Ottoman regime and the Bedouin. After this, Ottoman policies shifted toward encouraging the Bedouin to settle around the new city and benefit from its administrative services.

Bailey (1990, 324–25) points out that although the Bedouin in the desert had ignored the existence of the Ottomans and carried on with their traditional way of life, they also benefitted from Ottoman weaknesses in the desert and had great success with dealings in the international arena, serving as guides and assistants for the French and acquiring money and other economic benefits. During the nineteenth century, Bedouin in the various districts effectively controlled the desert trade routes, levying charges on traders and peasants who passed through their regions while transporting goods (such as wheat) to other places (Gottheil 1986, 216–17).

### *Ottoman Weakness: Intertribal Disputes in the Nineteenth and Twentieth Centuries*

With the departure of the Egyptians, the Ottomans were again in nominal control of southern Palestine and began to pay greater attention to the local dynamics of what had become a strategic border area with Egypt. In addition, as the empire passed through the modernization and bureaucratic reforms that typified the Tanzimat Era (1840–1861), the Ottomans set out to impose tighter control over the Naqab and southern Palestine. Initially, some of the older styles of interaction continued, and the policies of some of the Ottoman pashas toward the Bedouin tended to be conciliatory. According to Maʾoz, "Many Turkish Pashas not only refrained from fighting the Bedouin tribes, but actually flattered them and even occasionally cooperated with their chieftains to share the fruits of misdeeds" (1968, 129). The newspaper *Falastin* (*La Palestine*) reported in 1916 that the Ottoman governors recognized that the Bedouin would refuse to accept any plans imposed on them and held that cooperation would be the best strategy to deal with their affairs (*Falastin*, June 7, 1916).

During this period the primary aim of Ottoman policies toward the Bedouin of southern Palestine was to prevent them from dominating key economic and desert routes. Ottoman officialdom therefore attempted to contain the Bedouin by trying to settle them, bribing their leaders, destroying their forces, or attempting to weaken them through military action. However, most of these policies were ineffective since the Bedouin, including those in southern Palestine, continued to disobey the authorities and to carry on their strategy of targeting Ottoman resources using a variety of tactics. Thus, "the powerful Sinai-Negeb Bedouin, the ʿAzazma, Tayaha, and Tarabin, made deep incursions into the area" (Maʾoz 1968, 146).

From around 1799, fresh tribal migrations into the Naqab had started to upset the balance, and disputes continued through most of the next century as the tribal confederations worked out new territorial boundaries. For example, according to Bailey (1980, 38), two major tribes, the Tayaha and the Tarabin, conquered the Naqab in 1799, and Maʾoz states that the area of southern Palestine, especially the Naqab and Sinai, was controlled by three leading Bedouin tribes, the Tayaha, Tarabin, and ʿAzazma, who were also active in the area of Beersheba and Gaza (Maʾoz 1968, 130–131). The Ottomans failed to have any influence over this intracommunal fighting. Commenting on Ottoman Bedouin relations during the Tanzimat, Maʾoz states that "[the] government was unable to gain the upper hand over the nomads" (148). According to oral histories from Bedouin elders, in order to prevent the disputes between the Tayaha and the Tarabin, the Ottomans established a police post in Qalaʾat Futeis aimed at securing the border between the two tribal confederations (interview with al-ʾAtaika, Rahat, May 2014). A British explorer, C. R. Conder, observed in 1875 that "the Tayaha Arabs are at war with the ʿAzazma" without any successful intervention or attempts on the part of the Ottomans to stop the conflict between the two confederations (Bailey 1980, 35). Avci sees this as a war for territorial control; in 1888, government officials were sent from Jerusalem and Gaza to mediate between the ʿAzazma and the Tayaha in an attempt to settle the dispute (Avci 2009, 974). Gerber (1986, 34) also identified the conflict as a prolonged attempt to control land in the southern district of Palestine. This dispute continued for many years since the absence of the Ottoman government in the desert weakened their efforts to control violent confrontations between Bedouin tribes in the southern district. As *Falastin* reported, only after the Ottomans had established Biʾr al-Sabaʿ and started to have a presence in the region did internal Bedouin disputes show signs of diminishing (*Falastin*, June 6, 1913).

More fighting erupted in the Tarabin-ʿAzazma dispute of 1887, once again because of a quarrel over cultivable land. After three years of fighting and considerable loss of life, the government mediated successfully between the tribes to stop the conflict (Shuqayr 1991, 587). The Ottoman reaction to this particular dispute was to punish the tribes by sending in troops under the command of Rostum Pasha, who used various policies to impose order, including beatings, imprisoning shaikhs, and other coercive tactics. The last significant intertribal conflict in southern Palestine under Ottoman rule was in the early twentieth century, in 1907, between the Zullam tribes and the Yatatwa (Yatatwa is used for the Palestinians living in Hebron area in the town of Yata). The confrontation arose between these two groups over the cultivation and ownership of a piece of land in Tal ʿArad, which Avci calls "Masfara" land (Avci 2009, 974). This conflict continued for seven years, being halted just before the outbreak of the First World War; the dispute ultimately concerned which of the two tribes would control an area of some 20,000 *dunums* of land at Tal ʿArad (al-Aref 1999, 194).

The dispute between the Zullam tribes and the Yatatwa remained strong in the collective memory of subsequent generations. My interviews with Bedouin in their seventies indicate that, in their opinion, the Ottomans had been particularly feeble and indecisive in bringing intertribal disputes to an end. The Ottomans used fraudulent tactics by inviting representatives of both parties to peace talks and then prosecuting, arresting, or exiling them. This showed Ottoman weaknesses in controlling such disputes (interview with ʿAbdallah al-Nasasrah, August 2011). Oral histories reveal that the Ottomans had adopted a number of policies in this particular war. One was to confiscate the disputed land and claim it as government property (or land of the sultan—*jiftlik*), and then lease it to other tribes (*Falastin*, June 6, 1913). A second tactic was directed at the leadership of the tribes. Some of the tribal shaikhs would be arrested, imprisoned, and taken to Istanbul, where some were then executed. After such arrests, the Bedouin would complain to Istanbul and push for the release their shaikhs (al-Aref 1999, 196; Avci 2009).

It is important to note that most of these intertribal conflicts ended of their own accord or after a process of mediation by other powerful tribes, without the intervention of the government. On the whole they were resolved by indigenous means, including adoption of a strict code that involved rules of honor and implementation of a tribal court system.

There were also other reasons why the Ottomans sought to end the intertribal fighting. One of the interviewees stated that Ottoman rule at the beginning of the twentieth century was ineffective since the Ottomans were busy elsewhere, were focused on their war plans, and were preoccupied with building roads and railways. Certainly Glubb Pasha (John Bagot Glubb), who had a long history of working with Bedouin tribes in the Middle East, took the view that the Ottomans did not control the Bedouin tribes: "The Turks had never been able to control the tribes . . . and their natural turbulence had been further increased by the excitement of campaigns fought over their country and the absence of any government" (MECA\GB 165-0119). Some Bedouin interviewees also mentioned the complexity of Ottoman-Bedouin relations, particularly with regard to the weaknesses of the Ottomans in the desert. In fact, the Ottomans were effectively absent from the southern part of Palestine until 1900, when they built the city of Biʾr al-Sabaʿ.

With the British occupation of Egypt in 1882, the Ottomans became even more focused on the border with Sinai and the development of a military infrastructure to protect it. This distracted the Ottomans from internal Bedouin related issues in which they were less disposed to become involved. Ultimately, the interconnectedness of the Egyptian/British occupations, the growing significance of the Suez Canal, the lack of any real governmental authority in the Biʾr al-Sabaʿ, and the new global strategic framework for military action meant that controlling Bedouin dynamics in the Biʾr al-Sabaʿ became important to the Ottomans in a way it had not been before. This was the beginning of a new period in the southern Palestine where the Ottomans began to impose themselves on the Bedouin in new ways. Up until this point whatever attempts had been made had achieved only limited success.

## New Attempts at Governance: Biʾr al-Sabaʿ as an Administrative and Economic Center

The period from 1900 until 1917 marked a new era in Ottoman attempts to integrate and control the Biʾr al-Sabaʿ Bedouin through different integration policies that linked the frontiers of the empire to its central authority in Istanbul.[1] Since their oppressive policies had not worked, they adopted a new approach toward controlling the Bedouin: facilitating their entry into positions of governance. This dramatic alteration in Ottoman policy was implemented in 1900 by founding the administrative center of Biʾr al-Sabaʿ and linking the Bedouin to the urban centers in Palestine through road and railway construction. Until the 1860s the Ottoman authorities had applied a power strategy as a tactic for settling intertribal disputes in southern Palestine (Avci 2009, 969). Since this proved ineffective their policies shifted. This was apparent in the hope that the power of the state would emanate from Biʾr al-Sabaʿ. Transjordan adopted a similar policy of establishing administrative centers in an attempt to rule the Bedouin (Rogan 1999, 52–55). Cultivating a stable relationship with the local Bedouin and their leaders across the region was a new strategy for the Ottomans (Deringil 2003).

During the four hundred years or so that the Ottomans had controlled Palestine the Biʾr al-Sabaʿ had been ruled from either Gaza or Jerusalem (al-Aref 1999, 31–32), with Gaza acting as the administrative center of the Biʾr al-Sabaʿ and the seat of the Ottoman governor during the nineteenth century (Bailey 1980, 75). According to Bedouin oral testimonies, Biʾr al-Sabaʿ was a central economic region for tribes from all over the Middle East and a vital watering place, though part of the land it occupied was owned by the ʿAzazma. Encouraging the tribes to settle and use the government facilities had become a key policy in the Ottoman approach to the Biʾr al-Sabaʿ Bedouin, along with arresting and even exiling or executing shaikhs (Avci 2009). Some policies worked; others were resisted. When Rashid Pasha, governor of Syria, initiated a new strategy in 1870 to force the Bedouin in the Gaza area to settle by providing permanent buildings and huts, the Bedouin resisted his plan and killed fifteen of his soldiers who had been sent to implement the scheme. As a result, a punitive force was sent to arrest certain shaikhs and to confiscate their livestock in the name of stopping Bedouin resistance (Palmer 1871, 389).

By the second half of the nineteenth century, the Ottomans began to find it difficult to control the Bedouin and put more effort into facilitating Bedouin settlement (Avci 2009). Their policies toward the Bedouin tribes in Transjordan also shifted toward sedentarization plans (Rogan 1999), fitting in both regions into the rubric of imposed settlement plans and suppression mechanisms. Toward the end of the century, in an attempt to impose order, the Ottomans began establishing police posts across the frontier (southern Palestine and Transjordan). For example, they built police barracks in Transjordan and in various towns in southern Palestine to enhance their own security and control the tribes (Rogan 1999, 67). In 1894, Rostum Pasha, governor of Gaza, tried to impose order in Southern Palestine by establishing Qala'at Futeis. This was a police and government outpost in al-Jahir,

FIGURE 2.2 The police post in Qala'at Futeis (Wadi al-Mlieh), built by the Ottoman governor Rostum Pasha, 1894. *Source*: Photo by the author, September 2014.

north-west of Beersheba. This new policy resulted from the failure of the old tactic of punishing the Bedouin. According to Bedouin oral stories, the Ottomans aimed at establishing a secure border between the Tayaha and the Tarabin tribes by establishing this police post (interviews with Haj al-Buhairi, Abu Samara, October 2014).

For political, administrative, and economic reasons the next logical step was to establish a larger and more permanent administrative center in the region. In June 1899 the Ottomans decided to transform Biʾr al-Sabaʿ into a new sub-district center for the Bedouin tribes and to separate them from Gaza (Avci 2009, 973). As a result, they were detached from the Gaza sub-district and from direct governance from Jerusalem. Biʾr al-Sabaʿ became a new sub-district (*kaza*) in 1901 with the new city of Biʾr al-Sabaʿ at its center (PRO, FO 195/2106). Tevfik Bey was in charge of forming the new *kaza* of Biʾr al-Sabaʿ (Deringil 2003, 334). With an area of some 3,144,000 acres, the Biʾr al-Sabaʿ sub-district made up approximately half of the country (PRO, FO 371/61868).

Concurrently, the Ottomans were building administrative centers in Transjordan, including such facilities as schools and mosques (Rogan 1999, 61). In southern Palestine, the city of Beersheba was built on ʿAzazma land, after the Ottomans had purchased 480 acres from Shaikh Hassan al-Malta, the powerful ʿAzazma chief (Abu Rabia 2001, 8–10; Abu Hussein and McKay 2003, 112–113; Nasasra 2011, 305–325). British archival reports confirm that 2000 *dunums* were purchased from the ʿAzazma shaikh for this purpose (Avci 2009, 977; Nasasra 2011b). The establishment of the government building (*konak-saraya*) was the most important symbol of Ottoman rule over the desert region of southern Palestine. As part of the project in Beersheba, the government built a railway station, a tribal court, a Shariaʾ court, schools, the governor's office, a post office, a police post, a Bedouin market, two schools for Bedouin boys, and an agricultural school (Nasasra 2014).

Naciye Hanim recorded how, following completion of the government building, "people flocked to [it] to register themselves and settle around it. They requested that a mosque be built alongside it as an imperial gift and that all the buildings should bear the name of the August Personage" (Deringil 2003, 334). The newspaper *Falastin* reported that Asef Beik al-Dimashqi, the Ottoman governor of Biʾr al-Sabaʿ, built the mosque on a waqf land donated by the Bedouin after collecting donations from Bedouin shaikhs. Although he had moved to Jaffa as the new governor, he completed the mosque project six years after he had left Biʾr al-Sabaʿ (*Falastin*, April 20,

FIGURE 2.3 The Ottoman train station of Biʾr al-Sabaʿ. *Source*: Photo by the author.

1913), indicating that he had devoted particular attention to developing this amenity for the Bedouin.

According to oral history, the creation of Ottoman Biʾr al-Sabaʿ can be viewed partly as a result of collaboration between the ʿAzazma Bedouin and the Ottoman administration to halt tribal confrontations and impose order in the area. When it came to building government bases, cooperation with the local Bedouin leaders was a key Ottoman policy (Nasasra 2011b). Other reasons included facilitating the collection of taxes from the Bedouin tribes.

FIGURE 2.4 The *Konak* (Saraya) of Biʾr al-Sabaʿ was the first government house to be built in Biʾr al-Sabaʿ in 1901 by the Ottomans. *Source*: PRO, FO 195/2106.

The Ottomans adopted a similar tax policy in Transjordan where tribes were asked to pay taxes on their economic activities (Rogan 1999, 188).

Beersheba started to grow rapidly, and by 1914 the town had a population of 1000 inhabitants, with 200 houses and fifty shops (Abu Rabia 2001). Merchants from Gaza and Hebron moved to the new town, building new houses and economic centers. A number of leading Bedouin shaikhs (such as Hamad al-Sufi, the chief of the Tarabin) also moved to the town and built new houses there. As in Transjordan, erecting other government buildings added to the administrative role of Biʾr al-Sabaʿ (Avci 2009, 977). An agricultural school for thirty Bedouin students was also built in Beersheba (PRO, FO 195/2287).

## The Dispute Between the Bedouin Mayor of Biʾr al-Sabaʿ and the Ottoman Governor

Although the establishment of Biʾr al-Sabaʿ was of great significance for administrative control in the region, I argue that it did not lead to total stability and control over the Bedouin. Many of the older dynamics of

Bedouin-Ottoman relations persisted, and the Ottoman governors continued to report unstable conditions in their districts. Hamad al-Sufi, the Bedouin mayor of Biʾr al-Sabaʿ, warned the Ottoman governors to amend their policies toward the Bedouin; otherwise, the tribes would rebel against them.[2] Similarly, Mahmud Nadim Bey, *Qaimmakam* of Biʾr al-Sabaʿ, informed Istanbul in 1913 of problems with the Bedouin under his rule:

> The idea of an insurrection against Turkish rule is gaining ground. There is a continual correspondence between the Arabs on either side of the frontier, and the leading shaikh of his district, a certain Hamad al-Sufi, who is also Mayor of Beersheba, has declared that, unless the officials mend their ways, there will be a rising similar to Yemen. Mahmoud Nadim Bey said that he was powerless to prevent the abuses that were practised before his eyes because he was not in favour at Jerusalem or with the Committee and he was himself a victim of constant persecution.
>
> (PRO, FO 195/2452/1153)

Hamad al-Sufi used his status as a powerful shaikh and as mayor of Beersheba to revolt against the Ottomans in southern Palestine—another example of the impossibility of controlling the influential Bedouin leaders. The Ottomans also faced uprisings among local Bedouin tribes in Transjordan where the Karak revolt against Ottoman rule in 1910 was indicative of Bedouin resistance. The Bedouin rebellion targeted the elements that represented Ottoman rule in the Karak region (Rogan 1999, 198).

Another Ottoman report from 1914 shows the complex relationship between the Biʾr al-Sabaʿ Bedouin and the Ottoman regime in southern Palestine. The main dispute involved securing Ottoman recognition of Bedouin land claims. The Bedouin in Transjordan and southern Palestine petitioned the government to acknowledge these claims (Rogan 1999, 87). The Bedouin clashed with Ottoman officials over both land ownership and taxes, and disputed claims escalated into direct confrontations with the officials. Sometimes the gendarmes treated the Bedouin harshly, which led to complaints and protests such as this one over

> the maltreatment by gendarmes some weeks ago of a shaikh belonging to the important Tarabin tribe inhabiting the country south of Beersheba. An agreement was recently arrived at and the Bedouin asked that their full rights

> of ownership should be recognized as of old; but the authorities at Jerusalem refused to do so notwithstanding the urgent representation of the present qa-immaqam. Gendarmes were accordingly sent to collect the produce as usual and, on finding the shaikh recalcitrant, they proceeded to beat him and use the customary methods of intimidation.
> (PRO, FO 195/2452/1153)

As confrontations like this escalated over land and Bedouin properties, the Ottoman government usually adopted the tactic of punishing tribes by using the gendarmerie. This was also true of southern Palestine and Transjordan. In response, the Bedouin often refused to cooperate with the Ottoman officials. They challenged the authorities by protesting, leaving their encampments, and temporarily crossing the borders.

Despite persistent disputes over tax collection, Ottoman archival reports show that Bedouin tribes paid taxes to the Ottoman authorities for securing their land ownership and for their crops. For example, an Ottoman report from Jerusalem stated that the Bedouin of Beersheba paid land agriculture taxes—the "tithe"—and taxes for their flocks. Sir Nicholas O'Connor (British Ambassador at Constantinople) noted that in June 1907 the Bedouin in Beersheba had paid taxes of TL10,000 (PRO, FO 195/2452/1153), compared with the sum of TL20,000 they had paid the previous year (PRO, FO 195/2255).[3] As interaction between the Ottoman government and the Bedouin in Biʾr al-Sabaʿ increased, *Falastin* continued to report on the increasing amount of money, or tithe (*aʾshar*), that was collected from the Bedouin.

The full cooperation of the Bedouin shaikhs with the *mutasarif* of Jerusalem was acknowledged by Bedouin acceptance of tithe collection. After the establishment of Biʾr al-Sabaʿ, the number of visits to the Bedouin encampments by Ottoman officials increased, which in turn increased the level of trust on both sides. In a speech in front of the *mutasarif* in Biʾr al-Sabaʿ, one of the Bedouin shaikhs declared that the Ottoman government had reached an agreement with the Bedouin about the amount of yearly tithe to be paid to the government (*Falastin*, June 6, 1913).

The fact that the Ottoman authorities collected land taxes from the Bedouin is a clear recognition of Bedouin land ownership (Kram 2012, 136). As Abu Hussain and McKay (2003, 122) point out, the Ottomans had recognized Bedouin land ownership even before the land codes of 1858 were enacted.

After Biʾr al-Sabaʿ was established in 1901, Ottoman policies concerning the frontier of the empire shifted toward integrating the Bedouin into the central government body in Istanbul and improving services for Bedouin communities. As a result, the Ottomans tried to interact more with the Bedouin and even asked them to pay taxes for their land and agriculture. The fact that the Ottomans managed to access Bedouin areas in 1907 and collect taxes from them confirms the strategic shift of their policies toward the frontier and its marginalized communities.

After the establishment of Biʾr al-Sabaʿ, *Falastin* also reported on the growing interest of the Ottomans in developing the Beersheba region and improving government services on the frontiers. In 1913, Jawdat Pasha, the Ottoman *mutasarif* of Jerusalem, visited Biʾr al-Sabaʿ and initiated plans for linking Biʾr al-Sabaʿ to the central government and to other urban centers. The *mutasarif* reinforced the Sultan's policies for developing the region by meeting tribal leaders and visiting Bedouin camps in Biʾr al-Sabaʿ. For instance, linking Biʾr al-Sabaʿ to the rest of Palestine would be accomplished by building new roads between Hebron, Biʾr al-Sabaʿ, Gaza, and Jaffa (*Falastin*, June 6, 1913). Digging wells was also central to improving agricultural methods and water supplies.

The *mutasarif* stressed the importance of training Bedouin boys in up-to-date farming techniques at the new agricultural school. He also proposed plans for improving the education system for the Bedouin and asked the tribes to send their boys to study in Biʾr al-Sabaʿ. According to *Falastin*, the Bedouin had already begun to donate money to be used for general government services and to improve the education system (*Falastin*, June 6, 1913).

The Ottoman government provided loans for the Bedouin for improving their agricultural methods. The Ottoman *mutasarif* encouraged the Bedouin to submit claims for loans from the agricultural bank via a policy that aimed to improve their economic situation and to prevent the selling of land to Jewish settlers. This was after the *mutasarif* of Jerusalem had been informed that there were a number of Zionist attempts to buy land from Bedouin shaikhs in southern Palestine (*Falastin*, June 6, 1913).

In conclusion, the relationship between the Bedouin and the Ottomans marked a turning point for Ottoman rule in southern Palestine and Beersheba after 1900. In the early 1800s, Ottoman involvement in the internal issues of the Bedouin was limited. Before 1900 Biʾr al-Sabaʿ did not occupy a place of any significance in Ottoman policies. According to oral history narratives, Ottoman rule is remembered by the Bedouins as a tough regime that mostly oppressed them by using power and deceitful tactics. This would suggest that there were constant attempts at control, even if these were always resisted. Bedouin natural resistance can thus be understood as a tactic for marginalizing Ottoman rule.

THREE

# British Colonial Policies for the Southern Palestine and Transjordan Bedouin, 1917–1948

BRITAIN'S EFFECTIVE CONTROL of Palestine lasted for over thirty years, from 1917 to 1948. This included occupation of southern Palestine during World War I, during which the British actively sought a relationship with the Bedouin that was different from what the tribes had experienced under the Ottoman Empire. However, before they could capture Biʾr al-Sabaʿ, the British had to take control of Gaza and defeat the Ottomans.

Archival reports indicate the difficulties of occupying Gaza. General Sir Archibald Murray of the Egyptian Expeditionary Force described the failure of two attempts in early 1916:

> It will be remembered that two attempts to take Gaza were made, one late in March, the second in mid-April. In the first, in which our losses were about 4,000, we got to the outskirts of Gaza, but had to withdraw; in the second, when we faced a stronger enemy, the casualties were heavier, numbering 7,000 and the force made less progress towards the town.
> (GB99, KCLMA ALLENBY 4/3)

Some months later, in June 1917, Lieutenant General Philip W. Chetwode, commanding the Eastern Force, commented that

> the Advantages which we should have in attacking the enemy's might at Gaza are our knowledge of the ground, the fact that our trenches are within assaulting

> distance of the enemy [and] good observation and sufficient water for the troops. The disadvantages would be those inherent in attacking the enemy at the point where he is strongest, undoubtedly a very expensive operation.
> (GB99, KCLMA BARTHOLOMEW 1/2)

On their third attempt, the British, now under the command of General Sir Edmund Allenby, successfully broke the Turkish Gaza–Beersheba defensive line, making the line an easy target. After this, Allenby and a powerful attacking force succeeded in capturing the town of Beersheba in a single day despite stubborn resistance by the Ottomans (GB99, KCLMA Allenby), causing heavy Ottoman casualties (GB99, KCLMA Ismay 3/2/108). The clashes between the two empires brought victory for the British and defeat for the Ottomans.

The British occupied Jerusalem on December 11, 1917, with Allenby officially entering the city on foot through the Jaffa gate as ʿIzat Bey, the Ottoman governor, was leaving it (McKernan 1993, 171). In Beersheba, the British began to exercise their new policies toward the Bedouin by choosing a number of leading shaikhs to act as representatives of the main tribes. The city continued its role as the capital of the southern district (*kaza*) of Palestine and the seat of the district governor (*qaimmaqam*) (interview with Lord Oxford, Somerset, July 2008).

With the creation of the British Mandate, Palestine was divided into districts and subdistricts, including Jerusalem, Jaffa, Gaza, Hebron, and Biʾr al-Sabaʿ (Abu Rabia 2001, 64). The first British military governor appointed in Biʾr al-Sabaʿ was Captain B. B. Ragless (al-Aref 1999, 262). By 1931, the city served about 100,000 people from the surrounding areas. By 1945 it had a population of approximately 5,570 including villagers from Gaza and Hebron and some Bedouin shaikhs (Abu Rabia 2001, 41–43). The daily newspaper, *Falastin*, reported that property buying by Bedouin in the town of Beersheba had increased dramatically as a result of improved economic conditions. The newspaper also reported that Bedouin and Gazan merchants in Biʾr al-Sabaʿ also supplied the Bedouin with wheat, barley, and sugar (*Falastin*, September 19, 1942). Bedouin elders stated that represented among the Bedouin families that purchased property in Beersheba were tribes such as the Tarabin, the ʿAzazma (Ibn Saʾid), and the al-Sufi, as well as Gazans and Bedouin families such as al-Sanne and Abu Qarnn (interview with Hajj Mosa Abu ʿAyesh, Lakiya, September 2014).

## Biʾr al-Sabaʿ After 1917: Bedouin Shaikhs and Colonial Authorities

Once in active control of Beersheba the British administered the Bedouin through a network of military governors. Beersheba remained the main economic center for the Bedouin, and the policy of making it the administrative and control hub for the Naqab region continued. Recognizing that the shaikhs represented their tribes and were responsible for keeping them in order, the British made the shaikhs their key contact points with the tribes. This reaffirmed the traditional power relationship within the community. In the initial stages of the occupation it was deliberate British policy to build good relations with the Bedouin through their traditional structures (Abu Rabia 2001, 31–32). Under the British Mandate it was common practice to rely on indirect rule to govern tribes as was the case in Transjordan (see Alon 2005).

During the early period of the Mandate, the Bedouin shaikhs continued in their intermediary role between the people and the state, particularly with respect to maintaining law and order and collecting taxes on behalf of the central government. In fact, the British appointed a succession of Bedouin shaikhs as Beersheba mayors. Abu Rabia (2001, 41) lists some who served in this position, including ʿAli al-ʿAtawna, Hamad al- Sufi, Frieh Abu Meddein, and Hussein Abu Kaf. Shaikh Salameh Ibn Saʾid of the ʿAzazma acted as an elected deputy mayor of Beersheba. However, Lord Oxford stated that some of the Beersheba mayors were also Palestinians. For instance, Taj al-Dein Shaʿath and Shafiq Mustafa were of Gazan and Hebron lineage respectively (Lord Oxford, personal papers, Somerset, 2009). Some of these shaikhs had held powerful positions under the Ottomans and continued to do so under the British Mandate. Taj al-Dein Shaʿath, for example, was employed as mayor of Beersheba until 1947 (Bell 1983, 117).

British recognition of their legitimate position within their communities allowed these and other shaikhs to gain power by utilizing their relationship with the Mandatory authorities. The Bedouin shaikhs also found opportunities to build strong relations with the British and to improve their status in the eyes of the Mandate governors. For example, some went to Jerusalem to greet the first high commissioner, Herbert Samuel. Shaikh Frieh Abu-Meddein also represented the Bedouin clans at the first meeting of the Advisory Council in 1920 (Wasserstein 1991, 90–93).

As a result of this growing relationship between the traditional tribal leaders and the new governors, the Bedouin shaikhs acquired new avenues of contact and new methods of raising their voices. Official confirmation of their positions enabled them to establish different ways of communicating with the British authorities, such as writing formal letters. For example, one memorandum presenting Bedouin needs to the Mandatory government was written by Shaikh ʿIzat al-ʿAtawna. It was sent by Shaikh ʿIzat on behalf of the Beersheba Bedouin to the Palestine Royal Commission on February 12, 1937, and laid out key Bedouin concerns that the Mandatory authorities were expected not to ignore. These included improving educational facilities, reducing land taxation, providing agricultural loans, increasing road construction, improving water resources, improving medical treatment, allowing free trade, and making sure that Bedouin traditions were preserved (PRO, CO 733/344/4). This list and the tone of the memorandum itself provide firm evidence of agency and organization among the Beersheba Bedouin. As a result of Bedouin official letters and demands, the Mandatory authorities put greater effort into improving education and other facilities in the Beersheba region.

## *Bedouin Demands for Improved Services and Educational Facilities in Biʾr al-Sabaʿ*

On the basis of oral history accounts, archival diaries, and Palestinian newspapers, it is clear that education was a key component of Bedouin life in the Naqab and Beersheba region. Since the establishment of Sultan Abdulhamid II's tribal school in Istanbul until the late Mandatory era an educated elite existed among the Bedouin (Rogan 1996). Educated Bedouin were taught in Istanbul, Jerusalem, Safad, Gaza, and Bethlehem. Some attended religious studies in al-Azhar or even studied at the American University of Beirut. The notion of Bedouin youngsters traveling to study outside the Beersheba territory and even abroad had existed since the late Ottoman era and continued until the end of the Mandate.

Once the British controlled the region of the Naqab and Beersheba, they took significant steps to improve educational, administrative, infrastructural, and health facilities. Improving roads and railways was a key policy in enhancing their trade routes. British reports show that they realized how building railways would connect the entire Transjordan and Sinai region with the Naqab and extend their colonial influence. They were eager to develop the strategic Beersheba region by initiating "a road connection between the Gulf of ʿAqaba and the Mediterranean [that] would prove an invaluable alternative to the Suez Canal, for the transport of mail, goods and passengers" (PRO, FO 371/20885).

Colonial Office papers and documents show that improving facilities for the Bedouin was another strategic British policy. The British continued to grant free education to Bedouin boys in Beersheba: "the precedent of granting free education in certain circumstances was established in Ottoman times and has continued under the present administration" (PRO, CO 733/225/5). A 1932 report by Sir Philip Cunliffe-Lister, Principal Secretary of State for Colonies, noted that the only education facilities provided for the Bedouin were the "semi-nomadic schools of Beersheba and Gaza . . . the standard is very low and the period of schooling so short" (PRO, CO 733/220/5). Some of the leading Bedouin tribes benefited from these early dealings with the British since their sons were able to obtain a better education. Bedouin children, both boys and girls, studied at various schools in Beersheba that had been built by the British assisted by the Bedouin. The five main tribal schools in the Beersheba district—Jarawin, Abu-Sitta, Zureiyʾ, ʿHanajreh, and Jabarat—played an important role as training grounds for the next generation (Abu Rabia 2001, 73). Sir Gawain Bell (1983, 118) mentions Farid Saʿd, a principal of one of the Bedouin boarding schools who was the Arab District Officer and had graduated from the American University of Beirut. *Al-Difaʾ* newspaper reported in 1935 that the subdistrict of Beersheba had sent Ali Mohamad al-Najdi, a student from Beersheba, to pursue religious studies at al-Azhar in Cairo. The intention was to educate a number of Bedouin students at al-Azhar who would return to their district as religious leaders or mufti for the community (*al-Difaʾ*, March 31, 1935).

According to the diaries of British officials, Bedouin who had established a strong relationship with government bodies benefited from receiving education for their children. During the early 1940s a Bedouin shaikh from Beersheba approached Lord Oxford and asked for his son to be sent to study at Oxford University (Lord Oxford, personal papers, Somerset, UK). Some Bedouin who worked for the British and Ottoman government pushed them for help in obtaining advanced education abroad. It is not surprising that the majority of the Bedouin educated elite fled in 1948.

The Ottoman elementary school (*al-madrasa al-ameriya*) that had been established in Beersheba for the sons of Bedouin shaikhs continued under the British Mandate. In 1935, the school was run by Jamil Afandi ʿAbed al-Hadi, who had been brought from Qalqilya for this mission. In 1934, the school's headmaster was Farid Saʿd, who had graduated from the American University in Beirut. It was estimated that there were 340 students who were from Beersheba and the Bedouin tribes. *Al-madrasa al-ameriya* for girls in Beersheba included 150 female students and in 1935 was run by Suraya al-Ahdam and four other female teachers (*al-Difaʾ*, April 27, 1934).

Wanting something better, the shaikhs pressed the British authorities for more advanced educational opportunities. Unfortunately, the government could do very little as they had limited funding with which to expand the education system. As a result, some Bedouin shaikhs sent their children to study in high schools in Gaza and Safad. During the 1940s, other Bedouin children of the elite studied in the traditional *kuttab* system of schools, a few of which were located among various tribes in the Naqab. For example, Julian Asquith (later Lord Oxford), who was assistant district commissioner of Beersheba in 1943, founded three Bedouin schools in the Naqab, located in ʿAraʾra, Jammama, and Kseifa. He helped the Bedouin to establish a better system of education and to send their children to Gaza to continue their high school education since there was no high school in Beersheba. In an interview with Lord Oxford (September 2009, Somerset, UK) he stressed that the Bedouin were very eager to educate their children but that their economic situation did not allow them to enroll all their children in higher education. Since there was no high school for the Beersheba Bedouin, their sons were sent to study in Gaza, at high schools further north, or in Beisan, Jaffa, and Safad. According to Bedouin elders, a number of Bedouin students gained their high school education in Fallujah and Jaffa (interview with Hajj Mosa Abu ʿAyesh, Lakiya, September 2014). Despite the relative success of education for women, the Mandate faced difficulties in recruiting teachers in the area of Biʾr al-Sabaʿ, so female teachers were brought from other regions in Palestine. As reported by a Bedouin chief in 1937, "the institution of tribal lower elementary schools for bedu girls is as yet impracticable since no suitable teachers are available" (PRO, CO 733/344/4).

As reported by *Falastin*, the Bedouin themselves contributed financially to setting up schools in the Beersheba region. Shaikh Hassan al-Ifrnaji, a leading shaikh of the Tayaha, contributed all the costs for establishing a

Bedouin school located in Wadi al-Baha for his tribe. Al-Ifranji informed the *qaimmaqam* and other officials from Beersheba that the school for his tribe was sponsored entirely by himself with a contribution of 500 Palestinian lira (*Falastin*, November 5, 1942). This case is an example of significant individual Bedouin efforts to improve the education system for their children.

The teachers employed to instruct the students were mostly from what later became known as the West Bank, as well as from Gaza, Jaffa, and Egypt. There were a few from the Bedouin community itself who were trained mainly in Jaffa (interviews with Hajj Ismael al-ʾAmor and Hajj Hassan Abu Bader, September 2009). Shaikh Wassil Abu Jaber, a Bedouin leader and refugee from the Jabarat tribe who today reside in the Biqaʾ camp in Jordan, told me that some of the school's teachers came from the village of Fallujah and others were Egyptians. He remembered some of the teachers who had taught him at the Abu Jaber school in the 1930s, including Salim Abu Habib from Egypt and Muhammad Abu Zaaʾra from Fallujah (interview with Shaikh Wassil Abu Jaber/Jabarat, Biqaʾ camp, Jordan, April 2014). Local teachers were also Bedouin from a number of families, including the al-ʿAtawna tribe (*Falastin*, June 30 1934).

Interestingly, several Bedouin elders among my interviewees spoke fluent English as well as Ottoman Turkish, since some of the shaikhs and their sons studied in Istanbul in the tribal school of Sultan Abdulhamid II (Rogan 1996). Other individuals of that generation had attended college in Bethlehem, Beirut, or Hebron. The Bedouin of the Mandate period clearly valued education, and this commitment to education was passed on to their children, who, in turn, sought educational opportunities after 1948. For example, I found that members of al-ʿAtawna tribes had undertaken higher studies in Beirut. Both ʿAli and ʿIzat al-ʿAtawna (prominent leaders from the Tayaha) left before 1948 to study law in the American University of Beirut; one later worked in Kuwait, the other in Jordan. Members of al-ʿAtawna family also pursued advanced studies and typified the desire among the elite of the time to be well-educated (interview with Daham al-ʿAtawna; Shaikh Wassil Abu-Jaber, Jordan; November 2014).

Roads, railways, medical services, and water supplies also received positive attention from the colonial authorities. The authorities built a Sinai-Beersheba railway to connect Beersheba to other regions with British colonial legacies (PRO, AIR 20/612). In 1937, British officials reported construction of a road from Beersheba to ʿAqaba via Wadi ʿAraba, an important step toward upgrading roads as the Bedouin were demanding. The colonial government also spent significant amounts of money on improving water resources. The 1937 report noted that "during the last three years government has spent sum of LP[1] 4,587 on improving existing water supplies. Schemes to cost an additional 7,450 Palestinian Pounds (LP) have also been approved" (PRO, CO 733/344/4). As an added benefit, the improvements to the railway system encouraged Bedouin pilgrims to travel to Mecca by train. *Falastin* reported hundreds of Bedouin traveling via trains from Beersheba to Mecca due to the efficient system that was available to them during the Mandate era (*Falastin*, November 5, 1942).

The colonial authorities also improved medical facilities in Beersheba. According to the 1937 report, there was a small hospital with eight beds, an outpatient clinic, medical services for the boys' and girls' schools, and a medical officer who toured among the tribes (PRO, CO 733/344/4).

### *Traditional Conflict Resolution: Bedouin Tribal Courts as a Governing Mechanism*

The British saw the Bedouin system of tribunal courts as significant and wished to cement it as a key system of traditional conflict resolution for the southern Palestinian and Beersheba Bedouin (al-Aref 1974, 109–110). As in Transjordan, where the British authorities had adopted indirect rule with respect to the Bedouin tribes, British governance in Palestine allowed the Bedouin to continue their indigenous way of life after 1917.

The Bedouin warned the British authorities not to interfere with the tribal court system. As Shaikh ʿIzat al-ʿAtawna (one of the leading Bedouin shaikhs of Beersheba) reminded the British Mandate authorities in his February 1937 letter, "Beduin traditions and customs should be safeguarded and enhanced and tribal courts should be reformed. A tribal judge who does the work of a magistrate, is only paid £P.20 per annum and this salary should be raised" (PRO, CO 733/344/4).

The Bedouin regarded employing Bedouin as tribal judges as conferring high status. An Assistant Commissioner on special duty in Jerusalem in 1937 noted in an observation report, "it is considered a great honour to be appointed as a tribal judge" (PRO, CO 733/344/4). According to Aref al-Aref, the British approach was to take Bedouin customs into account and allow them to deal with their internal affairs according to their own practices (al-Aref 1999, 263; Shepherd 1999, 70). The fact that the British Mandate, like the Ottoman administration before them, recognized the Bedouin tribal courts confirms that Mandatory officials were keen to become familiar with Bedouin indigenous customs. Lord Oxford spoke about this in an interview:

> We, the British, did not solve the Bedouins' daily problems. However, we worked side by side with them and with the legal court which we established and supported, and we took tribal customs into great consideration. During my services as an assistant district commissioner in the early 1940s, I appointed eight Bedouin tribal shaikhs and judges to operate in the tribal court of Beersheba. I got to know the Bedouin shaikhs very well, and in many cases I used to follow their recommendations. Sometimes it was extremely difficult to judge cases by the British legal system, and the Bedouin did not accept this. They asked us to take their laws into account in advance in order to accept the final decisions. The Bedouin kept many secrets about tribal affairs which they did not want to bring to the British to deal with. With some particular honour and blood dispute cases, the Bedouin dealt with them and solved the cases without reporting them to the government.
>
> (INTERVIEW WITH LORD OXFORD, JUNE 2009, SOMERSET, UK)

This testimony confirms the notion that Bedouin-British relations were stable with mutual respect between the colonial power and the colonized people. To avoid clashes with the Bedouin, the British decided against working with them in a manner that might have been better suited to their own administrative systems. It is obvious that the Mandate government officials were willing to understand how the native tribunal system worked in order to avoid any friction between themselves and the Bedouin. *Falastin* reported that under British rule the tribal courts in Beersheba dealt annually with hundreds of dispute cases. The *qaimmaqam* Aref al-Aref and Ishaq al-Nashashibi, who were both Palestinians, were active in attending the tribal court meetings in Beersheba (*Falastin*, November 15, 1942). The direct intervention of the governor of Beersheba in cases of conflict resolution encouraged the courts and gave them official government status. Empowering the tribal court in Beersheba to deal with hundreds of disputes every year was a successful British tool for allowing an indigenous system to function according to local traditions and norms.

## Interterritorial Tribunal Relations

British colonial officials gave special attention to strengthening the role of Bedouin tribal courts beyond the Beersheba region. Transborder collaboration was reinforced among the region's Bedouin. The specific policy adopted by the British Mandate was to organize tribal judges from Sinai and Transjordan to work with southern Palestine judges in cases where critical internal problems needed solving. For the British, the importance of southern Palestine maintaining their connections with Transjordan and Sinai was related to securing frontier areas and controlling cross-border tribal movements.

Major John Bagot Glubb's (a.k.a. Glubb Pasha) colonial perception of the Bedouin was characterized by his desire to strengthen the relationships between Bedouin tribes under his charge. In referring to the Bedouin, Glubb Pasha argued that "[in] this tribal world (the Bedu) is not alienated or hostile and may yet, if well handled, be kept loyal and contented." (Liddell Hart Centre for Military Archives, Kings College London, GB99 KCLMA O'Connor 3/4/44). Thus, British policy was to keep the Bedouin happy and not to clash with them primarily to maintain stability in the region (Glubb Pasha letter, HQ Arab Legion, to Lord Oxford, October 1945: Lord Oxford papers, Somerset, UK). Lord Oxford and Sir Gawain Bell both spoke of the importance of the tribes of Palestine maintaining their tribal relationships (interview with Lord Oxford, June 2009, Somerset, UK). Arriving in Beersheba as assistant district commissioner, Bell wrote, "We needed to re-establish a working liaison with the neighbouring Trans-Jordanian tribes and with the Arab Legion . . . further it would be necessary to re-establish contacts with our neighbours in Sinai" (Bell 1983, 104). In order to rule the frontiers, British officials in Transjordan, Sinai, and Beersheba cooperated with each other over various matters related to Bedouin tribes.

British officials reported that the tribes were encouraged to settle their own problems and disputes according to their own methods of conflict resolution. Lord Oxford emphasized that "we, the British did not solve the Bedouins tribes' daily problems. However, we worked side by side with them in critical cases of blood feuds and outstanding disputes between tribes in the frontier regions" (interview with Lord Oxford, June 2009, Somerset, UK). His views on dealing with Bedouin disputes and resolving daily issues also reflected British policy toward other tribes in Sinai, Beersheba, and Transjordan.

To stabilize the frontier areas in Transjordan, Sinai, and southern Palestine, the British adopted cross-border tribal meetings that involved shaikhs from three different regions. The movement of Bedouin tribes across borders between Transjordan, southern Palestine, and Sinai had created different forms of tribal dispute. Mr. A. Saunders, Inspector General of the Palestine Police, reported in 1939 that Bedouin migration from southern Palestine to Transjordan and vice versa was causing disputes among the tribes in the region (Liddell Hart Centre for Military Archives, Kings College London, O'Connor 3/4/31). Writing about the subject, the *al-Difaʾ Egyptian Gazette* (June 18, 1932) gave a detailed account of tribal disputes in frontier areas where a special Transjordan police force that included Bedouin camelry had been sent to secure the borders and ʿAqaba.

The British authorities also encouraged cooperation through formal and informal tribunals for dealing with and settling outstanding disputes between tribes. Meetings took place between tribal shaikhs and police officers from Transjordan, Sinai, and Palestine to resolve disagreements over areas of cultivation used by tribes in the three regions (Alon 2009, 132).

British policy was to consolidate the role of tribal courts and turn them into a more workable mechanism for conflict resolution. The British developed new types of cooperation between the Bedouin tribes by creating a cross-border network for a single interterritorial tribunal system. These tribunals would be recognized by the British and would maintain peace, order, and good government for the tribes:

> Under Article 17 of the Palestine Order in Council, 1922, as amended by the order in council of 1923, ordinance may be made for the "peace order, and good government of Palestine", and there would not appear to be any objection in principle to an ordinance providing for the enforcement in Palestine of the judgement or orders of these inter-territorial tribunals (whether given in Palestine, Trans-Jordan or Sinai) in so far as they affect tribes in Palestine or their property there.
>
> (PRO, CO 733/205/12)

Establishment of the interterritorial tribunal courts was approved by the British Mandate in 1929. British archival reports from 1931 suggest that the intertribunal courts were as powerful as the civil courts. "Bedawi custom," which had no defined limitations, was crucial in the tribunals. Lord Passfield wrote, "It has been the practice since 1929 for such Inter-territorial Tribunals to settle outstanding disputes, raids and blood feuds between Palestine, Trans-Jordan and Sinai Peninsula." Tribunal representatives met every six months in southern Palestine, Sinai, or Transjordan where the strengthened tribal system was dominant. These representatives were empowered to give decisions and issue orders to be applied to tribes in the three regions (PRO, CO 733/205/12). The British announced the establishment of the interterritorial tribunal by inviting representatives of the three regions to a conference in Beersheba in 1930. A number of Bedouin leaders from Sinai, southern Palestine, and Transjordan were present, along with British military officers (such as Major Gravis of Sinai) and colonial officials from the three regions (*Falastin*, March 26, 1930).

The high commissioner for Palestine and Transjordan explained the intertribunal system and the interest of the Mandate as being "the enforcement of the decisions of inter-Territorial Tribunals Ordinance." According to the 1931 report, the intertribunal courts were structured as follows: a meeting involved the assistant district superintendent of police or his representative and three Bedouin shaikhs appointed on each occasion by the District Officer, usually from the members of Beersheba's tribal court; Aref al-Aref, the district officer of Beersheba, represented the Beersheba subdistrict; the president of the Bedouin Central Board of Transjordan, the officer commanding the Arab Legion, and three Bedawi shaikhs (appointed on each occasion by the president of the Control Board) represented Transjordan; and the *Mamur* of Central Sinai and three Bedawi shaikhs (appointed on each occasion by the district officer) represented Sinai (PRO, CO 733/205/12). Meetings could take place in Transjordan, Beersheba, or Sinai.

Cases were judged according to Bedouin customs, mainly by copying the same tribal regulations applied in the Beersheba court. The report stressed that "the control board in Trans-Jordan and the Mamur of Central Sinai have powers to execute the judgment given by the Tribunals," further empowering these intertribunal courts. To support the decisions and orders made by the interterritorial tribunals, the British issued the Enforcement of Judgment Ordinance in 1931. As their reports stated,

> Any judgment or order of an inter-territorial tribunal for the payment of money or the delivery of movable property affecting tribes or sub-tribes in Palestine or their property, whether given in Palestine or Trans-Jordan or Sinai, and whether before or after the date of this Ordinance, shall be executed in Palestine in the same manner as a judgement or order of a Civil Court. (PRO, CO 733/205/12)

The fact that Bedouin shaikhs reported certain existing border disputes between tribes in southern Palestine and Transjordan to the British officials in Beersheba reinforced the need for these interterritorial tribunal courts. For example, in 1943 a number of leading Bedouin shaikhs in Beersheba sent letters to Lord Oxford stating the important role of Glubb Pasha in settling disputes with the Transjordan tribes. This British policy was recognized as significant in stabilizing the relationship with Bedouin tribes on both sides of the border (Attia Saʿd Jumaaʾ, letter to Lord Oxford, March 2, 1955, Lord Oxford papers, Somerset, UK). It meant that the British officials needed to work closely with the shaikhs by using the interterritorial tribunals as a form of conflict resolution and ensuring that their decisions were enforced. Hundreds of cases were dealt with and executed by the interterritorial courts annually (*Falastin*, November 5, 1942).

According to archival reports, the Mandate government encouraged this policy in order to avoid clashes with the existing Bedouin structure of cross-boundary relations (PRO, CO 733/205/12). Lord Oxford confirmed the significant relations maintained by the British between tribes in Transjordan, Sinai, and Beersheba, "mainly through the inter-territorial tribunal and the existing relationship between Bedouin judges across the borders" (interview with Lord Oxford, June 2009 Somerset, UK). In the 1940s, for example, Bedouin judges from Jordan, Sinai, and Palestine met in tribal conferences to deal with specific cases related to Bedouin tribes. They also consulted the tribal court of Beersheba to deal with disputes that the British had failed to resolve. Similarly, Gawain Bell reported tribal meetings for settling cross-border disputes through the interterritorial tribunal court. In 1940, Bell, accompanied by neutral tribal judges and Bedouin shaikhs from Beersheba, met Transjordanian tribes to settle a tribal dispute.

This interterritorial meeting included the governor of Maʿan District, important tribal leaders of the Huwaitat, and neutral tribal judges from Transjordan. Both parties stayed for some time, dealing with cross-border tribal cases. In such cases, tribal judges and respected shaikhs from both regions played the most important role in judging the disputed circumstances (Bell 1983, 111).

The Jerusalemite newspaper *Huna al-Quds* provided comprehensive coverage of cases dealt with by the tribunal regarding cross-border relations between Bedouin tribes in Beersheba, Sinai, and Transjordan. In 1942, a bloody dispute over land ownership escalated between two tribes, al-Wuheydat and Tarabin Abu Muʾeliq, led to the intervention of the interterritorial tribunals. The Mandate government indicated that the interterritorial tribunal would deal with the case by bringing representatives of these tribes together for a formal meeting. The Mandate government then invited a leading expert to deal with the case: a Bedouin judge (*qadi*) from Transjordan, Shaikh Odeh ibn Jad, head of all the Huweytat tribes. The meeting included representatives from the two quarrelling tribes, representatives from the Beersheba Bedouin tribes (Shaikh Jaduaʾ al-ʿAssam, Shaikh Hussein Abu Jaber, Shaikh Ibrahim Abu Jaber), the Beersheba *qaimmaqam* (Ishak al-Nashashibi), and some British government officials. The role of Odeh ibn Jad as a leading Transjordanian was the key to resolving the dispute. After lengthy debates in the Beersheba tribunal, the judges negotiated an agreement between the two tribes over the disputed land. After declaring the final resolution, both the tribes met for a traditional lunch that included all the tribal, police, and government representatives, and signaled the end of the dispute (*Huna al-Quds*, June, 6, 1942).

Many other examples of cross-border cases were brought to the tribunals from Gaza and Sinai. The interterritorial tribunal also participated in settling other tribal disputes that were reported on the Sinai frontier (Bell 1983, 111). Likhovski (2006, 42) notes that the District Commissioner of Gaza reported in 1945 about existing tribunal relations between the Bedouin in the region, remarking that "every few months the Bedouin courts in Beersheba held informal joint meetings with the Bedouin tribal courts of Transjordan and Sinai to decide matters in which Palestinian Bedu were involved." The Mandate authorities stabilized the frontier regions as a result of enhancing the relations between Bedouin judges and courts across the borders with Sinai, Beersheba, and Transjordan.

## *Unsettled Disputes: Bedouin Land Ownership and Taxation*

Land ownership and taxes comprised one of the most heavily disputed issues between the Mandate authorities and native Palestinians (see Essaid 2013; Bunton 2007). To avoid direct confrontation, the British mandatory authorities took into account Bedouin demands for recognition of their land on their terms. By using every opportunity to secure ownership, including sending formal letters and complaints to the authorities, the Bedouin safeguarded their land ownership.

For the Bedouin, the land tax issue was central. Due to harsh economic conditions and persistent drought years, they consistently requested the British to reduce their land taxes, with the constant refrain that "land and animal taxation should be mitigated." British reports suggest that the Bedouin sometimes paid limited taxes, and because of difficult economic conditions avoided repaying loans throughout the 1920s (PRO, CO 733/344/4). Tax reductions for the Bedouin were mentioned by Palestinian newspapers in connection with Beersheba's municipal taxes. The Bedouin desire for reduced taxes was central to the Great Revolt. *Al-Difa*ʾ newspaper noted the Beersheba municipal council's announcement that the municipality would not collect taxes from the residents due to the unstable economic and security situation. The municipality usually collected taxes on properties and for cleaning services (*al-Difa*ʾ, September 26, 1936).

Bedouin elders mention that both the Ottomans and the British had collected taxes from the Bedouin for their flocks, crops, and land. As an al-Azazma shaikh remarked, "the British officials used to come every year to our encampments accompanied by members of the Bedouin police to count our flocks and to ask for money accordingly" (interview with Ahmad al-ʿAzazma, June 20, 2014). Similar methods had been used by the Ottomans who would sometimes send an official (called *al-mukhamin*) to calculate how much the Bedouin would be asked to pay for their crops. The taxes were collected by the Ottomans using a traditional method (*dafater al-hbal*), according to which the Ottoman official calculated the land taxes. Lord Oxford confirmed that as a result of harsh economic circumstances and drought years, and because the Bedouin were not rich, the government sometimes reduced the taxes that they collected from the Bedouin (interview with Lord Oxford, September 2009).

Approval of the Bedouin as taxpayers is covered in various Ottoman documents found in the British archives. For instance, Ottoman archival reports show that Naqab Bedouin paid land and agriculture taxes (the "tithe") and even taxes for their animals and properties. As noted, in June 1907 the Bedouin in Beersheba had paid TL10,000 (Turkish lira), compared with the previous year's sum of TL20,000 (PRO, FO 195/2255). Colonial Office archival reports confirm that the Bedouin paid taxes and support Lord Oxford's later claim that taxes were reduced in the southern district because of economic conditions. In January 1940, Secretary of State Malcolm MacDonald confirmed that the Beersheba Bedouin paid taxes to the Mandate authorities: "In the circumstances and on the recommendation of the District Commissioner, I propose to authorize the remission of commuted tithes payable on the crop in this sub-district (southern Palestine); on this basis will amount to £P.3,860, of a total value commuted tithes of approximately £P.9,000" (PRO, CO 733/403/17). MacDonald approved recognition of the "tithes" paid by Beersheba district Bedouin as signifying land ownership. Again, the archival records state that because of economic conditions, the British occasionally reduced the amount of taxes that the Bedouin were asked to pay.

The British tried to address concerns about land ownership and taxation. For example, Abu Sitta (2008) notes that when Winston Churchill and High Commissioner Herbert Samuel met the Bedouin shaikhs in 1921, they recognized land ownership based on Bedouin customs and tribal laws.

One important aspect of the land issue for the Naqab Bedouin that arose again and again in their representations and memoranda to the Mandatory authorities was the problem of land purchase by Jewish settlers in the Naqab. Like other Palestinian leaders during this period, some of the shaikhs tried to persuade the British to prohibit land sales to settlers. A report signed by Shaikh ʿIzat al-ʿAtawna in Beersheba stated unequivocally that sales of land to Jews and Jewish immigration had to end: "Land sales to Jews should be prohibited, Jewish immigration should be stopped, and a legislative council in which Beduins should be proportionately represented should be established" (PRO, CO 733/344/4). Al-ʿAtawna petitioned the British authorities after Jewish settlers had managed to purchase a significant number of land tracts from the Bedouin. Bedouin petitions to the Colonial Office were made after several land brokers had sold thousands of *dunums* to Jewish millionaires who had begun to visit the Naqab. *Al-Difaʾ* reported that in 1935 around 30,000 *dunums* of land were for sale in the

Beersheba region, mainly by *samasira* (agents) accompanied by Bedouins. In some cases, land deals were made in Jerusalem in the presence of Bedouin and land brokers (*al-Difa*ʾ, May 11, 1934).

Even though the British recognized Bedouin lands according to their culture and norms, they failed to establish a land registry office in Beersheba. Reiterating that Bedouin land was recognized according to Bedouin laws, Lord Oxford confirmed that the British were very careful in dealing with Bedouin land since the Mandate authorities in the Naqab knew that land was always a sensitive subject:

> We recognized Bedouin land ownership without asking them to register it or to pay high taxes due to their economic conditions. Bedouin land was the property of the tribe as a unit and not for individuals. All the tribes knew their land naturally without registering it with the government as the Ottoman codes of land asked. . . . We did not oppose Bedouin land ownership, nor did we force them to register it. For example, the town of Biʾr al-Sabaʿ land belonged to a very well-known Bedouin tribe [al-ʿAzazma]. As a result we did not confront the Bedouin about the way they perceived their properties. Because the Bedouin were not very rich, we preferred for economic reasons not to ask them to pay high taxes, but in fact some did pay tax. The economic situation of the Bedouin did not encourage the British to impose harsh taxation policies, so we were really helping them to survive. Only the Ottomans enacted land codes; we, the British, did not have any land registration system in Beersheba region.
> (INTERVIEW WITH LORD OXFORD, JUNE 2009)

Lord Oxford's assessment of the situation was correct. British archival reports concerned with Ottoman land codes indicate that while the codes had been enacted to encourage people to register their land as property, the Ottomans were not sufficiently firm about compelling the Bedouin to accept their laws. In 1858, as part of the Tanzimat reforms, the Ottoman authorities had decided to undertake large-scale land reform (Rogan 1999). An October 1948 memorandum from J. F. Spry, a former assistant director of land registration in Palestine, reported that "land registration law was introduced into the Ottoman Empire in 1858, however it does not appear to have been applied to the Palestine area until 1869 to 1873" (PRO, CO 733/494/3). The Ottomans' failure to impose their land codes on the Bedouin meant that a relatively limited number of them registered their land under Ottoman law.

Some Bedouin interviewees emphasized that the Bedouin knew their land without having to register it officially under the British system: "We lived in our land for generations; this is the best proof of Bedouin land ownership." As Suliman Sbayeh Abu Rabia explains:

> The Bedouin tribes clashed with each other sometimes for years in order to maintain their land and to prove ownership. The Bedouin means of proving their land was by an indigenous way of life and not by state papers. The British officials understood the system very well, and avoided opposing our land ownership.
>
> (INTERVIEW WITH SULIMAN SBAYEH ABU RABIA, AUGUST 2013)

Another significant proof of Bedouin land ownership was the continued cultivation of their land. Archival and newspaper records refer to land cultivation by Bedouin owners in southern Palestine and even provide details about the number of *dunums* cultivated. *Huna al-Quds*, reported in 1942 that the cultivated land in southern Palestine was estimated at two million *dunums* (*Huna al-Quds*, June 6, 1942). A British report from January 1947 shows that the area of Khalasa in northern Naqab was already cultivated by its Bedouin owners: "These Bedouin are keen farmers and very much alive to the possibility of improving their agricultural methods. Tractor ploughing has made considerable strides within recent years and an increasing area is being planted each year with fruit trees" (PRO, FO 371/61868). Lord Oxford, who lived in both Gaza and Beersheba as an assistant district commissioner, confirmed that he had helped the Bedouin to improve their agricultural methods by buying modern tools for cultivating land (interview with Lord Oxford, July 2008).

The urgency of Jewish immigration and land sales led Bedouin leaders to organize conferences with the Palestinian leadership as a means of securing southern Palestine from Jewish settlement. Local Bedouin shaikhs in the Naqab together with the Jamiʾyat al-Badu al-ʾArabiya (a local Bedouin organization) played a significant role in the campaign. A conference for this purpose was organized in 1935 in Wadi al-Shariaʾ, Western Naqab. During my interviews with the Bedouin elders they confirmed the al-Shariaʾ conference and its proceedings, and also spoke of other meetings that had taken place during 1935 in the Naqab involving Hajj Amin al-Hosseini (the grand mufti in Palestine) and tribal leaders who had attended the Wadi Al-Sharia᾿ conference (interview with Aliyan al-Sanne, August 2014).

Jewish settlers succeeded in purchasing large tracts of land from some Bedouin tribes and shaikhs (Kark 2002, 102; Shepherd 1999, 118; Cohen 2008, 48). *Falastin* reported in 1934 that around 30,000 *dunums* were officially pronounced as land for sale in the Beersheba region (*Falastin*, May 1934). It also reported that by 1934 a Jewish organization had managed to rent two houses in Beersheba with the aim of buying land and encouraging Jewish immigration to the southern region (February 10, 1934).

During the conference the shaikhs were asked to forbid the sale of land to Jews. Bedouin oral histories relate that the tribal shaikhs swore an oath in front of Hajj Amin al-Hosseini and banned any tribe that sold land to the settlers (interview with Aliyan al-Sanne, August 2014). Lord Oxford noted that the Beersheba Bedouin maintained contacts with Hajj Amin al-Hosseini, whom they admired as a leader: "The Bedouin in Beersheba had great sympathy toward Palestinian leaders, in particular Hajj Amin al-Hosseini" (interview, June 2008).

Another significant effort by Bedouin leaders to secure land ownership involved sending delegations to Jerusalem for negotiations with the British high commissioner. Several Bedouin shaikhs from the Beersheba region raised a number of important issues concerning their land at a meeting during the initial stage of the Great Revolt of 1936–1939. The delegation included Shaikhs Frieh Abu Meddein, Hussein Abu Sitta, Hamid al-Sanne, Abed Raba Abu Hossein, Hassan Abu Jaber, Hassan al-Wheidi, Mosa Abu Me᾿leig, Eʿid Ben Rabia, Salameh Ibn Saʿid, ʿEdisan Abu ʿAbdon, ʿAbdallah Abu Sitta, Hassan al-ʿAtawna, and Mosa Abu Shonar (*Falastin*, May 1, 1936: 4). They asked the High Commissioner to stop Jewish immigration and to avoid land sales to Jews. They also spoke about Beersheba Bedouin land ownership, the formation of a national parliamentary government, and the release of prisoners following recent incidents during the revolt in Palestine. They insisted that the British government should take notice of these claims and put them into effect, reiterating that if the British did not take these issues seriously the Arabs would take the lead in all these matters. *Falastin* also reported that the Bedouin leaders of Beersheba had intervened politically to secure their land and to support the Palestinian cause.

In the early 1940s, Bedouin leaders made another significant attempt to secure their land from the settlers at a local conference initiated by Shaikh

Hajj Ibrahim al-Sanne, a nationalist Bedouin leader (see Hutchison 1956). Bedouin shaikhs from the Qdirat signed a document confirming that they agreed that anyone who sold land to Jews, or mediated in selling land, would no longer belong to their tribe but would be expelled or killed in order to save their tribal lands and what they described as the land of *al-watan*, the "homeland." The shaikhs who signed this agreement included Hajj Ibrahim Al-Sanne, Muhammad Hassan Al-ʿAssam, Hajj Harb Abu Rqaiq, Muhammed Abu Kaf, and Salameh al-Hawashla (CZA S71/500).

Some of my findings clearly contradict the claim that the Bedouin tribes in southern Palestine played an active role in selling land to settlers and Jewish agencies. Examination of primary sources, many of which have not previously been consulted, reveals the active role of the Bedouin tribes in boycotting settlers and using political tactics to protect their land. Although a number of Bedouin shaikhs were undoubtedly involved in selling an extensive acreage of land in Palestine's southern district to Jews (Kark 2002, 102; Shepherd 1999, 118; Cohen 2008, 48), there is sufficient evidence that other leading Bedouin boycotted land sales and even managed to stop them from happening. Jamiʿyat al-Badu al-ʿArabiya (the Bedouin NGO), and local Bedouin organizations in Beersheba led by members of the Abu Sitta Bedouin organized a community conference in Beersheba in 1936 that included the leading Bedouin shaikhs. Palestinian Bedouin officials in Beersheba campaigned to raise awareness, made speeches about Jewish attempts to buy land in the region, and tried to block the land brokers (*samasira*). Such meetings gained support from the Arab Higher Committee in Jerusalem (*al-Difaʾ*, June 15, 1936).

According to a variety of archival reports and interviews, the Bedouin of the Naqab did not acknowledge a need to prove their land ownership and fought a political battle to protect their land. They petitioned the Mandate authorities for recognition of their land, met in tribal conferences to secure their land, sent tribal delegations to Jerusalem and, most effectively, rejected the 1939 White Paper as a means of preventing their land from being shared with Jewish settlers.

## Bedouin Representation in Palestinian Official Bodies

Reviewing Palestinian newspapers from the 1930s (*al-Difaʾ*, *Falastin*, *al-Carmel*, and *Huna al-Quds*) reveals that the Bedouin played a significant role in Palestinian politics and in protecting the Biʾr al-Sabaʿ region during the Great Revolt. The Bedouin were not excluded from official representation in the various Palestinian political bodies.

During the 1930s the Beersheba subdistrict received significant coverage in Palestinian newspapers. The newspapers reported on land issues, Jewish immigration to southern Palestine, the active participation of the Bedouin in Palestinian conferences and their attendance in meetings in Jerusalem, and the role played by the Bedouin in the Great Revolt of 1936–1939. One of the clearest instances of Bedouin representation in Jerusalem was in official Palestinian bodies. In the early days of the British Mandate, Bedouin shaikhs represented the Bedouin community in country-wide dialogs and discussions with the British about the future of Palestine. These discussions often arose because of outbreaks of violence and frustration on the part of the Palestinian community over Zionist immigration and British policies for Jewish immigration and land purchases. For example, Shaikh Frieh Abu Meddein represented the Bedouin in 1929 in secret talks held between H. C. Luke, chief secretary of the government of Palestine, and leaders of the Palestinian factions (Wasserstein 1991, 224). Such Bedouin participation demonstrated their active engagement with the political situation at the time. It revealed a clear message about the Bedouin view of the incidents in Palestine in 1929 that had given rise to the anti-Jewish and anti-British uprising.

Seeking to create a community-wide response to the British during the early 1930s, the Palestinian political leadership held numerous conferences that Bedouin leaders attended. They also served as members of the Arab Higher Committee and the Supreme Muslim Council in Gaza. Several Bedouin shaikhs representing the Beersheba tribes, including Shaikhs Hajj Ibrahim al-Sanne and Hussein Abu Sitta, participated in a conference in Jerusalem on March 25, 1935, with the aim of forming a Palestinian Arab Party (Ghuri 1972, 196–97). *Al-Difaʾ* reported that the Bedouin were represented in official meetings in Jerusalem. In 1936, members of Beersheba's National Committee (*al-Lajnah al-Qawmiya*) met to elect Bedouin representatives who would speak on their behalf in the Arab Higher Committee in Jerusalem (*al-Lajnah al-ʾArabiya al-ʿUlya*). Committee members that were elected in Beersheba as representatives included Taj al-Dein Shaʿath, Hussien al al-Sharaf, Hassan ʻAli Jaradeh, Saeed Bsiso, Salameh Ibn Saiʿd of the ʿAzazma, and Rashad al-Saqa. A number of representatives came originally from Gaza but lived in Beersheba or had official administrative roles in the town.

Representatives of the National Committee (*al-Lajnah al-Qawmiya*) of Beersheba went to Jerusalem a few times during the revolt to report about the situation in Beersheba to the Arab Higher Committee (*al-Difa'*, September 26, 1936). The Beersheba Bedouin were also represented on the Higher Islamic Council in Jerusalem: according to *al-Carmel* newspaper, one of the Council members was a Beersheba Bedouin (*al-Carmel*, June 22, 1929).

Archival reports and Palestinian newspapers clearly indicate that the Bedouin were organized both in interterritorial tribunals (which the British adopted as a mechanism of control) and in nascent Palestinian national and political organizations. While the British documents stress their "Bedouin-ness," i.e., a representation of the Bedouin as distinct and needing to be ruled separately, the Palestinian newspapers focus on the Bedouins' "Palestinian-ness," emphasizing more strongly that they were part of the broader Palestinian community resisting Zionist immigration.

## Bedouin Resistance to British Colonialism, 1936–1939

Though the Bedouin often cooperated with the British, they also demonstrated signs of resistance to British rule. Of particular importance were their continued contacts with their relatives across borders, their participation in Palestinian conferences, and their involvement and protest in the Great Revolt of 1936–1939.

Bedouin shaikhs represented the Bedouin community in Palestine-wide dialogs and discussions with the British about the future of Palestine. These discussions often arose because of outbreaks of violence and frustration on the part of the Palestinian community over Jewish immigration and land purchases. Bedouin women participated in the first Palestinian women's congress in the 1930s, "the first time that Arab women in this district [Beersheba] shared men's struggle" (Fleischmann 2000, 25). Such participation demonstrated active Bedouin engagement with the political situation, attempts to influence its trajectory, and a clear message about the incidents in Palestine during the anti-Jewish and anti-British uprising in 1929.

Seeking to create a community-wide response to the British during the early 1930s, the Palestinian political leadership held numerous conferences in which Bedouin leaders took part. They also served as members of the Arab Higher Committee and the Supreme Muslim Council in Gaza.

Significantly, the Beersheba Bedouin showed their communal strength during the Great Revolt of 1936–1939 through various forms of involvement. Details of the Great Revolt have been inherited through the memories of the older generation of Naqab Bedouin, one of whom remembered how the Bedouin would not cooperate with the Peel Commission in 1937:

> For the second year of the Great Revolt, we saw the Peel Commission committee in the Naqab. Many cars and military jeeps passed by our encampment, trying to investigate the violence between Arab and Jews. When some Bedouin shaikhs went to meet them, they realized that this was the special commission which wanted to divide the land between the Arabs and Jews. I also remember that the Bedouin shaikhs refused to cooperate with the Peel Commission, arguing this was our land and we would not move from here.
> (INTERVIEW WITH HAJJ MOSA ABU AL-KEYAʾAN, JULY 2009)

During the second phase of the revolt, Naqab Bedouin contacted Hajj Amin about possible roles that they could take. According to Rosemary Sayigh,

> A group of Bedouin gathered in Beersheba telephoned to the Mufti asking what action they should take in support of the uprising that was beginning to spread through the country in the wake of the killing of the District Commissioner for Galilee. The Mufti's reply to them was to do whatever they thought fit.
> (1979, 50)

ʿEid Al-Sanne (Tarabin), one of the leading Bedouin rebels in Beersheba region, is still remembered among the older generations of the Naqab Bedouin as a local Bedouin hero. Edward Horne describes how Inspector A. H. Leeves was sent to Beersheba in 1932 as second-in-command on a mission against a Bedouin rebel group led by ʿEid Al-Sanne (possibly somewhere east of Beersheba). Leeves set out to seize and arrest the rebel leader with the camel corps:

> On 16th October 1932, only a month after his arrival, he led a patrol that brushed against a gang of Arabs half a day from Beersheba. They were led by Eid el Sane, who had long been wanted by the police for robbery and other crimes. There was a sharp action in which Leeves led his constables with considerable gallantry and much credit to himself.
> (HORNE 1982, 109)

Leeves did not succeed in arresting ʿEid al-Sanne.

Presumably this was not the only case in which the Bedouin fought against the British in southern Palestine and formed rebel groups. *Al-Difaʾ* reported on Bedouin activities against the Mandatory Government during the early days of the revolt involving peaceful student-led demonstrations in Beersheba, as well as clashes between Bedouin rebels and police. One such incident was the attack on the police station in the Jammama (Rohama) colony (*al-Difaʾ*, September 26, 1936).

The rebels in Beersheba gained limited but strategic success during the Great Revolt. As indicated in secret reports from the British archives and mentioned in oral history testimonies, Beersheba was occupied by Palestinian rebels in September 1938. One account states that Bedouin shaikhs joined the groups of rebels from Hebron and Tulkarm and helped them to occupy the city. Other reports downplay the Bedouin role in defeating the British. According to C. E. V. Buxton, district commissioner for Gaza–Beersheba, the Bedouin were involved:

> The Beersheba shaikhs feel an unwholesome awe for the Hebron rebel groups which virtually secured the withdrawal of Government control from the whole of their area last September. Consequently they thought it wiser to be very vocal in their show of loyalty to the rebels. The district officer, who may be responsible for this vocality on the part of the shaikhs, is an astute man and may think it desirable to keep up political pressure while there is still doubt about the issue . . . the fact remains that 75 percent of the male population near the railway did pull up the line last September. Thereby they identified themselves with active rebellion. . . . They maintain that the population will help the rebel agents rather than the government forces.
> (GB99, KCLMA O'CONNOR 3/4/44)

Former Inspector General R. G. B. Spicer commented on the occupation of Beersheba by the Hebron rebel groups and the burning of government buildings and police stations in *The Times* in October 1938. According to Spicer, a rebel group of 300 armed men invaded Hebron by night; they then continued to Beersheba and destroyed government buildings (GB99, KCLMA O'Connor 3/2). Beersheba was retaken by the British Second Battalion in November 1938, having been briefly under the full control of Palestinian rebels. It should be noted that there was no governance in the city while it was under occupation since the Beersheba district was a rebel base and the British authorities had little influence there. Government offices were seized and destroyed by rebels who controlled police weaponry (GB99, KCLMA O'Connor 3/14/53).

Gawain Bell notes that government buildings were destroyed by rebels from Hebron with tribal support and that the British sometimes expected local shaikhs to help them capture members of the rebel groups who had found places to hide among the tribes (Bell 1983, 116–17). In the case described by Bell, the Bedouin knew when to cooperate with the British authorities even though they attacked British bases when they felt threatened. According to El-Nimr (1990, 173), certain heads of tribes in Beersheba were themselves leaders of rebel groups during the Great Revolt. Bedouin tribespeople sometimes collaborated with merchants from other Palestinian villages who brought in arms from Egypt and Sinai to sell to rebels in the Gaza and Beersheba area. It was extremely hard for the British to restrict the movements of Bedouin smugglers.

Some Bedouin interviewees remember the Great Revolt. They confirmed that Bedouin rebels had made life difficult for the British and recounted how some Bedouins who had worked for the Palestine Police suddenly began using their weapons and experience against the British:

> The Bedouin rebels made real problems for the British Mandate in Beersheba. Some Bedouins joined the Palestinian rebels in the 1936–1939 Arab Revolt, attacking the British bases in Beersheba.
> (INTERVIEW WITH ODA ABU SRIHAN, JUNE 2009).

British reports mention that Bedouin in the Beersheba subdistrict were armed and that it was difficult to get them to register their weapons. The British tried asking the Bedouin to register their arms. When that failed, they would attempt to disarm the Bedouin while trying to enforce British law on them. Neither strategy worked. A secret report on February 7, 1939, from A. Saunders, commander of the Palestine police force, noted the complexities of trying to impose laws and disarm the Bedouin:

> The considered opinions of Sir Charles Tegart and myself are that the control of gun-running and the disarmament of the Bedu [is imperative]. . . . There should be a frontier zone between Palestine and Trans-Jordan within which

> no firearm or ammunition can be carried without a permit . . . registration of all arms in the Beersheba Division must be enforced . . . the carrying of firearms or of ammunition is an offence punishable with the penalty imposed elsewhere in Palestine . . . it is imperative that carrying of arms must be subject to registration, in order that where it is determined that disarmament shall be enforced, such an order is capable of implementation.
> (GB99, KCLMA O'CONNOR 3/4/31)

This indicates the problems confronting the British authorities. The view was that the Bedouin should be deterred from participating in the Great Revolt in Palestine and disconnected from the rest of the Palestinian community, and that there should be efforts to stop tribal raids and clashes with other Bedouin groups. The difficulty of enforcement remained.

Once the Great Revolt had settled down, the Bedouin reacted to British decisions announced in the 1939 White Paper. According to Aref al-Aref (district administrative officer of Beersheba, 1929–1939), following a visit to the Tarabin tribe by the high commissioner in July 1939 the Bedouin shaikhs "refused to accept the White Paper and said they will accept only what the High Arab Committee and the Grand Mufti Hajj Amin Al Hossaini says" (MECA, AR-0016). This clearly shows the political resistance of the Bedouin and their rejection of a shared Arab/Jewish state in Palestine.

Aref al-Aref records in his diaries that he was told by Shaikh Hussein Abu Sitta in September 1939 that a letter had been sent to the British government by a number of Bedouin shaikhs from Beersheba declaring their loyalty and support to the British government in the war against the Germans (MECA, AR-0016). The Bedouin managed thus to play a very important political role. They supported the British in their war against Germany and also boycotted Britain's plans for Palestine as set out in the 1939 White Paper.

## The Palestine Police and Bedouin Camelry

The British incorporated several leading Bedouin tribesmen in the Palestine Police Colonial Force as another form of cooperation with the Bedouin and as an effort to impose order and security in the southern district. The strategy of recruiting natives to the colonial police and the army was not unique to Palestine; it was common in other regions under British colonial authority, such as Somalia (Porter 2013, 42–43). In Palestine, the police force was created in July 1921 with the overall aim of meeting order and security requirements (Horne 1982, 35). I argue that the police played a central role in creating order in different areas of Palestine, including the Beersheba region. Once established, the Gendarmerie included sixty-three officers and 1,247 other ranks, of which two-thirds were British. The Arab portion of the police was increased later on in 1926 (PRO, WO 106/5720). Colonel Alan Saunders was the inspector general of the Palestine police force and was succeeded by Captain Rymer Jones of the Metropolitan Police (Martin 2007, 136). The Palestine Police included former members of the British Gendarmerie, Jewish officers who were responsible for securing settlements in remote places (Kolinsky 1993, 95; Sinclair 2006, 107), a Bedouin camel corps section, wireless operators, and mounted police. All of them were important components of the force (Martin 2007).

In the southern subdistrict of Palestine the area was policed by Bedouin camelry. These mobile Bedouin forces became essential for securing the subdistrict. MacDonald, then colonial secretary, reported that, "Prior to September 1938, that area was policed by the camelry under the administration of the Inspector General of Police. The establishment consisted of eighty-eight men who were distributed in a number of outposts with their headquarters in Beersheba" (PRO, CO 733/390/1). The Bedouin police who were in charge of the region would rightly cover "that part of Beersheba subdistrict south of a line drawn from Naqab Zweira on the east to Raʾfa on the west. A small area north-west of this line will be included, stretching as far as Jammama" (PRO, CO 733/390/1).

The Bedouin were mainly recruited to the Palestine Police in camel corps and mobile police positions. MacDonald maintained that southern Palestine was entirely policed by Bedouin camelry (PRO, CO 733/390/1). The eighty-eight Bedouin police from the Beersheba region and Gaza employed by the Mandate were based at various police posts distributed throughout the Naqab region, including ʿAsluj and ʿAuja al-Hafir, Kurnub, Khalasa, ʿAyn Hosb, ʿAyn Ghadhyan, Tal al-Malah, and Biʾr al-Sabaʿ (Lord Oxford personal papers, Somerset, UK). Wireless telephones were maintained to connect the posts with Beersheba (Nasasra 2011b; Abu Rabia 2001; Kark and Frantzman 2012, 66). In 1921, a very experienced ex-military officer, Hassan Faiz al-Idrissi, was appointed to the camel corps in Beersheba as the first subinspector (Horne 1982, 399–400).

FIGURE 3.1 Bedouin-British meeting at the Tal al-Malah police post. *Source:* Earl of Oxford and Asquith, Somerset, UK.

The British relied on the tribal chiefs (shaikhs) as their main contacts with the tribes for the purpose of recruiting Bedouin to the Palestine Police in the Beersheba region. One of the most striking forms of collaboration between the Bedouin and the British could be found in the Palestine Police or Bedouin *Hajjaneh*, with leading Bedouin shaikhs encouraged to send their sons to join the mobile police forces (interview with Hajj Salih al-Nasasrah, Kseifa, June 2009).

Most of the Bedouin who enrolled in the police underwent intensive training courses in order to work as policemen or wireless operators in the service of the Mandate. According to elderly Bedouin who had served in the police, wireless operators were sent to Jerusalem to continue their wireless studies for several months. Police members were sent to a special training outfit (the Palestine Police Depot Training School) established in Jerusalem in 1921 (Horne 1982, 316; El-Eini 2006, 64). After completing the courses, they and other Bedouin boys were sent back to the Naqab to be employed by the British as wireless operators and border police throughout the region (interview with Suleiman Abu Sbayeh, Kseifa, June 2009).

FIGURE 3.2 ʿAtiya Ibn Rabia, a member of the Bedouin police from Eastern Beersheba. *Source*: Lord Oxford papers, Somerset, UK.

The main mission of the Bedouin police was to carry out special assignments in the desert and to patrol the borders. The Hajjaneh Bedouins were employed in various ways: they policed remote sites, reduced cross-border economic activities, acted as trackers, and served as wireless operators (Nasasra 2011b, 318). Enforcing law and maintaining order were also significant duties for the Bedouin police (Horne 1982, 401: Nasasra 2011b).

In a 1939 report, MacDonald referred to the crucial role of the Bedouin police in securing the area, and how "the camelry with their intimate local knowledge proved to be an effective means of maintaining law and order in this part of country under normal conditions" (PRO, CO 733/390/1).

### *The Bedouin Camelry in the Beersheba Region*

Creating order among the tribes was one of the main challenges facing the Mandate authorities in different situations. In this regard the Bedouin camelry played a marginal part in imposing order and securing the borders, and Bedouin police were used to restore order during riots and rebellions.

In September 1938 during the height of the Great Revolt of 1936–1939, rebels attacked outposts that the police were unable to defend. Furthermore, they could not secure Beersheba itself. As MacDonald reported, "In September 1938, after attack by armed bands, it was considered prudent to withdraw the camelry outposts[, which] might have been unable to defend themselves against determined assault; and since that time only a nucleus of the camelry has been retained at their head-quarters in Beersheba" (PRO, CO 733//390/1).

During the Great Revolt most of the Palestine police left their posts after being targeted by rebels (Shepherd 1999, 143). Meanwhile, Bedouin police stayed in their region and helped the rebels to seize police posts (Nasasra 2011b). Elsewhere in Palestine, police posts were destroyed by rebel leaders such as Eissa al-Battat, a Palestinian regional commander (Martin 2007, 63; Nasasra 2011b). As a result of being unable to secure their posts or defeat the rebels attacking Beersheba, most of the camelry left their posts and went back to their tribes (Horne 1982, 415).

The British used Bedouin police as a colonial strategy for settling riots and imposing order on other regions in Palestine. For example, in the 1933 riots in Jaffa, around twenty members of the police camel corps were brought specially from the Beersheba region (Horne 1982; Imray 1995, 93). *Al-Difa'* reported that Bedouin police were sent to suppress the student demonstrations that took place in Beersheba during the Great Revolt, killing one student (*al-Difa'*, June 6, 1936). The camelry also played an important role in imposing order during the Great Revolt. Key missions included fighting Arab bands and rebels and securing government houses and police posts in the Beersheba region (Horne 1982; Bell 1983; Nasasra 2011b).

Lord Oxford maintained that it would have been impossible to govern the Bedouin and maintain order without employing them as mobile police forces (interview with Lord Oxford, August 2009, Somerset, UK). However, despite being an effective force for maintaining order and security in southern Palestine, the Bedouin Police failed to defend Beersheba. In September 1938 the main city of the Naqab fell into rebel hands and the main police headquarters station in Beersheba was taken from the British (Dabbagh 1965, 360). Palestinian rebels, joined by Bedouin tribes and sometimes Bedouin police themselves, managed to occupy Beersheba in 1938: a significant step toward the temporary defeat of British colonial power (Nasasra 2009; Bell 1983; Horne 1982). The colonial strategy of using the Bedouin police was not always successful.

### *Reestablishing the Bedouin Police After the Great Revolt*

During the Great Revolt, police posts and Palestinian/Bedouin camelry policemen in the Beersheba region and elsewhere were targeted by angry Palestinian rebels (Cohen 2008). British officials made significant efforts to reestablish the Bedouin police and restore order and immediately after the Great Revolt set about repairing the damage. Naomi Shepherd (1999, 206) notes that Sir Charles Tegart, a chief of police, recommended replacing the posts that had been destroyed by the rebels in 1938 and reforming the entire police system. A similar policy of recreating the Bedouin police was applied to the Bedouin camelry in the Beersheba region. Although the Bedouin police had not been very effective in maintaining security and order, the Mandate authorities put significant amounts of money toward re-establishing them. They began recruiting Bedouin for a reconstructed police force immediately. According to proposals submitted by the high commissioner of Palestine, the aim after the revolt was to recreate "a former force of camelry which [had been] withdrawn and reduced when resistance to the forces of the government became so intense that camelry in isolated posts were no longer secure" (PRO, CO 733/390/1).

As noted by Lord Oxford, reestablishment of the Bedouin Gendarmerie was along the lines of the Arab Legion (interview with Lord Oxford, June 2009, Somerset, UK) and involved close cooperation with Glubb Pasha and other British officers in the legion (Bell 1983, 105). Sir Gawain Bell was given the task of overseeing the reconstitution of the Bedouin Camel Gendarmerie police in the Beersheba region and reopening the destroyed police posts (Bell 1983, 104; Horne 1982, 419). Bell was an assistant district commissioner with an excellent knowledge of Arabic and was transferred to Beersheba in June 1938 (PRO, CO 733/390/1). According to his post-revolt assessment, a number of camelry posts needed attention, including ʿAyn Hosb and Wadi ʿAraba. The Gendarmerie posts of ʿAsluj, ʿAuja al-Hafir, and Um Rash-Rash on the Sinai frontier were in similar sorry states (Bell 1983, 105–106).

The High Commissioner recommended strengthening the existing camelry to include thirteen noncommissioned officers, seventy-two constables, and nine wireless operators. In addition to re-establishing four outposts (ʿAyn Hosb, Um Rash-Rash, ʿAuja al-Hafir, and ʿAsluj), a small patrol post would be set up in Tal al-Malah. The two posts in Imara and Jammama would be reopened, despite a possible increase in overall costs, and four desert vehicles would be attached to the force to support the camelry. The rebuilding work took four months and was completed in March 1940 at a total cost of LP 4,183 (PRO, CO 733/390/1). Once the posts were secure, Alan Saunders, inspector general of police, supplied the Gendarmerie with arms. Some of the police who had served before the Great Revolt were re-recruited (Bell 1983, 108), and the members of the camelry were carefully selected for fitness and tribal connections. Training for the Gendarmerie took place in Beersheba while the police headquarters remained there, as in pre-revolt days (Nasasra 2011b).

In 1946, the Government of Palestine's Forestry Department undertook a fact-finding survey of the southern region, which involved census taking and observations of historical sites. The officials reported from Jerusalem that various posts, including ʿAyn Hosb and Kurnub, were operating normally, as previously. They also passed on the names of experienced Bedouin frontier police who had returned to serving in ʿAyn Hosb and Kurnub and whose views on the region's history they had listened to (Government of Palestine, Jerusalem, July 31, 1946: "Preliminary Report on Arid Pasture Investigation." Lord Oxford papers). As Lord Oxford noted, some of those working in ʿAyn Hosb had previously been enrolled in the Arab Legion with Glubb Pasha, indicating another form of cooperation between the Bedouin camelry in Beersheba and the Arab Legion. Following reorganization, the camelry became subject to close scrutiny. Lord Oxford confirmed their

FIGURE 3.3 Touring Wadi Murra in the frontier area after the reestablishment of the Bedouin police, 1943. *Source*: Lord Oxford papers, Somerset, UK.

efficiency and competence by reporting about them and referring to their outstanding intelligence, energy, and abilities (Lord Oxford, personal diaries of camelry inspection, Somerset, UK).

It is important to understand what happened to the Bedouin Gendarmerie after the Mandate ended. Lord Oxford confirmed that the Bedouin who had served in the camelry remained in close contact with their British officers after 1948. Letters from ʿAtiya Eʿid Bin Rabiaʾ, who lived in Hebron, stated that some of the Bedouin camelry had moved to different regions including ʿAqaba, Amman, Gaza, and Rafah, and that only a few of them remained in the Beersheba area. ʿAtiya even provided a list of camelry names and reported about them to Lord Oxford (letter from ʿAtiya Bin Rabiaʾ to Lord Oxford, Hebron, March 1955, Lord Oxford papers). Other letters were sent from Bedouin camelry who had moved to Jordan, recalling the "old good days" of serving under British officials (Farid Saʾad Jumaa, letter to Lord Oxford, Amman, 1950, Lord Oxford papers).

In late 1947 the relationship between the British and the Bedouin shifted toward its final phase with a formal meeting in Beersheba between the representatives of the tribal shaikhs and British officials:

> Sir Alan Cunningham, the High Commissioner, repeated that the British would be responsible for law and order in any area as long as they remained in control. His Excellency assured a meeting of over 20 tribal chiefs after he had unveiled a monument in memory of Lord Allenby. . . . There is no government which is perfect and no government which cannot be criticized, but they were not mistakes of intention. . . . Hoping that the people of Beersheba would consider it a monument to the good things the British and the Arabs had experienced together, Sir Alan wished them good luck and hoped that the seeds sown by the British administration in Palestine might grow and lead to increased prosperity and peace.
> (*PALESTINE POST*, NOVEMBER 28, 1947)

The British forces eventually withdrew from Biʾr al-Sabaʿ on May 14, 1948 in a ceremony attended by Bedouin shaikhs and government officials. The flag of Palestine was immediately raised at the city's Ottoman Saraya building by Shafiq Mustafa, mayor of Biʾr al-Sabaʿ, signaling the beginning of Palestinian rule over the city. This, however, lasted for only a few months. In October 1948 the Israeli army occupied the city.

FOUR

# Envisioning the Jewish State Project

> Negev land is reserved for Jewish citizens, whenever and wherever they want. . . . We must expel Arabs and take their places . . . and if we have to use force, then we have force at our disposal not in order to dispossess the Arabs of the Negev, and transfer them, but in order to guarantee our own right to settle in those places
>
> —DAVID BEN GURION IN A LETTER TO HIS SON, AMOS, OCTOBER 5, 1937

## The Founding Vision of the Jewish State

THE FIRST CRITICAL STEP toward the birth of a Jewish state was taken at the first World Zionist Congress, held from August 29–31, 1897, in Basel, Switzerland, and attended by around 197 delegates from Zionist groups in at least fifteen countries. Only two of the delegates were Palestine-born, confirmation that only a minority of Jews lived in Palestine at that time (Herzl 1958, 214). The primary goal of the gathering was to achieve the Jewish people's dream of living in one nation-state.

Theodor Herzl, born in Budapest in 1860, was the visionary and founder of Zionism, and the prime mover behind the Basel Congress. Describing its primary goal, he said: "We want to lay the foundation stone of the house which is to shelter the Jewish nation." On September 3, 1897, three days after the World Zionist Congress, Herzl, who had been elected as President of the World Zionist Organization (WZO) noted in his diary, "If I were to sum up the Congress in a word—which I shall take care not to publish: at Basel I founded the Jewish state" (Herzl 1958, 224). Herzl encapsulated the Zionist movement's target to establish a Jewish state as his ultimate goal, thereby solving the problem of life in the Jewish Diaspora. By the Basel Declaration of 1897 he showed his eagerness to transform Palestine into a monoreligious Jewish state. His method of achieving supremacy in Palestine was to adopt military power and promote massive Jewish immigration.

Jews faced problems and unstable situations wherever they lived. Herzl noted: "No one can deny the gravity of the situation of the Jews. Wherever they live in perceptible numbers, they are more or less persecuted" (Herzl 1946, 22). He depicted them as victims, and aimed to solve the Diaspora problem by bringing them together in one state: "Zionism seeks to obtain for the Jewish people a publicly-recognized, legally-secured homeland in Palestine" (Herzl 1958, 214–215). Avi Shlaim (2000, 4) notes that Herzl did not deny the fact that Palestine was already populated by indigenous Palestinian people; however, he saw them as "primitive and backward." This might have been another reason for establishing a Jewish state since colonizing Palestine would free it from its native Palestinian people.

The dream of establishing a Jewish state did not stop with Herzl, the leading figure in political Zionism. Many other Zionist leaders had a desire to implement the Basel declaration on the ground. For instance, the right-wing revisionist Zionist leader Vladimir (Ze'ev) Jabotinsky saw that a Jewish state could be achieved by a Jewish majority (Gorny 1987) and made creating such a majority in Palestine one of Zionism's fundamental aims.[1] Known as the founder of Revisionist Zionism, Jabotinsky wrote in his manifesto:

> Zionist colonization, even the most restricted, must either be terminated or carried out in defiance of the will of the native population. The colonization can, therefore, continue and develop only under the protection of a force independent of the local population—an iron wall which the native population cannot break through. This is, in toto, our policy towards the Arabs. To formulate it any other way would only be hypocrisy.
> (BRENNER 1984, 74–57)

Jabotinsky was clear in presenting his ideas that achieving a Jewish state meant using force and not negotiating with the indigenous population. Jabotinsky saw that Palestine was the ultimate solution for the Jewish people since they "had a moral right to return to Palestine" even if native Palestinian people populated the area (Shlaim 2000, 15). He presented his primary ideas for establishing a Jewish state in his famous paper "On the Iron Wall," which became the bible of his political and moral thinking.

Other prominent Jewish leaders pursued this concept of creating a Jewish state. Chaim Weizmann, who became president of the World Zionist Organization and later the first president of Israel, and David Ben Gurion, who became the first prime minister of Israel, played central roles in the state project.[2] As president of the WZO, Weizmann was adept "at enlisting the British government's support for the Zionist project in Palestine" (Shlaim 2000, 6).

Ben Gurion spoke of his vision to the joint secretariat of the main Zionist grouping in the *yishuv* on November 10, 1929: "The Arab must not and cannot be a Zionist. He could never wish the Jews to become a majority. This is the true antagonism between us and the Arabs. We both want to be the majority" (Masalha 1992, 18). Ben Gurion's goal was to create a Jewish majority in Palestine in order to achieve the final vision of a Jewish state. He did not care very much about the native Palestinians. Ben Gurion, referred to by Ilan Pappe as "the architect" (2008, 23), played a central role in creating the Jewish state. He raised the banner of a Jewish state at every possible opportunity. In an article, he stated clearly that "A Jewish state in Palestine would not only finally solve the world's most painful problem, but would contribute one of the principal guarantees for peace and progress in the Middle East. . . . The independent Arab nations [that surround] Palestine will have no closer, more loyal or useful friends than the independent Jewish nation" (*Palestine Post,* March 2, 1945). But although he spoke about mutual ties and possible alliances with the Arabs in the Middle East and in Palestine and perceived that the Jewish state would be a bridge between the West and the Arab world, he missed the point that his project would face Palestinian resistance.

To achieve their goal, the Jews needed to create a majority in Palestine by increasing the ratio of settlers. They used the biblical concept of "Eretz Israel" or a Hebrew state for the people of Israel. They argued that their charter was a divine promise, or used the Bible as the Jewish Mandate to establish their homeland. Geographically, "Falastin," as the indigenous Palestinians call it, and "Eretz Israel," as it is referred to by the Jews, was the place that would host the migrant Jews from all over the globe.

> Palestine is our ever-memorable historic home. The very name of Palestine would attract our people with a force of marvellous potency . . . we should there form a portion of the rampart of Europe against Asia, and outpost of civilization as opposed to barbarism . . . we should as a neutral State remain in contact with all Europe, which would have to guarantee our existence.
> (HERZL 1946, 30)

However, the vision that the Zionist movement sought to achieve in Palestine faced obstacles since it was "married to another man" (Karmi 2007). It clashed with the concept of "Falastin," held by the indigenous people of Palestine. The Palestinians saw Palestine as their home, where they lived in their villages and practiced their culture, religion, history, language, and beliefs. The same applied to the Naqab region where the Bedouin could narrate the long history of their ancestors going back centuries. Edward Said supported the argument of Palestine as a Palestinian holy place populated by indigenous Palestinian people: "The land of Palestine gave rise to one of the most ancient of all civilizations . . . before Hebrew tribes migrated to the area. . . . Palestine became predominantly Arab and Islamic by the end of the seventh century" (Said and Christopher 1988, 235).

From its earliest beginnings, Zionism was a settler movement, adopting a strategy intended to increase the number of Jews to the highest possible level through intensive immigration, and to uproot the Palestinians who populated "Falastin." Nira Yuval-Davis (1989, 94–95) shows that demography became a central tool in Zionist thinking. Weizmann's vision was to create facts on the ground: "Immigration must go on; there were, he reckoned, a million Jews in Europe who must be brought in within ten years" (PRO, CO 733/462/12).[3]

## *The Zionist Vision for the Naqab and Biʾr al-Sabaʿ Region*

In writing about the Naqab region in the 1930s, Major C. S. Jarvis, the governor of Sinai, noted: "The principal importance of the Negeb in Byzantine times was its value as a trade route. Situated . . . between the Mediterranean and the Red Sea, and by land between Palestine, Egypt and Syria, it was the key to three or four of the most important trade routes of the Middle East" (PRO, FO 371/20885; Levin. 2010, 1–18).

The Naqab and Beersheba continued to play an important strategic role for the Zionist movement. The Naqab seemed to complete the Zionist ideology of settlement, since in Zionist thinking it was an empty and unexploited territory that needed Jewish brain power to make it bloom. For David Ben Gurion, father of the Jewish state, the Naqab was central to the project:

> The southern border of our land is the same as it was in Shlomo's time: the Gulf of the Red Sea is the Arava [*Wadi ʿAraba*] or ancient Eilat. By the Mediterranean

> Sea, Eretz Israel is joined to Europe and by the Red Sea it is connected to India. . . . Until the tenth century Eilat was a central commercial city according to the Arab geographer Shams Al Din. The trade of the Negev crossed the Gulf of Eilat to India.
>
> (ASIA 1994, 9, MY TRANSLATION)

Ben Gurion argued on the basis of the narrative that the Naqab had been populated by Jewish people and was their commercial center, and that the southern borders of the Jewish state included the Gulf of Um Rash-Rash. To support his idea of including all the Naqab within his plans for "Eretz Israel" he framed it around the biblical Hebrew tribes. He wished to restore the commercial route with India by including Eilat within the borders of the Jewish state. He also wanted a corridor in the West via the Mediterranean in order to remain in contact with Europe. Since 1918 Ben Gurion had a specific vision of the Naqab, and of settling the Naqab. As a result, purchasing land was his ultimate aspiration. Merely to mention the history of the biblical Naqab was to colonize it: Hebrew history started in Beersheba, and Beersheba was based on one of the main central routes between the south and Egypt.

One reason the Zionist movement focused on the Naqab was its significant potential for settlement. Early on during the British Mandate, the Jewish National Fund (JNF) and the Zionist Commission had purchased land in the Naqab in order to build Jewish settlements. Weizmann was just as eager as Ben Gurion to fill the Naqab with Jewish settlers and recognized that the shortage of water in the desert might be an obstacle. In 1945, he spoke of "the possibilities of irrigating the Negeb and [how] they could settle there at least a million" (PRO, CO 733/462/12). However, his vision did not come to pass. Today only 8 percent of Israel's total population lives in the Naqab.

Ben Gurion wanted the Naqab as one of the main regions for settlement because it encompassed some 12,000,000 *dunams* and was "almost unpopulated and only slightly cultivated." In 1935, he commented that "This country is No Man's Land. It has no legal owners and anyone who cultivates it with the permission of the government is entitled to become its owner, according to a Turkish law, which will prevail in Palestine" (Kark 1981, 344).

Ben Gurion appears to have regarded the Naqab as a barren wasteland, left undeveloped by its inhabitants. In conceptualizing the notion that no one existed in the Naqab he victimized the indigenous Bedouin in order to facilitate his task of colonizing the region. Recent research shows that around 2 million *dunams* were being cultivated by their Bedouin owners in the Biʾr al-Sabaʿ region at this time (Nasasra 2012; Amara, Abu Saad, and Yiftachel 2012). Palestinian newspapers also report Bedouin cultivation efforts in the Naqab at this time (*Huna al-Quds*, 1942).

Efraim Karsh (1997, 50), who interprets Ben Gurion's vision for the Naqab as vital, acknowledges that Ben Gurion saw the creation of Jewish settlements in the Naqab as a possibility. However, Karsh rejects the view that Ben Gurion wanted to evict or drive the Arabs off the land. Yet as early as 1935, Ben Gurion expected to incorporate the Naqab into the new Jewish state. In 1935, he toured the eastern Naqab and traveled to ʿAqaba to check whether the area was populated by Bedouin. Returning to Washington, he spoke to Louis Brandeis about building settlements in the Naqab and investigated funding possibilities. Brandeis duly donated an amount of $25,000 to invest in settlement opportunities. His financial support was the first crucial step on the way to achieving Ben Gurion's vision of establishing settlements in the Naqab (Teveth 1987, 494–497).

During discussions on the White Paper in 1939, Zionist leaders argued for ownership of the Naqab as part of the future Jewish state. Missions were sent to the Naqab to explore opportunities for Jewish settlement. The leaders put pressure on their British supporters to include the Naqab in the Jewish state. Writing in the *Jewish Chronicle* in 1940, Sir Frank Sanderson (a member of the Conservative Party in the British Parliament) described the Naqab as "an empty territory in Palestine." He claimed that this area should be colonized by the Jews, and that the time had come

> for the Jews to colonize the Negev. . . . I cannot understand why Jews should seek a *Lebensraum* in the most unlikely places of the world when they have the wide and empty spaces of the Negev to look to. I know that for Jews one square mile in the Promised Land is worth a thousand square miles anywhere else.
>
> (*JEWISH CHRONICLE*, APRIL 9, 1940)

Sanderson promoted this myth of the Naqab as an "empty" and "wasted" land in other newspapers, arguing in the *Daily Telegraph* that "this is an area of 4,400 square miles, an area as great as that of Northern Palestine and seven times greater than that already owned by Jews in Palestine" (letter, *The Daily Telegraph*, March 11, 1940).

Interestingly, there were other British individuals who did not deny the existence of the Bedouin in the Naqab. For example, Sir George E. Kirk (a Middle East expert), writing a few days later in the *Daily Telegraph* on "Settlement in the Negev," responded to this eagerness to colonize the Naqab:

> I do not deny that some settlements in the northern and western Negeb is possible. It is vitally important, however, in that case that the Arab cultivator-herdsmen, who now inhabit the district to the number of several thousands, should be adequately protected. Like all primitive people they are attached to their tribal lands, and I have heard them express their dread of Jewish settlements
>
> (*DAILY TELEGRAPH*, MARCH 15, 1940)

Like other British commentators at the time, Kirk did not regard the Naqab as a wasted and empty land. Instead, he felt that there was a need to protect its indigenous people (still a colonialist attitude) and to consider possible resistance by the Bedouin to colonization. British diplomats took a similar line in a report from the field, which said: "the statement, so often made for propaganda purposes, that nearly half of Palestine (Naqab) is still empty and available for settlements is roughly speaking true as regards its emptiness but altogether false and misleading as regards its availability" (PRO, FO 371/61868).

## *Establishing Settlements in the Naqab, 1911–1936*

The first kibbutz settlement in Palestine had been established in 1878 in Pitah Tikva, called *Mlabbas* by the local Arabs (Pappe 2006, 2). Having succeeded with the initial settlements, the path toward expansion further into the south became easier. In the Naqab, the first piece of land (6,000 *dunams* of mainly Rohama/Jammama land) was purchased in 1911 from Bedouin of the Tayaha tribe (al-ʿAtawna) with the intention of setting up the first kibbutz in the Naqab (Kark 2002, 44). The Jewish buyers had problems with registering this land since the Ottomans refused to allow it. Eventually, Kibbutz Negba, the first kibbutz in the southern Naqab, was established in 1939. After this Jews managed to establish many other colonies, particularly in the northern Naqab, during the early 1940s.

Joseph Weitz of the Jewish National Fund reported that up to 1946 fifteen Jewish colonies had been created in the Naqab and the Maritime Plain, including Nirim, Mivtachim, Urim, and Shorashim (PRO, CO 537/2311). Weitz's reference to Jewish settlements as "colonies" strengthened the colonial aspect of the Zionist project in the south. By March 1947, according to Weitz's list, the JNF owned 55,960 *dunams* in the Naqab. (Weitz 1947, 196)

TABLE 4.1
Jewish settlements in the Naqab to 1947

| SETTLEMENT | NATIVE ARABIC NAME[a] | DATE ESTABLISHED (MONTH.DAY.YEAR) | POPULATION (MARCH 1947) | SETTLEMENT LANDS IN JNF OWNERSHIP (*DUNAMS*) |
|---|---|---|---|---|
| Urim | Qurien | 10.6.46 | 81 | 2,300 |
| Ba'ri | Nakhabir | 10.6.46 | 108 | 5,400 |
| *Beit-Eshel* | | 8.9.43 | 60 | 6,000 |
| *Gvulot* | | 5.12.43 | 75 | 5,000 |
| Hatzerim | Qalta | 10.6.46 | 55 | 2,500 |
| Kfar Darom | Deir Al Balah | 10.6.46 | 25 | 260 |
| Mivtachim | | 2.7.47 | 33 | 2,500 |
| Mishmar ha-Negev | Beir Abu Mansour | 10.6.46 | 52 | 2,200 |
| Navatim | Madsus | 10.6.46 | 30 | 2,300 |
| Nirim | Danqur | 10.6.46 | 56 | 2,200 |
| Alumim | Khaza'li | 2.7.47 | 25 | 8,000 |
| *Revivim* | *'Asloj region* | 7.28.43 | 125 | 12,000 |
| Shoval | Beir Zballa | 10.6.47 | 61 | 1,300 |
| Shorashim | | 2.7.47 | 25 | 2,600 |
| Tquma | Zummara | 10.6.46 | 30 | 1,400 |
| Rohama[b] | Jammama | 1911 | — | — |

*Notes*: Names in Arabic by the author.

[a]In October 1946, the head office of the Keren Kayement (KKL) (the Names Committee) decided on the ultimate names of the settlements established in Judea and the Naqab. According to the committee, the new kibbutzim names in the Naqab would replace the Arabic names of the villages.

[b]Rohama was the first kibbutz to be established in the Naqab in 1911 (during the Ottoman period). The Bedouin village called al-Jammama (al-ʿAtawna village).

New waves of Jewish migrants had begun to arrive in Palestine following the establishment of the first settlements in 1878. From 1882 until 1903, there was massive immigration (*aliyah*) with the aim of creating a Jewish community in Palestine. One of the first "to make *aliyah*" to Palestine was Herzl. The second *aliyah* from 1904 to 1914 was equally intensive. This second *aliyah* included young pioneering revolutionary individuals motivated by Zionist ideology. Among these new immigrants were some of the most effective Jewish leaders: David Ben Gurion, Moshe Sharett, and Levi Askhol (Gorny 1987, 13–16; Shapira 1992).

The metaphorical birth of a Jewish state occurred with the issuing of the Balfour Declaration in 1917. In one night, Zionism changed from dream to fact. Zionism had won a crucial victory with formal support for the Jews to build a national homeland in Palestine through this special mandatory license. Zionist plans to transform Palestine into Eretz Israel became a crucial element of conflict in the history of the Arab Middle East.

## UN Plans After 1947: Two States in Palestine

After the Peel Commission and the White Paper failed to settle the growing conflict in Palestine, an imposed partition emerged in 1947 as the best tactic for resolving the violence in the region. Weizmann succeeded in pressuring the Americans to include the Naqab in the Jewish state. On November 29, 1947, the United Nations General Assembly (UNGA) recommended a Partition Plan that divided Palestine into two countries, one Jewish and the other Arab, based on Resolution 181. According to this UN plan, a Jewish state was suggested that would include Eastern Galilee, the Ha Sharon region, the Coastal Strip, and the major part of the northern Naqab region. The Arab state was to include the West Bank, the Gaza Strip, and Upper and Western Galilee. Jerusalem and Bethlehem were to remain under international rule. In the south, a substantial part of the Naqab was due to come under the administration of the Jewish state, except for Beersheba, which would be included in the Arab state.

Neither the Jordanians nor the Palestinians were satisfied with the Partition Plan. The Jordanians sought to subject the Naqab to their control (as had been the case in 1937 with the Peel Commission). Jordan's King ʿAbdallah and Glubb Pasha, commander of the Arab Legion, were eager to bring the Naqab under their command since both regarded the area as Arab and were determined that it should remain Arab under their rule. However, Jewish lobbying was again successful in getting the major part of the Naqab included within the Partition Plan's Jewish state borders.

During the Partition Plan negotiations Glubb Pasha acknowledged that the Jews were eager to have the Naqab:

> I have never [*sic*] referred to the possibility of giving a part of the Southern Desert [i.e., the Negev] . . . to the Jews . . . but I see in the press that the Jews demand this area. Perhaps they have knowledge of some mineral wealth there, but this seems unlikely. The statement that this desert is agriculturally valuable (or could be made so) is almost certainly false, and conceals some other motives, probably of political or strategic nature.
> (MORRIS 2002, 88–89)

His analysis suggests that the Zionists had a strategic plan to control the Naqab for settlement purposes and possibly for mineral resources. At the same time it would give a future Jewish state a corridor to the port of ʿAqaba and prevent a continuation of Arab territory between Egypt and Transjordan.

With the acceptance of the Partition Plan in New York by the UN General Assembly on November 30, 1947, the Jewish state officially came into being. Zionist leaders saw it as a great achievement for their newly-independent country, whereas the Palestinians, as anticipated, refused to accept the division of their native land into two countries to be shared with Jewish settlers. The Arab Higher Committee declared its resistance to the UN decision resulting in a resumption of fighting in Palestine between the Palestinians and the Jews. The situation began to resemble a civil war, with sporadic but significant violence between the two sides. The fighting spread throughout the region, escalating to air strikes on Arab villages and Jewish settlements. Meanwhile, the British were busy packing up and preparing to withdraw from a region that was exploding; they eventually pulled out in May 1948.

In the southern district of Palestine, the Naqab Bedouin shaikhs played their part in the political crisis by clearly stating their position. Gathering in Beersheba on November 25, 1947, the shaikhs tried to shape their future by making certain crucial decisions. A message to the Arab Higher Committee following their meeting stated that "The Bedouin of the Negev constitute an independent segment [of the population] and politically their shaikhs are not connected to any other element . . . the Bedouin themselves will decide about the stand they will adopt regarding the development of events in Palestine, and will not take orders from above" (Morris 2004, 26). This meeting showed Bedouin ideology toward and interest in what was happening in Palestine.

Violence spread to the Naqab immediately after the UN partition plans became fact. In the early stages of the war, the Bedouin were encouraged by some Arab leaders to attack Jewish settlements in the Naqab. Active operations were launched against the *yishuv* in particular by targeting main water pipelines in isolated settlements in the eastern Mishamar Hanegev and southern Tkoma. John Bitzan notes that the Bedouin were responsible for many victims on the Jewish side, particularly among patrol units of the Palmach Brigade. They also targeted Jewish settlements in the Naqab. In December 1947, for example, they attacked Kibbutz Nivatim. Israel retaliated by taking military action, and the Bedouin assailants were bombed in an air strike directed from Beit Eshel. Bitzan records that the kibbutz was shocked by the violent actions of the local villagers (Bitzan 2006).

### *May 1948 and the Defeat of the Egyptians in the Naqab*

Jews and Arabs pursued civil war until March 1948 when sporadic clashes between the two sides intensified into more violent actions. The Palestinians received arms supplies from Arab countries and for the next six months were supported by volunteers from Iraq and Syria. Meanwhile, the Haganah, who had obtained arms and support from Czechoslovakia, started massive offensives against Palestinian villages, occupying several of the strategic ones.

As planned by Ben Gurion, the Jewish strategy of defending the *yishuv* proved very effective. In the initial stage of the war—until March 1948—his strategy had mainly involved defensive fighting since his refusal to abandon a single yishuv meant that the Arabs were prevented from occupying settlements. During March 1948, the Arabs managed to isolate the central territories in the Galilee and the Naqab and to disconnect them from the central area of the Jewish state. In April, there was a critical change of direction in Jewish war tactics starting with the Nahshon operation and Haganah's policy of occupying Arab neighborhoods in Haifa and Tiberias. After several months of fighting, a minority of well-organized Jewish communities successfully defeated the Palestinians, over half of whom were driven from their homes. The British completed their withdrawal from Palestine in May 1948. Jewish independence was pronounced at 4:00 p.m. on May 14, 1948, when David Ben Gurion read out the Declaration of the Independence of the State of Israel (Medinat Yisrael) at the Tel Aviv Art Museum.

The United States officially recognized Israel as a state on May 14, 1948. By doing so the United States became the Jewish state's most visible ally. The second country to recognize Israel as a new state in Palestine was the Soviet Union. Described as "godfathers" by Shlaim (2000, 33), these two international imperial powers provided the new state with real support from the first moments of its existence.

The day after the announcement of an Israeli state in Palestine, armies from five Arab nations (Egypt, Jordan, Syria, Lebanon, and Iraq, as well as two military groups from Saudi Arabia and Yemen) entered Palestine in an attempt to defend its people. The Egyptian forces invaded from the south and targeted Tel Aviv; the Iraqi army advanced from the East, attacking Kibbutz Gesher and aiming to invade Emik Yisrael; the Arab Legion crossed Transjordan and headed to Jerusalem; and Lebanese and Syrian forces invaded from the north (Morris 2002). The war between the new state of Israel and the invading Arab armies intensified and was pursued on all fronts. The Israel Defense Force (IDF) made efforts to target the Arab Legion and to release Jerusalem from the siege. Israeli forces occupied Lydda airport and Ramle in July 1948 following the launch of Operation Danny, thus opening the corridor to Jerusalem. However, at this stage the IDF failed to occupy either Latrun or Jerusalem. On the Galilee front, al-Qawiqji's Arab Liberation army was defeated and withdrew, which meant that Operation Hiram had successfully occupied central Galilee. Subsequently, both Western Galilee and Nazareth were occupied. The Syrian army remained stubborn and was not totally defeated.

On the southern front, Egyptian sources reported that the Fourth Brigade, which included the First, Second, and Sixth Battalions, would undertake the main role of the Egyptian army in Fallujah. These battalions entered Fallujah on June 20, 1948, and successfully besieged central bases in the Naqab. The First Battalion advanced at 06:00 a.m., from al-Majdal, occupying Iraq Suwaidan, Iraq al-Manshiya, Fallujah, and Beit Jibrin. They proceeded to Deir Nakhhas. In this advanced position the Egyptian army was just a few miles from al-Khalil (Hebron) and close to the new route that led to Jerusalem (Hussein 1949, 5). On October 14, the Israeli foreign minister, Moshe Sharett (who became Israel's second prime minister), approved the IDF's occupation of the Naqab. This marked the beginning of Operation Yoav, the main objective of which was to besiege the Egyptians who were still fighting in the Naqab. In air and ground operations, the IDF targeted the Egyptian bases that were spread all over the Naqab—at Beersheba (which had come under Egyptian army control in May 1948 and became their military headquarters in the south), at Gaza, al-Majdal, Fallujah, Beit Jibrin, Iraq Suwaidan, Iraq al-Manshiya, and others.

It proved difficult to overpower the Egyptians. The Egyptians had managed to isolate the Naqab from the Jews and control it along the main line of Majdal-Beit Jibrin and Hebron. The IDF's main policy involved isolating the transport routes to prevent supplies from reaching the Egyptian troops. The Egyptians successfully attacked settlements in the Naqab, such as Kibbutz Nirim and Kfar Darom, occupied Gaza, and afterwards headed toward al-Majdal and Sdud on the coast (El-Edross 1980).

Israel's crucial attack on the Egyptian army began at 6:00 a.m. on October 16, when the Israelis began a general offensive against the Fourth

FIGURE 4.1 Remains of the destroyed village of Iraq al-Manshiya (2008), where the Egyptian army was besieged in Fallujah. *Source*: Photo by the author.

Brigade aimed at occupying Fallujah. After five days of heavy shelling, the Israelis had still not defeated the Egyptian position. However, the capture of Beit Jibrin by Jewish forces isolated the Egyptian Fourth Brigade from the rest of the Egyptian army (Hussein 1949, 6). Operation Yoav, which had begun on October 15, 1948, ended with the anticipated defeat of the Egyptians. The Egyptians abandoned the city. Beersheba collapsed and felt into the hands of the Israeli army on October 21, 1948. In the space of a week, the IDF had managed to conquer Beit Jibrin and Beersheba. In the eyes of the Bedouin, the fall of Beersheba was a black day in their history. They referred to the occupation of Beersheba in 1948 as *kasret* Biʾr al-Sabaʿ, meaning in Bedouin dialect the "Nakba of Beersheba." Bedouin oral histories concerning the fall of Beersheba produced a different perspective.[4]

After Operation Yoav had successfully conquered Beersheba, Fallujah remained as the Egyptian army's most stubbornly resistant base. Following the conquest of Iraq Suwaidan, the Egyptians were then besieged in Fallujah, eventually withdrawing from Ashdod/Sdud and al-Majdal to Gaza. However, with the start of the armistice talks, the Egyptian army surrendered and marched out of Fallujah on February 26, 1949. The IDF's success in besieging the Egyptian army in Fallujah and Iraq al-Manshiya and isolating them in al-Majdal represented the turning point in the war over the Naqab and sealed its destiny as part of the future of Israel.

Because they lived just a few miles from Fallujah, the Jabarat Bedouin, who populated the area of Tal Abu Jaber, saw the clashes between the Egyptian and Jewish armies at close quarters. They were the first Bedouin tribe to pay the price of the war, since most of them fled their village when the war reached them. According to one of the survivors of the war, a Bedouin shaikh of the Jabarat who today lives in the Biqaʾ camp in Jordan,

> It was Ramadan and most of my tribe was trapped due to the clashes between the Jewish and the Egyptian armies. As a result some of the houses were bombed and members of various families were killed. On the 9th day of Ramadan, just after the war had calmed down, we headed East to Dawaiyma, then to Beit Jibrin and Qubaiba, then to Jericho where, together with hundreds of my tribe, we settled down and tried to build our lives in the middle of nowhere.
>
> (INTERVIEW WITH SHAIKH WASSIL ABU JABER, BIQA' CAMP, JORDAN, APRIL 2014)

Israeli forces finalized the takeover of the Naqab when they moved south and occupied Um Rash-Rash after the armistice agreement with Egypt had been signed on March 10, 1949 (PRO, FO 371/128154).

## *The Fall of Beersheba, 1948*

Before the fall of Beersheba, a leading Bedouin shaikh from the Tayaha had held secret talks with the Egyptians during the war. He met Hilmi Juma, the Egyptian governor of the area, and various Egyptian security officers near the village of Lakiya (secret report from Rehovot to the prime minister's office and the Defense Ministry, August 12, 1953: ISA/ GL 13904/14).

The future of the remaining Bedouin was decided quickly during the final stages of the war. Israeli leaders and the army were divided over whether to exile the Bedouin or to issue them with citizenship.[5] One group favored keeping the "loyal" Bedouin, particularly for recruitment to the army. Others supported exiling the remaining Bedouin. Moshe Sharett and Shimoni, for instance, were in favor of encouraging them to leave the country (Morris 2005, 327). Rhoda Kanaaneh (2009, 12–13) confirms that despite the small percentages, loyal Bedouin tribes were encouraged to volunteer for the Israeli military forces in different positions, such as trackers.

On November 18, 1948, sixteen Bedouin shaikhs sent a formal request to be left on their land. As a result, the defense minister set up a committee, and a discussion ensued on November 30 about the future of those Bedouin remaining within the borders of Israel. The committee, which included Yousef Weitz (KKL official), General Yigal Yadin, and General Yigal Alon, agreed that only "friendly" Bedouin tribes would be left:

> The *friendly/loyal* Bedouin will be concentrated, by tribe, in three centers, at least ten km [six miles] from one another . . . two tribes to inhabit no man's land east of Rohama and Shoval, close to the Dawaiyma border line, and a third tribe to stay north of the Nivatim-Kurnub line. . . . Most young men of military age will be enlisted in an appropriate combat unit [the minorities unit of the IDF]. . . . Michael Ha-Negbi [military governor of the Negev] will be responsible for Bedouin affairs . . . the tribes will be required to commit themselves to a particular policy, as well as to obligations regarding their land. (CZA: A 246/36, EMPHASIS ADDED)

This meeting between Jewish leaders and military officers shows that only loyal Bedouin would remain under Jewish rule. Oral history testimonies mention that Bedouin who agreed to these terms did manage to stay. As one respondent put it: "If you want to submit, come to the military government offices in Beersheba to get yourself registered, otherwise you must leave the territory" (interview with Shaikh abu Ahmad, September 2013).

In the Naqab, only 12,500 of the 95,000 Bedouin that had lived there before the Nakba remained on their land. Like their fellow Palestinians they faced very harsh consequences as a result of the war, including transfer activities (Saʿdi and Abu-Lughod 2007; see also chapters 6, 7, and 8). Reporting on army operations in the Naqab between July and October 1948, Morris records testimony of the early expulsion of Naqab Bedouin by the Negev and Yiftah Brigades:

> We opened fire at close quarters. Some of the camels were killed and under cover of darkness, the Arabs fled. Later the patrol ambushed two more caravans, killing additional camels . . . the Negev Brigade continued harassing the Arab inhabitants and Bedouin tribes . . . the brigade carried out full-scale clearing operations in the Kaufakha–al-Muharaqa area. The village inhabitants and Bedouin concentrations in the area were dispersed and expelled . . . Elsewhere in the Negev, Yiftah 51st and 53rd Battalions were ordered to cleanse the areas of the enemy [i.e. unfriendly Bedouin tribes] and to destroy his possessions . . . five days later, the Battalion duly reported that all the Arabs [in these areas] had been expelled.
>
> (MORRIS 2004, 446–447)

Morris described the army's operations against Bedouin in the Naqab as "cleansing." Some Jewish settlers who lived in the area criticized these "cleansing" activities. Certain *mukhtars* (village headmen) among the settlers, including those from Kibbutz Dorot, Nir-ʿAm and Rohama, complained to Ben Gurion and requested that cleansing the Bedouin and sabotaging their properties should stop (Morris 2004, 447). I came across some interviewees who confirmed that Jewish settlers had mediated between them and the army:

> We helped some Kibbutz to survive prior to the war by supplying them with smuggled food. Economically, the kibbutz relied on Bedouin supplies which were smuggled and sold to them by neighboring Bedouin. Some tribes sold

> land to their neighboring kibbutz, which created good relations between Bedouin and settlers. Some Bedouin used to complain to the Kibbutz settlers by saying "we helped you to survive, and we want you to mediate between us and the army in order to leave us on our land and to treat us differently."
> (INTERVIEW WITH ABU AHMAD, AUGUST 2009)

Some Jewish *mukhtars* maintained good relations with Bedouin tribes and also mediated between them and the military governors after the war (Porat 2015, 66). Many Bedouin oral accounts recount supplying the settlers with smuggled goods during the first stages of settlement. As the elders explained, the Bedouin in return asked the settlers to mediate between them and the army so they could be left on their land. Because of the stable relations that had emerged between these settlers and the Bedouin, some settlers helped the tribespeople to remain in Israeli territory. According to Bedouin elders, the mediation of the *mukhtar* of Kibbutz Shoval prevented the expulsion of Bedouin during and after the war (interview with al-Haj Saud, October 2014).

Sasson Bar Zvi, the military governor of the Naqab in the 1960s, indicates that Beersheba was empty of Bedouin after the war. Almost all of them had gone, and not a single one remained in the city:

> In the war, people were exiled or else left to many other places. By the end of the war the main Bedouin city of Beersheba was empty of Bedouin. No Bedouin, no Gazan businessmen, no shopkeepers, and not even any birds remained in the city. After the war had ended some new Jewish immigrants started to come to the city.
> (INTERVIEW WITH SASSON BAR ZVI, JULY 2007)

During the war, a new form of treatment of Bedouin in the Naqab by soldiers appears in an unpleasant story recounted by Ben Gurion. This incident, in which a Bedouin girl was raped and killed by soldiers, remained secret for a long time. Ben Gurion himself noted in his diaries that the rape and murder of the Bedouin girl was a "horrific atrocity":

> In August 1949, an army unit stationed at Nirim in the Negev shot an Arab man and captured a Bedouin girl who was with him. Her name and age remain unknown, but she was probably in her mid-teens. In the following hours she

> was taken from the hut and forced to shower naked in full view of the soldiers. Three of the men raped her. . . . She was forced into a patrol vehicle with several soldiers, two carrying shovels, and they drove off into dunes. When the girl realised what was about to happen she tried to run, but only made a few paces before she was shot by a Sergeant Michael.
> (*GUARDIAN*, NOVEMBER 4, 2003)

## Armistice Agreements: A Jewish State Recognized by the Arabs, 1949

The first round of armistice agreement negotiations began on the Greek island of Rhodes in January 1949. This marked the formal end of the fighting between Israel and the Arab armies. The first armistice agreement was signed on February 24, 1949 following a marathon round of talks between the Jewish state and Egypt that ended with the Egyptians withdrawing from the Naqab and the Gaza Strip being left under Egyptian rule. As expected, the people of the Naqab were critical of these Egyptian-Jewish negotiations, mainly because the Egyptians had controlled Beersheba and other strategic parts of the Naqab since 1948. In the end, Israel secured control over the Naqab and strengthened its position in the Bedouin land.

Lebanon started armistice negotiations with Israel on March 1, 1949, by asking Israel to withdraw from parts of southern Lebanon. An armistice agreement signed between Israel and Lebanon on March 23 marked the end of mutual hostilities. Stability returned with the withdrawal of Israel from occupied villages in Lebanon.

After the armistice agreement signed with Jordan, Egypt lost parts of the Naqab. Negotiations between Jordan and the Jewish delegates started on March 4, 1949 in Rhodes and continued in Jerusalem as well as in Jordan at al-Shona. While the negotiations were proceeding, the Israelis took active steps to conquer more areas in the southern Naqab, mainly Um Rash-Rash, which would become part of the Jewish state. British archival reports show that Israel wanted to secure more land in the southern Naqab and therefore sent forces on March 10, 1949, to occupy Eilat. Since the Israeli forces had entered the southern Naqab from Egyptian territory, it appeared that by occupying Eilat Israel had breached the armistice agreement with Egypt (PRO, FO 371/128154).

Reports by the United Nations Observers during the negotiations in Rhodes show that the Jordanians complained about Israel's violation of the truce. They also stated that the Israelis were continuing to conduct military operations, on Jordanian land. Their complaint included Israel's operations against the Arab Legion in Wadi ʿAraba as well as incursions by Israeli aircraft into Jordanian territory. These details were contained in a cable containing a supplementary report on the situation in the southern Negev dated March 22, 1949, from the acting mediator (Ralph Bunche) to the UN secretary-general (PRO, FO 371/128154).

By the end of these armistice negotiations, Israel fully controlled the Naqab. King ʿAbdallah of Jordan signed an armistice agreement with Israel on April 3, 1949 (PRO, FO 371/128154), in which the Jordanians made various concessions over certain pieces of territory. The Little Triangle (Wadi ʿAra region) became subject to Israel, and in return the Jordanians acquired the West Bank. The case of Jerusalem remained open (Shlaim (2000); Ali El-Edroos 1980). Israel established its recognized eastern and southern borders by signing the two armistice agreements with Egypt and Jordan, with its strategic gain being the Naqab.

Syria was the fourth and last Arab country to sign an armistice agreement with Israel. The process took longer (March to July 1949) than any other Arab-Israeli negotiations, as Syria was asked to withdraw its military forces and build a demilitarized zone around the Jordan River. Following the Syrian withdrawal, the armistice agreement was signed with Israel on July 20, 1949. Shlaim notes that after all the armistice agreements had been signed, the map of Israel had expanded from 55 percent (according to the Partition Plan) to 79 percent of Mandatory Palestine (Shlaim 2000, 47).

FIVE

# The Emergence of Military Rule, 1949–1950

WITH THE CREATION of the state of Israel in May 1948, most of the Bedouin became refugees in neighboring Arab countries, with around 13,000 remaining in the Naqab. Following Israel's establishment, a system of military rule was designed and imposed on the Palestinian Arab minority who remained under the control of the new state. As Sa'di (2014) notes, the lives of the Palestinian Arab minority were monitored under military rule via a surveillance system. According to Sabri Jiryis, this military rule was legally created in January 1950 (Jiryis 1976, 16). I argue that the system of control lasted until 1967 and cruelly restricted the lives of the Arab minority. In order to achieve its aims as a new settler state Israel needed to accumulate more territory for the use of its Jewish citizens, a process that Ghazi Falah identifies as an "enclavization of space" (Falah 2005, 1,343).

The founding of Israel created the phenomenon of a Palestinian indigenous minority within its borders. After the Nakba, Palestinian Arab inhabitants lived across a broad area of the new state: the Galilee, the Naqab, and the Little Triangle. However, considerable numbers of Arabs also lived in mixed cities such as Acre, Haifa, Jaffa, Ramle, and Lydda, in which they were subjected to regulation. Military rule was imposed on Palestinian Arab Israeli citizens regardless of where they lived, yet the military regulations did not apply to citizens who lived outside the closed zones.

## Palestinians in Israel under Military Defense Regulations

The overall aim of the Israeli military rule was control (*shlita* in Hebrew) according to Penhas Amir (military governor of the Naqab in the late 1950s). Military rule was based on the British Emergency Defense Regulations that had been used during the Mandate to fight Jewish militant groups and to suppress Palestinian revolts. While the regulations were intended to maintain Israel's security, their use enabled Israel to restrict daily life among the Arab minority with the intent to force them to abandon their belligerent attitude toward the state of Israel (Robinson 2013).

Israeli military rule exercised its legal power on the basis of the 1945 British Emergency Defense Regulations. Initially adopted against the Arab minority in Israel during the era of government rule (1948–1967), these regulations were subsequently maintained by the state for security reasons. Some remain in force up to the present against the Arab minority between Israeli opponents and proponents. These regulations were mostly implemented without recourse to the courts and constrained the lives of the Palestinians in Israel at all levels. The regulations or Takanot Haganah (the Hebrew term) included almost all the categories for punishing and restricting the Arab minority in Israel. According to Ted Gurr (1993), states oppress minorities in order to achieve their goals. His analysis applies to the way Israel oppressed the remnants of the Arab population in order to achieve its ultimate vision. James Scott (1998, 2) also agrees that states use coercive power to achieve their aims. Certainly Israel would not have succeeded in manipulating the Arabs without the use of coercive power and control tactics. Settler states also use internal colonialism to dominate minorities (Zureik 1979; Yiftachel 2003, 2013).

The same regulations had been opposed by the Jewish leaders and the yishuv during the British Mandate. However, immediately after 1948, they became a lens of power used by Israel against its Arab minority citizens. The emergency regulations that had been drawn up by the British high commissioner in Mandatory Palestine in 1937 to put down the Great Revolt of 1936–1939 had allowed the British army authorities free use of power in various positions and were not restricted by any body of law (Jiryis 1976, 9–35; Korn 1996, 2000). Jewish militant groups (Lehi) were pronounced as being outside the law according to the regulations. Many Jewish leaders were prosecuted, such as members of the Etsel group.

Some were even exiled to Africa. In reply to proposals for the abolition of military government, a press statement on February 20, 1962, from David Ben Gurion highlighted the importance of using the emergency regulations for Israeli security:

> The Defense Regulations of 1945 and the military administration system are essential for the security of the state and the peace of the Arabs in Israel who wish to live in tranquility and hope for peace between Israel and her Arab neighbors.
>
> (ISA/ GL 7128/7)

The prime minister was aware that use of the emergency regulations combined with a military government was essential for governing the Arab minority in Israel. He justified this for security reasons as did many other Jewish supporters of military rule.

According to a report from the Department of the Military Government, the British Mandatory Defense Regulations of 1945 represented the only legal foundation of the military government. On that basis, all the activities of the military government before 1950 were illegal. Some of the regulations were cancelled or watered down after the creation of the state of Israel, such as Articles 102–107, which prevented immigration (*aliyah*). This served the Jewish community by bringing in more immigrants. Articles 114–118, which dealt with land holding, were also cancelled for the same reason. The professed goals of the Takanot Haganah were to protect the safety of the public, to protect the state, to maintain public order, to quell rebellion or riots, and to secure the supply of essential services. To secure these goals, the military authorities were granted power of attorney to use the regulations in various cases. A report from the military government department summarizing the functions and the authorities of the Haganah regulations and other positions stated:

> The Haganah regulation "emergency time" does not recognize the term "military governor"; this phrase does not provide the person who holds it with any authority according to the law. The official authorization of the military governors derives from the power of appointing them as military governors according to *Ha* Haganah regulations only.
>
> (ISA/ GL 13904/9)

## Palestinians under Surveillance

Israel identified the Palestinian minority as disloyal and needing to be ruled tightly under a strict surveillance mechanism. Gurr's (1993) observation that state policies tend to oppress minorities in order accomplish their targets is confirmed by the fact that immediately after the Nakba, the indigenous Palestinians who had stayed in Israel became in the eyes of the state a suspect group without a sense of loyalty to the new state. Palestinians were perceived as a potential fifth column and a security threat to Israel that had to be controlled. James Tully (2000) and Elia Zureik (1979) both refer to the development of a system of "internal colonialism" to separate minorities and indigenous people in order to control them. This is what Israel created in order to control the Bedouin and the entire Palestinian Arab minority. Similarly, Ian Lustick (1980) mentions that the political system used to control the Arabs included segmentation, co-optation, and dependency.

Most recently, Ahmad Saʾdi and Nadera Shalhoub-Koverkian have referred to surveillance methods of controlling the Palestinian Arab minority (Saʾdi 2014; Shalhoub Kovorkian 2015). Saʾdi emphasizes surveillance strategies and tactics of population management as key mechanisms adopted to govern the minority in referring to the techniques of political control and Israeli policies during the early decades of the state. The establishment of the military government marked the beginning of a system of rule aimed at separating the Palestinian Arab minority from the Jewish majority so that the Naqab could be "Judaized" (Falah 1989a, 1989b; Yiftachel 2003). These Judaization policies were evident in other areas such as the Galilee, in which a majority of Arabs living in Israel were located (Kanaaneh 2002).

The Palestinian Arabs who remained after the Nakba inhabited three main districts of Israel—the Naqab district, the Little Triangle, and the Galilee. Even though a number of Jewish settlements were included within the military government areas, the regulations applied solely to Arab citizens. Arabs were not allowed to travel to Jewish towns without holding a special permit. From time to time curfews were imposed on Arab villages and people were arrested for security reasons. One of the military government's main tasks was to control the Arab minority and to prevent Palestinian infiltrators returning to the lands from which they had been uprooted. Yair Bauml argues that the chief mission of the military government was in fact civil, involving "special surveillance on the Arab minority" (Bauml 2002, 133).

Alina Korn claims that the Israelis adopted three main methods of control toward the Arabs under military government: surveillance, administration, and registration (Korn 2000, 162). Abu Saad (2006), following Lustick (1980), suggests that Israel used a three-pronged system of control toward the Arabs based on segmentation, dependence, and co-option. A summary of the justification for the military government cited in the Ratner Committee's report stated that the Israeli authorities felt the Arab community in Israel was not loyal to the state and represented a threat because of a "common interest with the Arab across the border" (Lazar 2002, 106). Thus, adopting a military government and policing system was considered the ultimate solution to governing the Arab minority. Other government offices and state agencies took part in controlling the Arabs, including the prime minister's office, the Shin Bet security service, the Israeli Defense Forces, political parties, and the Histadrut labor federation.

A report titled "The Present Status of Arabs Resident in Israel, and Plans for Their Future," sent by the U.S. Embassy in Tel Aviv to the State Department in Washington, DC, on June 20, 1950, explains the framework of the military government:

> The country has been divided into four Arab Districts: Western Galilee, Eastern Galilee, the Little Triangle (that portion of Central Israel and the Lower Galilee which lies contiguous to the central Arab Palestinian frontier) and the Negev. The Arabs and their villages in each of these districts are under supervision of a resident Military Governor. The four military Governors, Majors in the Israeli Defense Army, are in turn under the direct supervision of a Military Governor-General who is directly responsible to the Prime Minister's Office. The Jewish towns, villages and settlements in all areas of the country are of course under civil government. There are one hundred inhabited Arab villages in the territory presently under Israel's control. . . . [This] does not include Bedouin encampments.
>
> (PRO, FO 371/82512).

The first of the military government districts was the northern region. This, according to Lazar and others,[1] was the Galilee, an area that included one million *dunams* of land and most of whose residents were Arabs (Lazar 2002, 104–105). The largest Arab city, Nazareth, was subject to military government, and the inhabitants under military rule were purely Arab. Until

1954, the region contained forty-five closed areas. Any movement from one area to another required a permit (ISA/ GL 7128/7).

In this northern region of military government the Arabs were the majority. There were few Jewish settlements and fewer than 150,000 *dunams* were under Jewish control. This fact has continued to annoy the Israeli authorities when they see the continuation of Arab towns in Wadi ʿAra. In this district the Arab community was thirty kilometers from the Syrian and Lebanese borders and outnumbered the Jewish population. About 90,000 Arabs lived in the area of the Galilee along with fewer than 45,000 Jews. In Haifa, a mixed city, there were between 5,000 and 6,000 Arabs living among 140,000 Jews. In Jaffa, some 4,000 to 4,500 Arabs lived alongside 50,000 Jews.

The second military zone was the central region, called the Little Triangle (*Memshal Zvai Techon*). This strip constitutes an area of fifty-five to sixty square kilometers, the overall area found in the length of the border of the armistice agreement with Jordan. This area extended over 320,000 *dunams*. There were no Jewish settlements, but the zone included around 30 Arab villages and towns inhabited by more than 36,000 people (ISA/ GL 7128/7).

The third military zone included the entire Naqab and Biʾr al-Sabaʿ region in the south, and extended across one million *dunams*. Some 13,000 Bedouin were concentrated within the region. They constituted the nineteen remaining tribes in three confederations. The military government in the Naqab included the entire southern region. However, the Bedouin were concentrated in a closed zone (*siyaj*) whose borders touched the Jordanian border from the north along a length of more than twenty kilometers and the Gaza Strip in the west (ISA/ GL 7128/7).

This land constitutes about 5 percent of the total Israeli territory. The average density of population in the military government zone was thirteen and a half persons per square kilometer and average annual rainfall was about 200 millimeters (ISA/ GL 17093/1). The area was considered and defined as a security zone by the military government since it was bordered by both Egypt and Jordan. By creating this security zone, they aimed to prevent any contact between the Naqab Bedouin and their related tribes or subtribes across the borders; to stop cross-border economy, infiltrators (*muhajareen*), and sabotage; and to maintain border security (ISA/ GL 17093/1). At that time, there were 8,000 Jews and more than 12,000 registered Bedouin in the Naqab.

Arabs also resided in other villages and in mixed cities, for example, in Haifa (5,000–6,000), Jaffa (4,000), Lydda (1,100), Ramle (1,400), Jerusalem

(5,000), Acre (3,300), and al-Majdal (2,500). In the mixed cities of al-Majdal and Acre, they were segregated from the Jews, who ran their municipalities separately (PRO, FO 371/82512).

About 145,000, out of a total of 165,000 Arabs lived under military rule in these three restricted zones. Others were segregated from the Jewish majority in mixed cities. Their freedom of movement was restricted. Since the geographic distribution of the Arabs in the three military regions made it impossible to control them without using a permit system, only those holding permits were allowed to move around, and then only for a specific purpose and for a limited time. In effect, the military government cut off the Arabs from the Jewish community as well as from the outside world. These security considerations isolated the Arabs and impinged on their daily lives.

> All Arabs under military jurisdiction must have permission from the competent military authority to move from one place to another. This permission is usually granted provided that the Arab has a legitimate and worth-while reason for leaving the area. He may obtain a permanent permit, renewed monthly, if he is a businessman legitimately engaged in the pursuit of his affairs or a Government employee whose work necessitates his travelling from one district to another.
> (PRO, FO 371/82512)

Around 165,000 Palestinian Arabs resided in Israel after the war and were therefore under the jurisdiction of the state of Israel. Military rule was implemented by Israel to control the Arabs as well as to reduce security risks. The Israeli authorities were alarmed by the fact that most of the Arab population in the north, south, and Little Triangle lived in frontier areas. The fact that some Arab towns in the Little Triangle were on the border was considered ample justification for the military government. Indeed, the existence of the Arab population on the frontier was highly sensitive and beyond security issues. Controlling these communities was a matter of urgency in obstructing the creation of relationships with Arabs beyond Israel's borders, such as Lebanon, Syria, Egypt, and Jordan. Controlling Israel's frontiers where Arab inhabitants had settled was similarly crucial in preventing infiltration and stopping refugees attempting to return to their land.

The fact that Jewish communities were a minority in all the frontier areas of the new state meant the presence of the police and the army in all Arab towns and villages. The existence of the Arab population in Israel and in the neighboring countries strengthened the possibility of *muhajareen* returning to their lands with help from the indigenous Palestinians in Israel. It was therefore vital for Israel to prevent any contact between the Arabs in its territory and those across the border primarily to prevent the return of refugees (Morris 2002). The reduction of smuggling and prevention of infiltration were further Israeli aims in setting up military rule, as a report from Tel Aviv in 1950 made clear:

> Smuggling, the age-old pastime of the Near East, is another bothersome feature. Many of the ancient smuggling highways from Lebanon to Egypt run through territory now under Israel's control. Constant vigilance is required on the part of Israel's army and police to make certain that smuggling is kept to a minimum. . . . In an attempt to keep infiltration to a minimum, the police now make periodic raids upon towns and villages in Israel, filter out the illegal visitors, and eventually return them to the country from which they came . . . with the military in control of all the purely Arab areas in Israel, and with the restriction placed upon the freedom of travel of most Arabs in these areas, it is possible to maintain a fairly efficient system of security.
> (PRO, FO 371/82512).

Arab citizens had to apply to the military governor for permits in order to move between villages or even to visit a doctor. All Arabs without exception, including "chiefs and shaikhs," were required to obtain permits in case they wanted to travel for any reason.

The 1956 report by the Ratner Committee noted that the military regulations included 162 articles, some of which were used against the Arabs in Israel.[2] The authority of the military governors and their officials derived from the use of these regulations. Those most frequently employed were Article 109 (forbidding individuals to be present in specific areas, i.e., restriction of movement); Article 110 (to detain by administrative order any person suspected of infringing security or incitement while exiling him from his permanent place of living); Article 111 (administrative detention); Article 124 (imposing a curfew in case of disturbance); and Article 125 (to declare certain areas as closed during army maneuvers or for other military considerations and restricting movement in or to these areas—this was the most effective article and was always employed) (ISA/GL 7128/7).

In security terms, surveillance was required in the areas where Arab citizens lived. Since these areas were geographically close to neighboring Arab countries, imposing military rule was a crucial security matter. The aim was to prevent any attempt by Arab countries to use these areas, to prevent infiltrators onto Israeli land, and to secure Jewish settlements and encourage immigrants to live there.

A report by Jon Kimche in the *Jerusalem Post* in 1950 stated that the Arabs in Israel were a suspect minority and compared their situation to Jews living in Europe:

> The Arabs in Israel are a suspect minority. Their loyalty to the new state, it is true, is almost embarrassingly demonstrative, much in the same way as it was once usual to find a certain type of naturalized Jew among the super-patriots in Germany or Austria, or even in England. But this show of loyalty has not—indeed cannot—removed the suspicion with which the Arabs are viewed by the Jewish majority in Israel . . . the Israeli government seems still undecided on what it proposes to do about this. At present it looks upon its Arab minority as primarily a security risk, secondly as a possible political warfare weapon, and thirdly as a minority requiring a degree of protection.
> (*JERUSALEM POST*, JULY 11, 1950)

Israel's justification for controlling the Palestinian minority was that it represented a visible mechanism for maintaining Zionist hegemony since the Arabs were suspected of having kinship ties with other Arab countries. Of course, the Arabs in Israel and under Israeli control were, and are, part of the Palestinian population that was uprooted from their land. These Arabs wanted to be reunited with their families across the borders. For Israel, such relationships threatened security and daily life. Israel therefore imposed a cruel mechanism of control to prevent the Arabs from contacting their exiled relatives.

Another justification for the military government was to encourage Jewish settlements in frontier areas and prevent the Arabs from living there. The aim was total separation of the Arab and Jewish communities. This motive was obvious since the Jews enjoyed freedom and only the Arabs suffered this collective punishment. Economically, the military rule system prevented the Arabs from entering the Jewish labor market since almost all jobs were secured by the new Jewish immigrants and the Arabs faced severe restrictions in seeking work outside their areas. Every week, long queues of people lined up in front of the military administration offices looking for jobs (Qahawaji 1972).

Controlling the Arabs at the frontiers in order to maintain security—the main objective of military rule—was extremely difficult. Penhas Amir commented that

> it was impossible to control the frontiers, especially in the Naqab. The military government had a limited number of staff and could not prevent or stop all the smuggling or subversive activities on the part of the Arabs, especially the Bedouin. In order to control the borders, we needed whole army units at that time, which was impossible. We were not able to stop people from crossing the borders, as there were members of families on both sides of the borders, "*mikabel ve noten*," which made it impossible to impose order there.
>
> (INTERVIEW WITH PENHAS AMIR, JULY 2008)

I conclude from Penhas Amir's remarks that the military government was not successful in providing security at the frontiers. The Naqab Bedouin continued to move back and forth across the Israeli borders.

## Moving South: Military Rule of the Naqab Bedouin

> In the Naqab and Biʾr al-Sabaʿ, it would have been impossible to be in contact with our relatives across the borders and with the rest of the Arabs in Israel without breaking military regulations through the border economy and cross-border relations.
>
> —ABU-AHMAD, A BEDOUIN FROM EAST OF BIʾR AL-SABAʿ

After 1948, the remnants of the Bedouin in the Naqab were distributed across the vast expanses of the Naqab desert, which made it difficult for the new Israeli state to govern them. For security reasons all the Bedouin who stayed were evicted from their land, which became a closed zone. These Bedouin were then concentrated instead into enclosed zones in northern and central Naqab. The Bedouin employed the term *al-mantiqa al-muharama* when speaking of the closed zone that they were forbidden to enter.[3]

The military areas of the Naqab in which the Bedouin were concentrated, called *sayeg* in Hebrew, extended over approximately 1,100,000 *dunams*. Of this, some 400,000 *dunams* were suitable for agriculture, and about 700,000 *dunams* were pasture and mountainous territories (IDFA 590/1961–60). The military government in the Naqab was responsible for the entire Naqab region. However, it maintained active control only in the region populated by the nineteen Bedouin tribes. The enclosed zone stretched between the Jewish towns of Dimona, Arad, Kibbutz Shoval, and the central city of Beersheba (the city was outside the *siyaj* zone).

This *siyaj/sayeg* subdivided into two subareas in which the Bedouin were concentrated. Territory A stretched from Kibbutz Shoval—near the current Arab Bedouin town of Rahat—down to the south and east to join the major area near the Hebron-Beersheba road. Territory B extended from the Hebron-Beersheba road east along the Jordanian border to Tal ʿArad. The border then went south until Kurnub and returned to Beersheba via Tal Yiroham (ISA/ GL 17002/13).

In the Naqab the military government received support from the army. They took over responsibility for operating in the desert and trying to control the Bedouin: "In the Negev, frontier and internal security are maintained exclusively by the army . . . except in the Negev, the civil police are entirely responsible for peace and security within the State of Israel, in the Arab as well as the Jewish areas" (PRO, FO 371/82512). According to an IDFA report, the major part of the military government's work in the Naqab involved patrolling, maintaining a presence in the area, establishing close daily contact with the Bedouin, collecting information, and registering activities against military rule, all because of the special nature of the Bedouin community (IDFA 590/1961–60). The army was the obvious choice for this kind of work with the Bedouin. Military units were put in charge of evicting them from one location to another and patrolling their encampments from time to time. The military government needed the army in the Naqab in a close relationship that was not evident in the Galilee or the Little Triangle areas.

Beersheba continued its role as the city of central governance even after its occupation by the Israeli army in October 1948. Although just outside the military-government region, the city was the base for the military rule headquarters (*mateh*) of the Naqab region. Some of the military governors in the Naqab, such as Sasson Bar Zvi, settled in Aref al-Aref's house as their main office. Others were based near the Beersheba railway station.[4]

FIGURE 5.1 One of the remaining military rule posts in the Naqab-west Rahat (Wadi Suballa). Built in 1943, this post served as a Palestine Police point/*hajjaneh*; it was subsequently used as a military rule post. *Source*: Photo by the author, 2008.

Administratively, four branches or military units existed in the Naqab at Laqiya-Um Batin, Tal al-Malah, Shoval-al-Huzayil, and Shqeib al-Salam. These branches were supposed to serve more than 12,500 Bedouin and to facilitate official contact with the tribes. Their offices were open to the public for dealing with their daily needs. A single military law court handed out speedy sentences supported by a section of the military police that was responsible for maintaining law and order and implementing instructions and security. There was also a Bedouin tribal court consisting of a secretary and nine Bedouin judges who were required to handle issues that Israeli law could not resolve and who dealt mainly with matters according to Bedouin custom and laws (IDFA 590/1961–60).

The military rule in the Naqab fulfilled two important roles in controlling the Bedouin community. According to an IDFA report, the mechanism used by the military government in the Naqab was based on intense supervision through issuing moving passes. The four main branches were open to the public to deal with their daily problems. One military law court existed to carry out quick sentences. A section of the military police was present and was in charge of implementing instructions and security and maintaining law and order. There was one Bedouin tribal court managed by a secretary and nine Bedouin judges who were required to deal with issues that Israeli law could not handle and who mainly resolved matters according to Bedouin customs and laws (IDFA 590/1961–60).

### *Staffing Positions in the Military Government*

The military governor of the Naqab was appointed directly by the Israeli prime minister. However, recruitment for jobs in the military government was carried out largely through personal contacts. The process was often unprofessional and corrupt. Reports from the ISA show that one of the military government's objectives was to offer professional training to employees so they could work for the military government since most of the military government's existing staff came from an army background and lacked civilian work experience. Their job was to act as an administrative unit linking the government and the army (ISA/ GL 13904/9; a military government department report summarizing the first four years of its work, August 14, 1952). Many military officials were Jews from an Arab background and most spoke fluent Arabic.

Most members of the military government's staff in the Naqab were appointed on the basis of personal relationships rather than through professional decisions and experience. Jewish individuals who had never previously worked in official positions were suddenly employed by the military government in the Naqab. The Bedouin now found themselves manipulated by some of the Jewish *mukhtars* and kibbutz members. From 1948 until the end of the military government period, a total of five military governors served in the Naqab: Michael Ha-Negbi, Bazil Herman, Yihoshua Verbin, Penhas Amir, and Sasson Bar Zvi, with the last military governor appointed in 1963 (interview with Penhas Amir, July 2008). A few of the governors and some officials had experience with Bedouin culture and spoke Arabic, which was a basic requirement for working with the Bedouin. Unfortunately, most of the officials employed in the military government lacked knowledge of the Bedouin, and few were capable of working with indigenous people.

I give a number of examples here: one is Penhas Amir (who the Bedouin knew as Abu Suliman), and the other is Sasson Bar Zvi (who was known by the Bedouin as Captain Freih or Abu Daood). I was able to meet them both and listen to their stories of interacting with Bedouin in the 1950s and 1960s.

Bar Zvi and Amir interacted with Bedouin and Arabs before taking up their military governorships. Penhas Amir recounted the story of how he met the Bedouin before becoming a military governor:

> I was born in 1915, and grew up in kibbutz Balforia. During my childhood, I had good relations with Bedouin after I had met some shepherds out in the fields. I worked especially with Al Kaʾabya and Zubidat Arabs in the northern part of Palestine, and at the village of Basmat Tabuʾn; there were also Al Heeb and Zarazeer Arabs. When Yitzhak Sheni was a military officer, he offered me work with the army in the south, and then I used to visit Michael Ha-Negbi who was a military governor of the Negev, and had the possibility of working with Bedouin tribes as part of my job. In 1956, I was appointed as the military governor of Negev and held the post until 1963, the only military governor who did this job for seven years.
>
> (INTERVIEW WITH PENHAS AMIR, JULY 2008)

Penhas Amir's story shows that he had contacts with the Arab community before he took office as a military governor in the Naqab in 1956 and that meeting Bedouin tribes in the north facilitated his eventual acquisition of a military governor position. Personal contact with Michael Ha-Negbi was crucial for Amir in enabling him to work with the Bedouin, as was his experience of Bedouin culture and knowledge of the Arabic language. It seems to me that personal relations were always a factor in obtaining a job in this military government, which was regarded as a business.

Another military governor of the Naqab whom I interviewed was Sasson Bar Zvi. One of the first Jewish settlers in the Naqab Bar Zvi had had a chance to observe Bedouin life long before the creation of Israel in 1948. He was one of the "Shai" men (the *Shirut ha-Yediʾot*) who played the role of the *mukhtar* of Kibbutz Revivim (one of the oldest kibbutz in the Naqab-Beir ʿAsluj). Bedouin whom I interviewed remembered Sasson Bar Zvi as a military governor and official before 1948. Some said they had never realized that he was a government official when he visited them. He was fluent in Arabic and knew how to communicate with the tribes. He was always asking questions and writing things down about the Bedouin at every opportunity, mostly for purposes of managing them. In some cases, the Bedouin were suspicious of his behavior and avoided meeting him. Bar Zvi described how the government dealt with the Bedouin after 1948 and the creation of Israel's authority in the Naqab:

> We copied the British exactly and used the same legacies to control the Bedouin by using police and the tribal system in the way the British did. We knew that it would be impossible to control the Bedouin without knowing their tribal structure (the Bedouin court system), and without the police. The tribal "shaikh" and the heads of the sub-tribes were certainly urgently needed to deal with the Bedouin.
> (BAR ZVI 1982, 28)

Gene Sharp called this type of Bedouin politics non-cooperation as a form of nonviolent action. The Bedouin resisted any collaboration with the military governors by avoiding meeting them and warning their relatives when the officials came to their *sheq*. Tully (2000) also identifies this as resistance when he speaks of "working with and against." The Bedouin sometimes cooperated with the military government officials and sometimes resisted and ignored them. Despite that, a number of Bedouin tribal shaikhs are well known of their full cooperation with the Israeli military government during and after the war. As Rhoda Kanaaneh (2009, 12) put it, loyal Bedouin were encouraged to serve in the Israel forces. Oral history testimonies and archival reports also provide details about recruiting Bedouin to the army during the war in 1948.

There were significant problems with the staff who served under this military government system. From Sasson Bar Zvi's account, Israel faced difficulties in dealing with the Bedouin during the early years of its existence. He seems to suggest that the only way to work with the Bedouin was through shaikhs and community leaders; otherwise, they would have been ungovernable. Sometimes military governors would be accompanied by Bedouin to facilitate visiting the tribes. From the experience of some interviewees, the Bedouin knew the weaknesses of the military rule and knew exactly when to avoid meeting the officials. They resisted meeting Bar Zvi for fear that he was a representative of the government.

One of the successful policies that Bar Zvi used was having contacts with many Bedouin in the area. He visited and socialized with them, which helped him build trust with the Bedouin. They treated him as an Arab rather than as a military governor, which helped Bar Zvi to get what he wanted from them: "I remember when people used to gather in the *sheq* as normal, if they recognized that one of the government men was on his way to the tribe; they used to announce for the people "Freih-Abu Daood has come" (interview with abu-Saʿd, June 2012). The Bedouin played things wisely. They resisted being manipulated by officials and even resisted welcoming them. One of Sasson Bar Zvi's missions was collecting data about the Bedouin, their tribes, and their lives. This settler colonial tactic was used in other contexts in the Middle East such as Morocco and Algeria. Gathering knowledge about the natives and trying to understand their internal dynamics and affiliations was a key feature of colonialism in the Middle East.

While Sasson Bar Zvi was in the Naqab, Bedouin managed to avoid giving him specific details about their tribes, refused to collaborate with him, and sometimes even sent their women to tell him that no one was around as a way of protecting their space. The military governor in some cases was weak and the Bedouin were powerful, hiding new smuggled clothes from him when he arrived at their public space. A member of one of the ʿAzazma tribes whom I met said, "We never recognized Sasson was Jewish; he dressed the same as we did, and even rode a horse and use to visit us a lot, and his name was Freih, which sounded Arabic" (interview with Abu Ahmad, June 2009). Of course, in order to build trust with the Bedouin, Sasson Bar Zvi had to behave like them, visiting and eating with them at various times throughout a month.

Bar Zvi admits and explains that the initial system of military government was not professionally run:

> The mission to establish the military rule in the Naqab was given to Michael Ha-Negbi, the first military governor, and other officials who worked with us were from kibbutzim in the Naqab. . . . When we look at the military rule staff in the early days we see something interesting. Michael Ha-Negbi was a member of kibbutz Negba; a few officers were available to work with us, like Yitzhak Shemesh from kibbutz Nivatim, Zaav Zrizi from kibbutz Gal-On, and Eliezer Fresh from Rohama. Sasson Bar Zvi was from kibbutz Revivim, Mesha Negbi from kibbutz Alumim.

Negbi chose to appoint people to work in the military government whom he knew and trusted and who knew the environment and the language. These staff lacked experience in working in an official system of control but did the work and gained experience according to the circumstances (Negev Archive [Tovyaho], Ben Gurion University, Israel, interview with Sasson Bar Zvi part 1, version 2: 12.02.1985–05.03.1985).

Only a few officials had experience living with Bedouin and getting to know their culture. While conducting interviews, I found many other people who had been employed in the military rule of the Naqab, such as officers, commanders, and police. These included Abraham Yaffe (Aluf Habikod, the commander of the southern district), Yitzhak Tsamah, Benjamin Gur-Arieh, Nissim Kazaz, Hayem Tzori (*mafkal* of Beersheba police), Zeʾev Shamai, Haim Tabori, and Kadori (Rav Samal; issuer of Bedouin permits). Amos Yarkoni (his Jewish name) was a special case from the Arab al-Heeb Bedouin, a Northern tribe. His original name was Abed al-Majeed, and he was the head of the Bedouin trackers unit. Bringing in a Northern Bedouin for this post indicates that sometimes the military government did not succeed in building trust with the Naqab Bedouin.

Yitzhak Tsamah was another important figure who worked with the Bedouin. Assisted by two other officers, Zeʾev Shamai and Benjamin Gur-Arieh, he was in command of regular desert patrols. Each of the three controlled a particular area in which the Bedouin lived, and each patrolled the borders from time to time in his assigned region. Ability to speak Arabic and knowledge of Bedouin culture was essential to working with the Bedouin. When I met Yitzhak Tsamah he recounted his story of being born and raised in Iraq and then later working with the Bedouin in Biʾr al-Sabaʿ region:

> I was born in 1924 in Baghdad and first met the Bedouin in 1959. I grew up and finished high school in Baghdad when I was 17, while the Keylani revolution was taking place. My family left Baghdad in 1936; however, I refused to leave—I stayed behind and lived with my sister. I emigrated in 1942 and lived for a while in a kibbutz, after which I spent some time living in Jerusalem and getting to know the Arabs and living in a nice environment which was similar to Baghdad. I knew Arabic very well and that enabled me to work in various fields such as teaching Arabic, and was also one reason for working with the Bedouin.
>
> (INTERVIEW WITH YITZHAK TSAMAH, JUNE 2007)

Yitzhak is fluent in Arabic and is very familiar with Bedouin culture, sometimes in great detail. He argues that the Jewish community and government will not understand the Arabs in Israel if they do not speak their language since without knowing Arabic, they will not be able to understand Arab culture. As he said, "We do not know each other very well, like two people listening to different radio channels. I do not know him, and he does not know me. Unless the situation improves, we will never understand each other." I saw something very important in Yitzhak Tsamah's comments here. In almost all cases when interacting with the Bedouin, he was accompanied by a known Bedouin figure (such as Shaikh Oda Abu Maʿamar from the ʿAzazma) while he patrolled the area. Having a Bedouin as his counterpart gave rise to different perceptions of them: "Without Bedouin it is impossible to operate in the desert" (interview with Yitzhak Tsamah, July 2007). In this case, governing the natives needed selected native individuals, such as Abu Maʿamar, to function as part of the system.

The point to be made here is that some of the military government staff of the Naqab had served as Jewish *mukhtars* of various kibbutzim before the war and had had dealings with the indigenous Bedouin. After the Nakba, some of these *mukhtars* became military governors and government officials. Sasson Bar Zvi, for instance, was the *mukhtar* of Kibbutz Revivim. Ha-Negbi was a member of Kibbutz Negba. Relations that had existed between Jewish *mukhtars* and the Bedouin during the Mandate took a new form after the Nakba. After the war, the balance of power changed with the Bedouin who had been the dominant power in the Naqab becoming a minority controlled by Jewish *mukhtars* who, just prior to the war, had only survived with Bedouin cooperation.

These *mukhtars* secured their position in the Naqab by creating good relations with their Bedouin neighbors, speaking Arabic, and even dressing as Arabs. A number of Jewish *mukhtars* who became part of the military government system adopted similar dress, clothing, horses, and camels as the Bedouin. They also hosted visitors in the same style as the Bedouin in order to secure their interactions with the indigenous community. One example is Sasson Bar Zvi, who had his own horse, dressed similarly to the Bedouin, and shuttled about between the tribes. Some Bedouin said they had thought he was Egyptian rather than Jewish. Military officials' adoption of Bedouin culture was a key policy to being able to rule them.

Some of the military government staff were not professionals, and very few were familiar with Bedouin culture. Therefore, the majority of government staff members had no training on how to work with Bedouin. As Bar Zvi noted, the authorities initially took kibbutz members and put them in military government positions where they dealt with different issues and problems in the Beersheba area, including security and dealing with

Bedouin tribes (Tovyaho Archive, interview with Sasson Bar Zvi). The military government of the Naqab was a model of corruption and failure to deal with the daily issues of the Bedouin.

The military government's interaction with the Bedouin was complicated. In my view, the shortage of professional staff caused the development of corruption in the system itself. Bedouin used the shortage of military government staff to their advantage. When this shortage was used against the military government, it became one of the obvious forms of resistance from which the Bedouin benefited. The military government failed to build up a permanent staff base; even the competent staff did not last long in their posts and resigned.

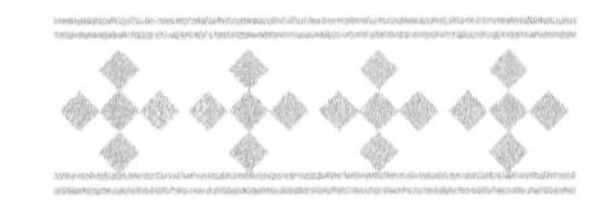

SIX

# Reshaping the Tribes' Historical Order, 1950–1952

## *Border Issues, Land Rights, IDPs, and UN Intervention*

IN THE FIRST FEW YEARS of the military rule, its concern was to establish a structure for manipulating the remnants of the Bedouin tribes in the *siyaj* region. New policies were framed to govern the remnant Bedouin in the *siyaj* as soon as the system had begun to stabilize. The Bedouin who had been "masters of the desert" (*al-sayid al-badawi*) before the 1948 war now found themselves controlled by military regulations. The military government attempted to govern them by shaping their future, framing them under a new tribal order, and using multiple legal tricks.

Israel developed a variety of strategies for controlling the Palestinian Arab minority under military rule, including surveillance tools and population management (Korn 2000; 1996; Sa'di 2014). The main policies that were applied to the Bedouin in the early 1950s after they had been concentrated in the *siyaj* included separating out the tribes, retaining the loyal tribes, expelling Bedouin tribes from the western Naqab into the *siyaj*, appointing new tribal shaikhs, expropriating Bedouin land by enacting land laws (Abu Hussein and McKay 2003), and repeated census-taking among the Bedouin to maintain tight surveillance.

### From Freedom to Military Control

Out of the ninety-five tribes that had existed during the British Mandate, only nineteen remained in Israel's territory. They were immediately concentrated in the closed area (called *sayeg* in Hebrew and *siyaj* in Arabic) in the northeastern Naqab. The number nineteen refers to Israel's understanding of the remnants of the recognized tribes after 1948. It also reflects the number of the nineteen recognized shaikhs. I do not regard this number as accurate: it was a state-created number because the Israelis forced the Bedouin to remain under these nineteen tribes, regardless of whether the individual Bedouins belonged to those tribes historically. In my view more than nineteen tribes remained in the Naqab. Israel's policies disturbed tribal order by encouraging the tribes to consolidate. While I was reviewing Israeli archive documents, sometimes eighteen tribes appeared. In other cases the number was nineteen, clearly indicating that this was an unstable framework.

After the Nakba, extended families (*ruba'*) or tribes (*ʿashair*) of three Bedouin confederations (*qabail*) remained in the Naqab:[1] the Tayaha, Tarabin, and ʿAzazma.[2] According to the Israel State Archives (ISA), the majority of the Tarabin *qabila* fled to Gaza, Khan Younis, and Rafah; only a few remained in Israel. This also applied to the Tayaha *qabila*, with most fleeing to Jordan. Some Tayaha remained in Israel, and another group left for the Gaza Strip. The majority of the ʿAzazma fled to Jordan. A large group of ʿAzazma moved to Sinai, and only a minority remained in Israel (ISA/GL 17002/13). Only certain families or tribes remained to be organized by the Israeli regime (Falah 1989b).[3]

Israel's policy toward the remnant tribes was to concentrate them in the *siyaj* after evicting them from their native areas of the Naqab. Israel did not leave any part of the remaining tribes on their native land but put them into enclosed zones, forcing them to live on the land of other tribes. The remnant tribes in the Naqab gathered the nineteen or so shaikhs who were recognized by the state, congregating in the northeastern Naqab. Ghazi Falah states that of the nineteen remnant tribes, eleven were evicted from the western Naqab region (between Beersheba and the Gaza Strip border) to the enclosed zone (Falah 1985, 38).[4] The Israel Defense Force Archive listed the tribes who remained in the Naqab, showing their original land and where they had been exiled to in 1951. The report indicates that five tribes were not moved from their native land and fourteen tribes were expelled from the western Naqab and forced to live in the *siyaj* region (IDFA 490/1956–125).

According to Sasson Bar Zvi, who was the military governor of the Naqab in the 1960s, "Only *blagim* or *belgi blagim* of the Bedouin tribes remained under Israel's control, and not full tribes."[5] He thus confirms that after the war, only sections or subsections of tribes were left in Israel's territory

TABLE 6.1
Remnant tribes in the Naqab as reported in 1951

| TRIBE | AREA POPULATED BEFORE 1951 |
|---|---|
| Najmat al-Sanne | Jbibat, Kharbit Abu Ghalyon, Wadi Gaza, Tal Jameh |
| Abu Blal | Abu Shʿar |
| Abu Srihan | Wadi Abu Msaʿid, Jur al-Jarm, Kharbit Abu Ghalyon |
| ʿAzazma (Masʿodin) | Khazaʿla, Martaba, Abu Shaʿr, Kharbit Abu Dhiban, Kharbit Abu Ghalyon |
| Qdirat al-Sanne | Wadi al-Sharia', Abu Sdeir, Laqiya, Jisr Abu Rqaiq |
| Abu Rqaiq | Zummara, Jisr Abu Rqaiq, Sdeir |
| Abu ʿAbdon | Wadi Fteis, Abu Sdeir, Meileha, Karkor |
| Al-Talalqa | Mishmar Ha-Negev region (Bir Abu Mansour), Twayel Abu- Jarwal |
| Al-Oqbi | Mishmar Ha-Negev region (Bir Abu Mansour), al-ʿAraqib |
| Al-ʿAtawna | Jammama |
| Saqr Al Huzayil | Shoval region (Wadi Suballa), Sefeiha |
| Al-ʿAssam | Abu Sdeir |
| Al-Afenish | Sfeiha region |
| Abu ʿAmrah | Kharbit Abu Ghalyion-Qurien |
| Abu Rabia | Tal al-Malah region |
| Abu Qrinat | ʿAraʿara |
| Abu Jweyaʿd | Sdeir |
| Al-Huzayil | Kharbit al-Huzayil |
| Al-Assad | Laqiya |

(interview with Bar Zvi, September 2008). According to some of the Bedouin interviewees, most of the tribes found that after 1948 their traditional structures, which had existed before the Nakba, had broken down. This was confirmed by most of the Bedouin whom I interviewed.

In referring to and defining the tribes remaining under military rule after 1948, Sasson Bar Zvi used the Arabic term *lamam* (literally "collection of tribes or families"). In this case, only some tribes or parts of them had stayed in Israel and had joined other big tribes under new shaikhs and registered in order to stay. This patchwork of mismatched new tribes or pieces of tribes who had joined others had never existed before. Bar Zvi described how these random groupings came together in the early 1950s:

> The war was the same as any other war; the Bedouin fled or were exiled to a variety of places. Some went to Jordan, or Egypt, and some stayed in

> the mountains waiting to see whether or not to return to their land. Those remaining in the Naqab were from three main *qabail*: Tayaha, Tarabin and ʿAzazma. Some were big tribes, (*ʿashair*), and others were parts and pieces of tribes. New tribes and parts of tribes, *ruba*ʾ, had been formed after the creation of Israel and this new post-war phenomenon put the remaining tribes in a very difficult position. Some elements of the tribes remained in Israel, but with no shaikhs or leaders. Many shaikhs left the territory of Israel; however, parts of their tribes remained
> (INTERVIEW, BAR ZVI, SEPTEMBER 2008)

In order to secure their stay, these remaining sections intentionally joined big tribes under the leadership of the newly recognized shaikhs. Sometimes they simply moved and lived with other tribes or established themselves close to where the main tribes were concentrated. In other cases, the government sent small families to join tribal groups under recognized shaikhs. In this way, "new tribes" were formed and came later to be recognized by the military government under Israeli administration. The new shaikhs were also recognized. Some tribes were eager to keep the name of their tribe alive; as a result, small tribes joined big tribes and were recognized by the state of Israel.

This system of tribes joining together did not last long since by the early 1960s, it was clear that many tribes had split off from the big tribe they had joined immediately after the war. The state also recognized other new shaikhs as a result of conflict between the shaikhs of the main tribe and of other tribes under his rule. Members of tribes did not like the orders set by the state and the recognized shaikhs, so they broke away and tried to revive their own tribe or family. For example, Shaikh ʿAwadd Abu Rqaiq joined pieces from all the *ʿashair* of al-Qdirat tribes and combined them under his leadership. In this way a new tribe was formed under the name of *ʿashirat* Abu Rqaiq al-Sharqi. According to Bar Zvi, before the war of 1948, the original *ʿashira* of Abu Rqaiq had been under the leadership of Shaikh Harb Abu Rqaiq. In a second case, the al-ʿAssam tribe behaved in the same way, with smaller tribes joining it to form a larger unit. In a third example, Oda Abu Maʿamar from the ʿAzazma gathered pieces from ten *ʿashair* of the ʿAzazma. In this way, sections of the remaining ʿAzazma formed a larger *ʿashira* of the ʿAzazma under his leadership. Other tribes from the ʿAzazma confederation had already left Israel, which was why Shaikh Oda Abu Maʿamar became the shaikh of a newly established tribe of the remaining ʿAzazma. The Abu Srihan tribe, which remained under Israeli control, consisted of a collection of al-Jarawin tribes who were expelled to Jordan. According to Bar Zvi, all the small groups that remained in Israel and felt unsafe joined the tribes of the new shaikhs, or "*ʿarab al-shaikh*" (interview with Sasson Bar Zvi, September 2008).

Some Bedouin tribes resisted the policies of the state to annex them to other remnant tribes or shaikhs. I heard many stories that illustrated Bedouin resistance to the policies of the military rule authorities. In 1951, the Abu Sayʿleik *ʿashira* sent a letter to the military governor complaining about the state's policy of removing them from the rule of a shaikh who had been their shaikh before 1948. The letter stated clearly that according to government orders, they were to be transferred to the leadership of a shaikh who was not their previous tribal leader. They requested the military governor to leave them in their usual *ʿashira* (ʿArab al-Shaikh Qassim Abu Sayʿleik) under their original shaikh. They stated that they opposed the new shaikh under whose authority they were to be placed and wished to be allowed to go back to their original *ʿashira* under their own shaikh (IDFA 834/1953–266).[6] Other cases show that parts of tribes were able to stay on their land because they resisted annexation under these recognized shaikhs. Some small tribes frequently had disputes with big tribes, something that the Israeli authorities had failed to anticipate. As a result, when they were asked to join other tribes, they refused. Ultimately, this meant that some tribes that refused to be annexed to other shaikhs were asked to leave the country.

These cases show that Israel's policy of breaking up the historical order of the tribes did not always succeed. The Bedouin operated according to their own interests, sometimes joining other tribes in order to secure their ability to stay and sometimes resisting the breakup of their historic tribal order.

## *Early Tribe-State Relations*

One of the key policies adopted by the Israeli authorities immediately after the war was to leave alone those Bedouin tribes and shaikhs who were willing to recognize Israel's new authority. The fact that Israel asked the tribes to swear a loyalty oath at the meeting in Beersheba in November 1948 showed its willingness to expel tribes that proved disloyal. Benny Morris highlights the discussion between army officials and Ben Gurion about the possibility of leaving friendly tribes to their own devices (Morris 2005).

The government officially recognized nineteen shaikhs as leaders of the remnant Bedouin. The recognition of just nineteen tribes created a new phenomenon of "designated tribes." Sections of tribes that remained without tribal affiliation or that had lost their leaders were encouraged to join other big tribes and to register under their shaikhs. After 1948, one method of choosing new tribal leaders was through their relations with the local kibbutz or recommendation by Jewish *mukhtars* (the term used in referring to elected Jewish kibbutz leaders in the old *yishuv*). John Bitzan notes that in many cases the recognized shaikhs had not necessarily been shaikhs before but instead were chosen according to their prior history of cooperation with the kibbutz *mukhtars* and the authorities:

> To construct this system, ha-Negbi and his officers drew on their personal networks and their experience managing patron-client relationships. Asked in November 1948 to find Bedouin shaikhs who would publicly pledge allegiance to the state of Israel, ha-Negbi and Bar Zvi used the occasion to appoint reliable allies. As a result, most of the individuals presented as shaikhs at the ceremony in Beersheba were chosen because they had helped the yishuv before and during the war, and because many of them were well acquainted with the *mukhtars*. In effect, the public ceremony in Beersheba allowed the *mukhtars* to revive their old personal ties and to reward those Bedouin who had acted as their informants and loyal allies when the yishuv had been under siege. (BITZAN 2006, 67)

Bitzan was not correct in this regard since Israel was surprised to find among the remnants of the Bedouin, disloyal tribes as well as shaikhs who had refused to swear loyalty to the new state. A number of Bedouin refused to accept Israel's plan to appoint them as shaikhs. In this respect, they resisted cooperation, which represented a significant challenge to the new system of control. I came across two individuals who had served as Bedouin shaikhs in the 1950s. Since they did not agree to become government-appointed shaikhs, they had instead been registered in the Ministry of Interior as tribal representatives. Other shaikhs, particularly those of the ʿAzazma subtribes, were categorized as problematic. They refused to swear allegiance to the state and thus were trapped between the borders of Egypt,

Jordan, and Israel. A report from November 24, 1949, addressed to the British Foreign Office indicates that some Bedouin (especially the ʿAzazma) had not declared loyalty to the new state and that 700 members of the ʿAzazma tribes had been expelled:

> Israel's version is that these Bedouin numbering 700 persons belonged to the ʿAzazma tribe who formerly lived in Al ʿAuja al-Hafir. They joined in with the Egyptians during the fighting and when a year ago the Bedouin tribes were gathered at Beersheba to swear loyalty to Israel, the ʿAzazma were absent; they were then on the other side of Israeli/Egyptian lines. They began to filter back into Israel later. As a result of complaints by other Bedouin that a hostile tribe had infiltrated, they were ordered to leave the country. They were reportedly given a choice of where they wanted to go, and are said to have turned north-eastward into the Hebron area. It is denied that any force was used and the tribesman are said to have taken all their possessions with them.[7]
>
> (PRO, FO 371/75355)

Letters from the United Nations indicate that Israel pushed between 7,000 and 8,000 Bedouin from the ʿAzazma subtribe across the border into Egyptian territory. According to Security Council Resolution of November 17, 1950, the following subtribes faced expulsions: "A number of Bedouins, estimated between 6000 to 7000 appertaining to the following sub-tribes of the ʿAzazma tribe have been expelled from the area under Israeli control and from the demilitarized zone across the international border into Egyptian territory; Subheyeen; Mohamadeen; Isbaihat; Sawakhneh; Imreaʾat, El Assayat" (IDFA 1338/1979–714).

Many of the subtribes of the ʿAzazma on the list faced real problems concerning where to settle. A telegram addressed to the Foreign Office titled "Expulsion of Arabs from Israel" gives a good picture of these events:

> The facts appear to be that a section of the ʿAzazma tribe which had remained on its lands at the time of the Israeli occupation of Beersheba moved into Arab territory recently with nothing but the clothes which they were wearing. They claimed to have been beaten up and robbed of all their possessions by Israeli troops and to have been told to make for Arab territory before worse befell them. They stated that they had no idea why the Israelis treated them

> in this manner. The net result was that Jordan has acquired another group of utterly destitute refugees.
> (PRO, FO 371/75355).

A meeting of Bedouin from Palestine, Israel, and Jordan was proposed in a telegram sent from Jerusalem to the Foreign Office on December 2, 1949. This telegram concerned Israel's rejection of Bedouins from the Beersheba area:

> Arab press yesterday reported that as a result of a meeting between Israel and Jordanian military representatives in the south, agreement had been reached to form a committee of four Bedouin shaikhs from southern Palestine to discuss the Bedouin problem as a whole. If this is the case the matter will no doubt be adjusted in due course [through] the medium of the Mixed Armistice Commission to which Jordanian complaints have been represented.
> (PRO, FO 371/75355)

Benny Morris claims that the IDF had driven the Bedouin off during the 1950s due to what he called their "Anti Yishuv." The ʿAzazma Bedouin were the IDF's main target, especially in the Naqab border regions. Morris estimates that between 1949 and 1953 17,000 Bedouin were expelled from or fled the Naqab (Morris 1993, 153–157). Such transfers happened; findings by Rhoda Kanaaneh (2009, 28) show that members of the ʿAzazma served in the Israeli military.

The ill-treatment of the ʿAzazma during the early 1950s was discussed by UNRWA (the United Nations Relief and Works Agency), which, as an international organization working for Palestinian refugees, examined the expulsion of the ʿAzazma and tried to find ways to donate money to alleviate their situation:

> At yesterday's meeting of the advisory Commission to UNRWA the ʿAzazma Bedouin case was discussed. This was raised by Colonel Gohar of Egypt. He repeated the old arguments and then informed us that UNTSO special committee, meeting on August 4, 1954, has decided in favour of Egypt. This means that it was finally established that these unfortunates were driven from Israel by armed force. After some discussion it was agreed that UNRWA would

> (without commitment) consider the possibility of making a grant in kind to the ʿAzazma to relieve immediate distress.
>
> (EXTRACTS FROM LETTER NO. 222/3/6, FEBRUARY 2, 1955, TO MR. SIMPSON FROM THE BRITISH MIDDLE EAST OFFICE, BEIRUT; PRO, FO 371/115627).

Another instance of Bedouin fleeing their land was reported in a telegram from Jerusalem to the Foreign Office on November 24, 1949: "On November 7th the Arab press reported the expulsion of 500 Bedouin families in circumstances described by the Jordan Foreign Minister" (PRO, FO 371/75355).

The military government's aim of keeping only friendly and loyal tribes did not work very well, mainly because Bedouin kept moving across the borders. Influential Bedouin shaikhs also helped to mediate with the government and encouraged weaker tribes to stay on their land. Secret reports in the Israeli archives suggest ways in which leading Bedouin shaikhs helped each other to stay. For instance, there is the case of the shaikh of *ʿashirat* al-Oqbi, which had been ordered to leave Muharaqa during the war. One of the influential Tayaha shaikhs intervened and by negotiating with the military rule officials managed to organize the return of al-Oqbi after they had been exiled (secret report sent to the office of the prime minister and the Ministry of Defense, April 12, 1953; ISA/GL 13904/14). This form of cooperation between different Bedouin shaikhs can be categorized as a form of resistance. As Hollander and Einwohner (2004, 536) remark, resistance can have a level of coordination. Rubin (1996, 239) also notes that resistance has "[some] degree of consciousness and collectivity."

Another tactic used by the Bedouin was to seek the mediation of Jewish *mukhtars* to help stop their eviction. For example, the role of the *mukhtar* of Kibbutz Shoval was critical in mediating between the government and local tribes. In a 1959 report, *Maʾariv* newspaper described the mediatory role of Kibbutz Shoval's *mukhtar*, who acted discreetly to stop the expulsion of an *ʿashira* of the Tayaha immediately after the war. This tribe had twice faced exile, but their friends from Kibbutz Shoval had prevented it from happening. The *mukhtar's* intervention at a critical moment stopped the army from expelling a whole tribe (*Maʾariv*, April 19, 1959). The story was widely reported in the Naqab, and is still remembered by the Bedouin.

### *Bedouin Refugees/IDPs and Property Claims*

Access to the properties of absentees and internally displaced peoples (IDPs) under military rule was one of the key concerns of the Palestinians in Israel.[8] As Sa'di argues, "the state prevented internal refugees from returning to their villages and confiscated their property, dislocated residents of several villages, and continued to expel Palestinians outside its borders for eleven years after the end of the 1948 war" (Sa'di 2015, 463). The same scenario was true of IDPs' properties and was also evident in the Naqab. In many interviews and archival reports, Bedouin have used the term *diyarna* to refer to their territory—mainly the land that they were pushed into leaving and to which they were not permitted to return.[9] Persistent Bedouin claims for the restitution of their property and for the right to return to their land in the western Naqab can be categorized as an identity issue. Even though most of the remnant Bedouin were not allowed to return to their native land, they sought to obtain their rights as refugees and IDPs by using different forms of complaint and legal claims. Those expelled from the western Naqab and forced to live in an enclosed zone had lost a large portion of their belongings. Along with the loss of their land, they faced the challenge of how to reclaim the property they had left in the western Naqab and elsewhere (Nasasra 2012).

Many of the remnant tribes, especially those from the western Naqab (*al-mantiqa al-gharbiya*, the term the Bedouin used to refer to their native land in that area), were ordered to leave their land and properties and move into the *siyaj* region. However, as archival reports reveal, the Bedouin shaikhs took measures to prevent this. According to IDFA documents, the bedouin resisted efforts to expel them from the western Naqab. The shaikhs of the Tarabin complained to the military governor about being moved from their land on November 25, 1950. When the remaining leaders of the Tarabin shaikhs (Suliman al-Sanne, Hlayel Abu ʿAmrah, Salman Abu Blal) sent a message to the military government in 1951, asking to be allowed to return to their land as they wished to cultivate it, the military governor (Michael Ha-Negbi) offered to assist them in other ways but refused them permission to go back to their land (IDFA 1953/834–263).

With the western Naqab turned into a restricted zone (*al-mantiqa al-muharama*), it was difficult to recover personal belongings. While I was conducting interviews in the Naqab, one interviewee stated that it had been impossible to return to their land in Western Naqab. Nonetheless, some Bedouin returned incognito for the purpose of collecting their property. In fact, many Bedouin who became IDPs tried to reclaim their property through legal action. One form of action involved writing letters to the military government seeking permission to collect their belongings or requesting compensation. The IDFA has documented several cases in which the Bedouin asked to recover their property from the western Naqab. In 1950, a leading member of *ʿashirat* al-Sanne sent a letter to the military governor claiming his family's property that had been left behind when they were expelled:

> The government expelled us from western Naqab to the enclosed zone in 1950, and as a result we left our property and belongings behind us. We left stone houses, wells, and seeds. After we were expelled, the military government announced ten days of curfew, and after that we returned, but did not find our properties.
> (IDFA 834/1953–263)

In many cases, properties left by the Bedouin were damaged or seized by kibbutzim. A leading Bedouin shaikh from the Tarabin wrote a letter to the military governor of the Naqab in 1951 requesting return of properties left behind when he had been obliged to leave: "When we lived in western Naqab *(al-manatiqa al-gharbiya)*, we stored some food for our flocks, and left food and property at our wells." He asked for a permit to allow him to return and collect what had been left of their property (IDFA 834/1953–265). Many other Bedouin letters reached the military government claiming their right to recover property or seeking compensation for lost possessions. One of the ʿAzazma shaikhs sent a letter in 1950 requesting either money from the government or the return of their stolen properties:

> You expelled us from our land, our land (*diyarna*), and prohibited our right to live on it. We made many claims for you to give us financial assistance or to issue us permits to collect our property or to pay us compensation instead. Until now we have not received any compensation, and we kindly request you to allow us to collect our property, as currently it has been confiscated by the nearest settlers.
> (IDFA 1953/834–262)

A couple of the remnant Tarabin shaikhs sent similar requests to find out what had happened to the personal belongings they had left behind when they were expelled from the western Naqab (IDFA 1953/834–263). Similarly, the shaikhs of *ʿashirat* al-Jarawin sent a request in 1950 to recover property that had been left on their land, complaining that their possessions had been seized by the Jewish Custodian of Absentees' Properties (interview in Tal al-Sabaʿ, June 2008). Some leading Bedouin shaikhs were active agents in claiming their rights and had been claiming property ownership since the early days of the military government. For example, Shaikh Musa al-ʿAtawna was sacked from his post because of campaigning for Bedouin rights and resisting military regulations. This shaikh was known to be active in calling for more rights for the Bedouin and for recognition of Bedouin land ownership. Al-Aref mentions how Shaikh Musa resisted the policies of military rule and as a result was sacked from his position of leadership (al-Aref 1956; 1962). This is a classic case of resisting military rule instructions and can be considered a form of noncooperation.

Clearly the Bedouin in the Naqab faced a situation similar to that of many other Palestinian IDPs who had lost their property. Most of them left their possessions behind in the western Naqab in 1950–1951 when they were expelled into the enclosed zone. But these cases also show how new settler states use a range of techniques against indigenous peoples, including exploiting their resources and property. As noted by Gurr and Harff (2004), the Bedouin did not submit but instead tried to protect what survived of their resources. They also used different avenues for claiming their property during the initial stages of military rule.

## The Early Stages of Expropriating Bedouin Land

According to Frantz Fanon, land is the "the essential value" for colonized people (Fanon 1963, 34). In the Naqab land, is the most important aspect of Bedouin life since it constitutes people's identity. However, during the first few years of military rule the Bedouin lost most of their land to the state. Wolfe (2006, 387) remarks that, "[land] is life—or at least, land is necessary for life. Thus contests for land can be—indeed, often are—contests for life." After the remnant Bedouin tribes were expelled from the western Naqab to the enclosed zone, they lost most of their historical land de facto.

During the 1950s the Israelis declared that all Bedouin land belonged to the state, relying on Ottoman codes to argue that the Bedouin had no land because they had neither registered nor cultivated it. Avinoam Meir (1997), Ghazi Falah (1989b), and Ronen Shamir (1996) note that Israel relied on the Ottoman Land Law of 1858, and particularly on the category of *mawat* land, as the legal basis for expropriating Bedouin land. Initially Ottoman land codes had been enacted to encourage people to register their land as property, but the Ottomans did not work hard enough at enforcing their laws on the Bedouin. A memorandum from J. F. Spry, a former assistant director of land registration in Palestine during the British Mandate, reported that "land registration law was introduced into the Ottoman Empire in 1858, however it does not appear to have been applied to the Palestine area until 1869 to 1873" (PRO, CO 733/494/3).

Israel also tried to benefit from the British Mandatory laws in order to assert that the Bedouin either did not own land or had not cultivated it. The Israeli government followed the 1921 British legislation to deny Bedouin land claims and continued to stick to their arguments in order to dispossess the Bedouin and control their land. They claimed that Bedouin had never owned land in the Naqab and did not register or cultivate their land according to the British ordinance of 1921, i.e., "the *mawat* law" (Abu Sitta 2008). To this day Israel claims that the Bedouin cannot produce official documents from either the Ottomans or the British to prove their land ownership (Segev 2010a, 2010b). However, many Bedouin have provided both Ottoman and British documents as proof of their land ownership.

According to Lord Oxford, assistant district commissioner of Beersheba in 1943, the British did not have any system in Beersheba to register Bedouin land and thus accepted traditional patterns of ownership. Bedouin land was the property of the tribe as a unit and was not only for individuals: "All the tribes knew their land naturally without registering it with the government as the Ottoman codes of land asked." He explained Bedouin land ownership further:

> We did not oppose Bedouin land ownership, nor did we force them to register their land. They were happy about the way they recognized their land, so we thought it better not to impose on them something they did not like and would resist. Only the Ottomans enacted land codes; we, the British, did not have any registration system for land in Beersheba.
> (INTERVIEW WITH LORD OXFORD, AUGUST 2008, SOMERSET, UK)

It is evident that under both Ottoman and British rule the Bedouin cultivated their lands continuously. Reports from the British Mandate era state that the Bedouin cultivated their land and maintained a strong agricultural presence. For example, a report from January 1947 indicates that the area of Khalasa, located on ʿAzazma clan land, was cultivated by its Bedouin owners: "These Bedouin are keen farmers and very much alive to the possibility of improving their agricultural methods. Tractor ploughing has made considerable strides within recent years and an increasing area is being planted each year with fruit trees" (PRO FO 371/61868).

The military rule authorities also used the 1949 British Emergency Defense Regulations—specifically Article 126 concerning security zones and closed zones—to expropriate Bedouin land. According to Article 126, such regions were closed to Arabs, with some of these closed zones secured for Jewish settlement. Another law used by Israel to control Arab land was the Absentees Property Law of 1950. Israel controlled most Bedouin lands with this law. For the Bedouin in particular, from the creation of Israel until 1964, only 220,000 *dunams* remained under Bedouin control. This land was constantly threatened by seizure (*Sawt al-Bilad,* April 10, 1985). Such legal maneuvers facilitated the expropriation of Bedouin land and concentrated the Bedouin in a shrinking space within the enclosed zone (Marx 1967; Abu Saad 2004; Shamir 1996; Falah 1989a; Yiftachel 2003, 2006).

It can be argued that Israel's policies in relation to Bedouin land claims are hypocritical. For example, Israeli archive reports dating to 1952 offer a snapshot of the early dynamics between the state and the Bedouin regarding land. As early records indicate, the Israeli authorities were initially very careful in dealing with Bedouin land claims. A now declassified secret report shows how Israel tried to deal with matters related to Bedouin land ownership immediately after the war. In this report, sent from Rehovot to the office of the prime minister and the Ministry of Defense on April 12, 1953, Michael Ha-Negbi (military governor of the Negev) wrote, "During 1950/1951, a total amount of 19,000 Israeli lira was collected from the Bedouin as land tax by the Negev military governor with the help of Bedouin shaikhs. Bedouin paid money for each *dunam* to be recognized" (ISA GL 13904/14). Almost all the Bedouin who remained in Israel in the 1950s paid land taxes that were collected by the military governor and Bedouin shaikhs.

The government set up a small but important committee, the Weitz Committee, to deal with persistent Bedouin land ownership claims.[10] This committee reported to the Ministry of Justice on its discussions around this contentious issue in 1952 (Nasasra 2011a). The committee proposed that it would be possible to "avoid recognizing Bedouin rights on their land even if they prove that they have cultivated it for a long and extended time" and recommended, among other things, delaying "the opening of a registration office in Be'er Sheva" to prevent any Bedouin from attempting to formalize their title. The committee called on the government to speed up the passage of a land purchase law "in order to facilitate the process of transferring the land that in the past was cultivated by Bedouin to Israel development authorities." In the same vein, the committee declared that the Bedouin "should be compensated if they can prove land ownership" (ISA G 5742/10).

From this we learn that the committee accepted that the Bedouin had populated the Negev before the founding of the state, recognized land cultivation as constituting evidence of ownership, and recommended compensation to Bedouin whose land was to be expropriated. If one examines the Weitz Committee's recommendations, one can argue that Israeli policies of dealing with Bedouin land ownership were disingenuous. On the one hand, they recognized that Bedouin had populated the Naqab before 1948, and on the other, they continued to use the Ottoman and the British land codes as the only legal justifications for denying Bedouin land claims and rights.

In summarizing how Israel seized Bedouin land, Emanuel Marx notes that the Israel Lands Authority (ILA), which controls 93 percent of Israel's land, allocates land to powerful groups—such as the army, Jewish settlers, and commercial interests—but not to the Bedouin. It is estimated that 80 percent of the land in the Naqab today has been allotted to the army for training and camps. All these policies of controlling Bedouin land are aimed at discouraging what Israel labels as "the encroachment of Bedouin on state land." In 1950, Israel declared and registered all the Naqab south of Beersheba as state land. This region, estimated at 10 million *dunams*, included 1.2 million *dunams* (around 300,000 acres) that had been owned and cultivated by individual Bedouin.

Abu Hussein and McKay also highlight the Bedouin confrontation with the state's policies over land. They point out that among all Palestinians within Israel, the Bedouin constitute the group most affected by Israeli laws and regulations, since they lost most of their land to the state for army and settlement use. Israel has continued to exercise harsh policies against the Naqab Bedouin, including house demolitions, as a means toward evicting them from their historical land. Nevertheless, "the Bedouin employ the most effective form of resistance in their power—their presence on the land" (Abu Hussein and McKay 2003, 84, 127–29). As one Bedouin stated, "we have lost part of our land, but we have not lost our honor." Of course, the state of Israel did not recognize these claims. Falk supports recognition of "indigenous peoples claims" (such as those of the Bedouin) and stresses that such claims clash with the state project and challenge its "territorial sovereignty" (Falk 1988, 18).

## Trapped Between the Borders: Bedouin Refugees and the UN

In 1952, a whole *ʿashira* of al-Sanne was expelled into Jordanian territory and became refugees in Jordan for months. The entire tribe of al-Sanne faced expulsion following an attack on a Jewish trader in 1952 in a border dispute. A curfew was imposed in Laqiya and negotiations began between the military government and the tribal shaikh. The army ordered the tribe to leave, but the tribal shaikh refused to do so:

> To begin with, a curfew was imposed on the tribe for a month, preventing any food or water from entering the tribal area. After that, the soldiers came with their trucks and military jeeps, and carried off our tribe by using force. They dropped us in the Rahwa area, and we built a refugee camp there, and remained there for two months.
> (INTERVIEW IN LAKIYA, AUGUST 2010).

Negotiations then took place between the army and Shaikh Ibrahim al-Sanne, who was recognized within the community as a Bedouin leader who had not submitted to the army's pressure to exile him and his tribe. During these negotiations, the army proposed that Hajj Ibrahim should move to the Tal ʿArad region, which he resolutely refused to do, saying "we will not live in Tal ʿArad."[11] He made the point that he did not want to live in a dry region without water resources. In the end, according to his daughter, Hajj Ibrahim said, "Open the border for me and my tribe to go to Jordan, to ʿAbdallah.

I do not want to live in exile in Tal ʿArad, and I would prefer to live in Jordan. However, ʿAbdallah refused to accept the Bedouin of the tribe in Jordan; as a result we were trapped between the borders as refugees for two months" (interview with Shaikh Ibrahim al-Sanne's daughter, *Sidreh*, no. 5, 2010). The Jordanians were nervous about offering al-Sanne a place to stay in case more Bedouin tribes came to join them. As a result, King ʿAbdullah of Jordan refused to offer them a place in his territory, which prompted their return to Israeli territory (*Akhbar al-Naqab*, May 12, 2009). It appears that more than thirty-one families from *ʿashirat* al-Sanne were exiled in 1952. The tribe remained in Jordan for forty days and was forbidden to return to Laqiya.

For the first time, the case was taken up to by the United Nations, which intervened in an attempt to settle the dispute. E. H. Hutchison, a Western military observer in Jordan, claimed to have counted one hundred families numbering 1,000 Bedouin who had been exiled by Israel, and described the *sumud* (steadfastness) of this tribe that had lived in exile in a refugee camp for more than two months (Hutchison 1956, 30–31). The reason Hajj Ibrahim asked for the mediation of Bedouin tribes from Jordan was because of his old relationship with them. After negotiations with the Israeli military governor had ended with al-Sanne tribe being sent back to Tal ʿArad the members of the tribe that did not accept the UN and Israel deal refused to return to live in Tal ʿArad. Some resisted and fled into Jordanian territory, not wanting to return with the majority of the tribe:

> It was October 26th before the es-Sanis [al-Sanne] were back in Israel. Seventeen of the tribe members had vanished deeper into Jordan and the search for them was not pressed. The crossing was a drama of frustration and despair driven by an unrelenting force. The Israeli court action was forgotten. By allowing the es-Sanis to cross to Jordan under threat of being sent to Tal ʿArad, the Israeli Military Governor had very cleverly been able to make credulous his claim that these were nomadic people who should not be allowed to control the more productive land.
> (HUTCHISON 1956, 35–36).

The disappearance of some of the tribe's members deep into Jordan was a sign of dissatisfaction about the deal and an indication that they were not willing to live in Tal ʿArad.

From Hutchison's description of the situation of al-Sanne living in exile in al-Rahwa, it is possible to realize the steadfast nature of these people (Hutchison 1956, 31–32). Women took an active role in feeding the tribe, employing a strong form of resistance in order to survive. Men followed the decisions of the shaikh of the tribe and stubbornly refused to move to Tal ʿArad, preferring to return to their land in Laqiya. These Bedouin ended up living in exile and resisting the military government's decision to move them to Tal ʿArad because of the tribe's strong leadership. Importantly, al-Sanne appealed to the Israeli Supreme Court in order to gain the right to move back to their original land. Negotiations took place among the UN committee, the Israelis, Shaikh Ibrahim al-Sanne, and the Jordanians in order to settle the dispute. Hajj Ibrahim also tried to use his old contacts with certain Bedouin shaikhs and friends from Jordan to intervene.

Described as a leading shaikh—wise, enthusiastic and nationalistic—a friend of Hajj Amin al-Hosseini, and a member of the Arab Higher Committee (ISA GAL 17002/13), Shaikh Ibrahim al-Sanne was well educated, having studied in Istanbul, and spoke fluent Turkish and English. He represents one of the outstanding symbols of Bedouin steadfastness. When he died in late 1952, Israeli newspapers acknowledged him as a leading figure of the Bedouin struggle.

The *ʿashirat* al-Sanne had spent more than forty days in Jordan, living between the borders of the two countries. At the end of the process they were transported on Jordanian trucks back to the Israeli border and then from there by Israeli trucks into Tal ʿArad. Significantly, Bedouin elders from *ʿashirat* al-Sanne remember that Israel charged them for the truck transportation and took their grain, leaving them without food. By late October 1952, the majority of the tribe's members had returned across the Israeli border into another form of exile in Tal ʿArad.

## Legal Maneuvers

The Ottoman Empire and the British Mandate faced difficulties in counting Bedouin tribes in the Naqab as the Bedouin were resistant to this policy (al-Aref 1999). British and French colonial states in the Middle East such as Algeria and Palestine devised strategies for collecting data about local populations, but native populations resisted these efforts. The French also faced obstacles to collecting statistical data about the Bedouin population in Syria and Lebanon. As Dawn Chatty notes, the French conducted the first national census in 1932, but "many Bedouin were not registered in this census either because they happened to be seasonally out of the Bekaa Valley at the time or because they refused to be registered, in opposition to the French colonial presence" (2014, 21).

Israel faced a similar challenge since the remnant tribes did not cooperate with the government in its attempts to count and register them as citizens. Having successfully moved all the remnant tribes from western Naqab into the closed zone, the Israeli authorities began to develop new policies to tighten control over them. One of the most important legal tricks was census and registration, a core tactic adopted by Israel to restrict and control the movement of Bedouin tribes. As Lustick points out, the Bedouin were asked to register according to their tribal affiliation, which broke up the big confederations (1980, 134). Between 1948 and 1954, Israel governed the Bedouin through a leading policy of tight control As Sa'di (2014) notes, after 1948 the state adopted population management and surveillance mechanisms to contain and govern the entire Palestinian minority.

It might be assumed that a census and registration system would be straightforward. However, Israeli government documents reveal a chaotic process. Israel attempted five times to count the Bedouin between 1948 and 1954, and only after the fifth census, carried out in 1954, was a number revealed. The 1954 census estimated the Bedouin at 11,463 people and was far from accurate.

The first official Israeli national census of the entire Palestinian Arab minority, who now found themselves within the border of the new state, took place immediately after the first stage of the war. Conducted in November 1948, it was justified as a positive move since it allowed Arabs to participate in the first Knesset elections (Lazar 2002, 103; Robinson 2005, 48). The first census in the Naqab was taken in December 1948 as part of the population management of the Palestinians in Israel (Sa'di 2014). This first census, administered by the army and the Department of Statistics, was a primitive count in which only 3,200 Bedouin were registered. All those registered were given blue army IDs (report by the Department of Minorities, Jerusalem, January 18, 1956; ISA/G 2218/4). Alina Korn (1996, 61) points out that the government decided to move the Bedouins to the closed zone in December 1948, which would have delayed the census. It was difficult to count the Bedouin immediately after the war since some were trapped between borders while others were filtering back and forth. In addition, the first attempt at counting the Bedouin was not completed because of financial difficulties.

A second attempt at a census of the Bedouin was made in late 1949. This time the census was carried out by the Department for Population Registration and managed to count about 16,215 Bedouin. However, the IDs were issued without photos and in the end were not distributed (although they were archived). This second census registered more Bedouin than the first, but administrative difficulties (such as a lack of equipment and photographers) affected its accuracy (ISA/G 2218/4). There was a third attempt to register the Bedouin conducted by the military government in 1950, but the problems were not solved, and the number of Bedouin was considered far from accurate (ISA/G 2218/4).

Further difficulties faced the military government in counting Bedouin during the fourth census in June 1951. This census also failed to count all the Bedouin accurately, this time registering 15,491 Bedouin and issuing them with civil IDs (ISA/G 2218/4). Only one large tribe of 1,800 people and another four small tribes were registered and issued IDs. The census remained incomplete, due in some cases to lack of private transportation or the nonaccompaniment of a military government representative. Furthermore, many trips to visit the tribes had to be cancelled because of administrative obstacles (ISA/GL 17099/16). A policy regarding Bedouin who did not hold IDs presented by the prime minister's Arab Affairs adviser, Yihoshua Palmon, favored exiling them (ISA/GL 17099/16).

Moshe Bar On argued that 600 Bedouin had not been counted and registered during the fourth census, thus proving that the census was a failure (ISA/GL 17099/16). Another report on Bedouin census problems and the issuing of IDs was given on February 7, 1952, at a meeting in the office of the military governor of the Naqab in Beersheba (ISA/GL 17099/16). The report argued that the Bedouin infiltration was a major factor in disrupting the counting process.

The fifth census attempt, which aimed at mapping the Bedouin and obtaining correct numbers, seems to have been the most accurate, but it still lacked crucial details. This time it was carried out in April and May 1954. In April 1954, *Davar* reported that the Naqab Bedouin census aimed to issue ID cards to Bedouin who had temporary IDs. It was meant to be completed before the Bedouin began to migrate for grazing purposes; otherwise, it would be difficult to finish as the Bedouin would be widely dispersed (*Davar,* April 21, 1954). *Haboker* newspaper reported that for the first time since the British Mandate, the Bedouin would start to receive ID cards and food vouchers. This time the registration process was agreed upon by the Bedouin shaikhs and was to include a survey of women and children. It was expected that the registration would include around 14,000 to 16,000 Bedouin (*Haboker,* March 28, 1954).

When the first full registration process ended in June 1954, the survey results from the Ministry of the Interior were reported in the Israeli media. *Al-Hamishmar* (May 27, 1954) noted that nineteen Bedouin tribes were registered in the Naqab (the three biggest tribes were the Abu Rqaiq tribe, which numbered 2,000 people; Abu Rabia, which numbered 1600; and al-Huzayil, which numbered 1450). According to government officials, this census was the most comprehensive of the five and included all the Bedouin in the Naqab since children had now been registered and some IDs had been renewed or replaced. It was found that only 343 individuals were not eligible to remain (probably Bedouin infiltrators who came and rejoined their tribes, but were not allowed to stay), ninety-six of whom were subsequently issued with IDs while another sixty-five were scheduled to be checked to see if they were legal or not (ISA/ G 2218/4).

The press release issued on May 23, 1954, by the Israeli Ministry of the Interior announced that the census had registered 11,433 Bedouins:

> On 20 May 1954, the census of the Bedouin tribes in the Negev came to an end. This census was the first which included all the Bedouin tribes in the Negev. In 1949, a similar census was carried among the Negev Bedouin; however, it lacked much missing information and it did not include all the citizens. After that, many changes happened in the structure of the Bedouin tribes, so this census was conducted in order to complete the missing information . . . this census included all the Bedouin: men and women . . . were registered under 19 tribes, 400 newborn children were registered, 220 marriage cases, 440 deceased, and 300 cases of amendment of ages . . . this census started on 28 March 1954, and ended on 20 May 1954. Nineteen tribes were registered according to the list. (ISA/G 5593/22)

A couple of changes had been made for the census of 1954, and new Bedouin were registered. A special committee dealt with those who had not registered or were absent during the census and with tribal leaders who insisted on registering more of their tribal members. After some changes, an updated list was released on July 15, 1954, including new families that had been added to the May 20th census. According to the new July list, 11,947 Bedouin had been registered in nineteen tribes (ISA/G 2218/4), most of which had been expelled from the western Naqab and now lived in the *siyaj* region.

Interestingly, it took the Israeli authorities six years and several failed censuses to count and register the Bedouin. This was due to significant Bedouin attempts at noncooperation. They used noncooperation techniques to resist efforts to count them and refused to allow their women to be photographed, actions that made life very difficult for the census staff.

Of the nineteen tribes recognized by the state in the 1954 census, fourteen belonged to the Tayaha, four to the Tarabin, and only one to the ʿAzazma. As table 6.2 shows, Israel used a tight system of registration, which meant

TABLE 6.2
Final list of tribes after the 1954 census

| TRIBE | PLACES | SHAIKH |
|---|---|---|
| Abu Rqaiq | Beir al-Hamam, Kharbit al-Watan, al-Mshash, Kurnub, Saʿawa | ʿAwadd Abu Rqaiq |
| Al-ʿAssam | Abu Tlol, al-Madhbah, Kharbit al-Watan | Muhammad al-ʿAssam |
| Qdirat al-Sanne | Khshom Biodd, Tal ʿArad | Mansor al-Sanne |
| Abu Rabia | Tal al-Malah, Qseima, Hdeiba | Hammad Abu Rabia |
| Abu Qrinat | ʿAraʿra, Um Mtnan | Ali Abu Qrinat |
| Abu Jweyaʾd | Am Sheiq, ʿAraʿara, Sdeir | Muhammad Abu Jweyaʿd |
| Al-Huzayil | Kharbit al-Huzayil, Abu Ayash | Salman al-Huzayil |
| Saqr al-Huzayil | Um ʿAllaq, Laqiya | Saqr al-Huzayil |
| Al-Assad | Laqiya | Faraj al-Assad |
| Abu ʿAbdon | Laqiya | Hassan Abu ʿAbdon |
| Al-ʿAtawna | Hura | Musa al-ʿAtawna |
| Al-Talalqa | Twayel al-Mahdi | ʿAmer al-Talalqa |
| Al-Afenish | Saʿawa | Muhammad al-Afenish |
| Al-Oqbi | Hura, Kharbit al-Watan | Salim al-Oqbi |
| Tarabin al-Sanne | Wadi Shqeib | Sliman al-Sanne |
| Abu ʿAmra | Wadi Shqeib | Hlayel Abu ʿAmrah |
| Abu Srihan | Tal Abu Mahfoz, Um Batin | Jaber Abu Srihan |
| Masoʿdin al-ʿAzazma (Abu Maʿamar) | Wadi Shqeib | Oda Abu Maʿamar |
| Abu Blal | Wadi Shqeib | Not specified |

that tribes were fragmented. The Tayaha was split into a couple of tribes in an attempt to create a new tribal system that would be easy to control. As a result of this census, the Bedouin were issued with formal Israeli ID cards, different from the previous era when they had held temporary military ID cards (ISA/G 5593/22; IDFA 490/1956–125).

Counting and registering the tribes was one of the state's primary tools for manipulating the Bedouin. However, as Sa'di (2014) shows, the use of the census as a manipulation tool was a failure. The census was delayed by technical problems, lack of knowledge of the tribal mentality, and the difficulties of operating in the desert. More importantly, the Bedouin were uncooperative. Many tribes and shaikhs would not cooperate with the census because they felt at risk from their numbers being known. Tribes also feared that the census would be used to expropriate their land and evict them from their encampments, and that it would threaten their women, which was against their culture and customs. Penhas Amir, military governor of the Naqab (1956–1963), confirmed Bedouin opposition to photos being taken of the women:

> The problem was that we were not allowed to photograph Bedouin women, it was not proper for a strange man to get a photo of a Bedouin women, so the Bedouin used this to their advantage, and we failed totally on this point, as there were no ways to identify whether the women were local Bedouin or filtered back.
>
> (INTERVIEW, PENHAS AMIR, SEPTEMBER 2008).

The newspaper *Davar* reported in April 1954 that Bedouin women were being issued IDs with no pictures on them. In the blank space were the words, "without picture, with permission of the Ministry of Interior." (*Davar*, April 21, 1954)

Noncooperation was one form of nonviolent action (Sharp 1973), and was also an attempt to prevent government interference in Bedouin tribal politics and affairs. Overall, Bedouin distrusted the official Israeli censuses. Many refused to cooperate with the data collectors for fear of knowledge about their private lives becoming public. Others were worried about urbanization or expropriation and expulsion.

In the end it seems that more Bedouin tribes than anticipated had succeeded in staying on their land. On April 12, 1953, a copy of a secret report marked "not for publication" was sent from Rehovot to the office of the prime minister and the Ministry of Defense. The sender's name was omitted, and it was addressed to the military government in the Negev. According to the ISA, the report questioned how these nineteen tribes had been recreated, adding that, based on the declarations of Bedouin shaikhs who had submitted to the authorities following the occupation of Beersheba, the remnant tribes had numbered only 4,000 individuals. The report indicated that these 4,000 persons belonged to tribes that had submitted to the army. The report also pointed out that, the policy of accepting those who returned and registered had continued even though some had been not friendly.

Interestingly, this secret report acknowledged the fact that the registration of the Bedouin in the Naqab had taken years and that this protracted process had enabled more families and even full tribes to stay (ISA/GL 13904/14). The report reveals not only that there was internal disagreement among the Israeli authorities but also that there was little consensus about methods of dealing with the Bedouin tribes. The registration and population management strategy (Saʾdi 2014) represents one of the key policies of surveillance and political control that was adopted toward the Palestinians in Israel after the Nakba.

SEVEN

# Traditional Leadership, Border Economy, Resistance, and Survival, 1952–1956

HISTORICALLY, TRIBAL LEADERS played a core role in managing tribal affairs and representing Bedouin throughout the Middle East. In referring to the strong political role of the tribal leader, Dawn Chatty argues that "he negotiates access, arbitrates disputes and generally represents the tribe in its relations with the central authority of the state" (2014, 18). In Israel during the period of military rule (1948–1967) the government saw the Bedouin shaikhs as a potential force for governing Bedouin tribes, mainly by co-option and fragmentation. Lustick (1980) notes that co-opting traditional Arab elites was a common policy of the Israeli state. Like the United States and Canada in the late nineteenth and twentieth centuries, the military rule authorities in Israel co-opted tribal leaders to gain control over indigenous people (Champagne 2003, 267). In the context of other Middle Eastern states, tribal heads were empowered, and their position was officially recognized by the government.

In Jordan, for example, tribal leaders were authorized by the king to deal with tribal issues on a variety of levels (interview with Shaikh Wassil Abu Jaber, Biqaᶜ camp, Jordan). In 1960s Syria under the Baᶜth Party, tribal leaders were considered part of the old order, and Bedouin shaikhs were challenged by the party with the possibility that their land and power would be stripped from them (Chatty 2014, 23). Israel's policies met with limited success in relation to the Bedouin shaikhs, who used what I call their "internal politics role" not just to serve the state as brokers but to acquire their own rights. In some cases, tribal shaikhs were recruited to the Labor party to collect votes from their tribes. In other cases, Bedouin shaikhs were leading the struggle for recognition.

## Bedouin Shaikhs as Brokers and Clients

According to Weingrod (1977, 323), patronage is the complex web of relations between those who use their influence to protect others and those whom they protect. In the first phase of military rule, the authorities created an interpersonal structure (patron-client relationship) with shaikhs in order to govern the Bedouin, a relationship that was based on both inequality and reciprocity. Sasson Bar Zvi recalled this relationship: "We recognized that it would be impossible to control the Bedouin in the accepted way without our need to understand the tribal structure and to work through it: in other words we needed the shaikhs and the heads of the tribes" (Bar Zvi 1973).

Marx (1967, 41) also emphasized the importance of the shaikhs for the military rule system, pointing out that the military governors were interested in working with decisive and charismatic shaikhs who were able to control their tribes and who could be relied on to implement the governors' instructions. As a result of government policies, the Bedouin shaikhs under military rule acquired significant political force among their tribes.

Similarly, archival material confirms that the role of the shaikhs was critical for governing the Bedouin. An anonymous secret report from 1953 shows the significance of the role of Bedouin shaikhs in the Naqab and Biʾr al-Sabaʿ for the government, confirming that in the eyes of the Israeli authorities the status of the shaikhs was crucial (ISA/ GL 13904/14). The report clearly indicates that a number of Bedouin were appointed to be shaikhs because of their close-knit relationship with the state and that the Bedouin shaikhs were good for the system. I found instances where tribes opposed the appointing of shaikhs without their agreement. One case showed that tribes resisted the military government instructions. The Tarabin tribe refused to accept the appointment of a shaikh for their tribe without their assent. They boycotted those who were appointed by the military government and refused to cooperate with them (*Al Hamishmar*, July 4, 1958). Bedouin shaikhs were not puppets in the hands of the military government, but benefited from every opportunity to gain more of their rights by exploiting the government.

Penhas Amir (military governor of the Naqab in 1956) described the relationship between Bedouin shaikhs and the military government:

> We worked very closely with Bedouin shaikhs to solve internal issues of their tribes. Shaikhs used to come to my office and raise their tribal problems and needs; they were very active. I tried to help them as much as I could, saying "your problems are my problems." The signature of the shaikh was that of the military governor; they were meant to tell the governor if there were some problems which had to be solved. In many cases Bedouin shaikhs also contested my decisions, especially in cases that they saw as not good for them. (INTERVIEW WITH PENHAS AMIR, AUGUST 2008)

This interview suggests that shaikhs and military governors created a patron-client relationship when they dealt with tribal affairs. The shaikhs knew what they wanted and did not submit their claims and the needs of the tribes. As a result, patron-client relationships granted these Bedouin shaikhs both power and wealth.

Based on military government perceptions, Bedouin shaikhs were supposed to do the following: confirm things about their tribes, undertake registration for their tribes, supply workers for possible jobs in kibbutzim, obtain permits for their tribal members from Beersheba, report on unusual incidents within their tribes, report infiltrations, charge fees for leased land, validate marriages, own properties such as shops, report on members of their tribes who left the country, and follow all instructions given by the military government. They became the agents of the military government, providing information and registering children, marriages, and deaths (in effect becoming, as one Bedouin shaikh commented, a branch of the Ministry of the Interior). The shaikhs were not submissive and passive as the military government had hoped, but instead were active agents in using the system, helping their tribes to gain more rights, and struggling to get their land ownership recognized.

This policy of co-opting leaders of the Arab community (not only Bedouin shaikhs) was discussed in the Koenig Report. Written by Israel Koenig, northern district commissioner of the Ministry of the Interior, the report dealt with the subject of how to handle the Palestinian Arabs of the Galilee. The report was published in the Israeli newspaper *Al-Hamishmar* on

September 7, 1976 (Hadawi 1989, 157). One policy that had been applied to the Palestinian citizens of Israel since 1948 was the creation of a new type of leadership unconnected with communists or nationalists and willing to collaborate with Israel (Saʿdi 2003, 53). One section of the report emphasized these cooptation policies as "imposing upon the Arabs a dishonest leadership in the form of a national Arab party administered secretly by the Israeli Intelligence Agency" (Hadawi 1989, 157).

The Koenig Report was employed with regard to the Naqab Bedouin shaikhs and the Arab leadership in the north. Although some shaikhs refused to serve the Israeli authorities as brokers in their community, other Bedouin shaikhs chose to mediate between their tribes and the military government (Lustick 1980), becoming the military government's main link in supplying services:

> The relationship was between the shaikh and the military governor only; no one else could go and get permits without the shaikh's knowledge, and no one except the shaikh was even recognized by the military governor. There were some shaikhs with very limited influence who were designated by the government and who applied the military government criteria in order to be shaikhs.
>
> (INTERVIEW WITH ABU ʿALI, AUGUST 2012).

I argue that Bedouin shaikhs actually benefited from the co-option policies of the military rule authorities. First, the only individuals to gain from the government's services were the shaikh's small family and immediate relatives. In this regard, a shaikh's close relatives enjoyed certain services more than other members of the tribe. However, sometimes shaikhs behaved independently and dealt with matters solely for their own benefit. Second, these shaikhs used their powerful status without the knowledge of the Israeli officials. When the shaikhs went back to their tribes, the military officials had no idea about their behavior. Third, they resisted military rule by recognizing its weaknesses. Fourth, many things happened within the tribes without government knowledge of them. Shaikhs reported what they wanted to the military government and concealed what they thought should be hidden. The military government had only one means of entry into the Bedouin tribes, and that came via the shaikhs.

As a result, by using their internal politics, the shaikhs knew exactly how to deal with military rule officials. They hid facts from the officials and reported only what they felt was good for their tribes:

> Normally, the military governor agrees with what the shaikh says. The military government did not get to know all the tribe; only shaikhs knew details about their tribes, and it was here that the shaikhs employed their power. The military governors know less about the tribes; they don't know me or you personally, but they only knew the shaikh, and everything the shaikh agreed with, the military governor could not say "no."
>
> (INTERVIEW WITH SHAIKH ABU SALIH, JULY 2012)

As this interviewee suggests, the military government ruled through the shaikhs, and the shaikhs were crucial to the system. However, the role of brokerage can be tricky for governments. Shaikhs were given a lot of power and were allowed to accumulate wealth and status. It is known that the military rule worked hard at controlling the tribes by co-opting shaikhs and leaders. However, the patron-client relationship that existed between the government and the shaikhs was problematic for all concerned.[1]

## *Shaikhs Caught Between Patron and Client*

One of the most important methods adopted by the Israeli authorities for co-opting the shaikhs was by leasing land to them. In this situation, patron-client ties served as a mediating mechanism. The Israeli authorities became the landlord, a patron who leased the Bedouin land. On the one hand, this policy empowered Bedouin shaikhs and raised their status; on the other, it weakened Bedouin land ownership claims.

Chanina Porat (1998) notes that until 1953 there had been no clear agreement among government officials as to the preferred method of leasing land to the Bedouin. After the tribes had lost the major part of their historical land, the government leased land to shaikhs according to their status. Big tribes were leased thousands of tracts of land via their shaikhs and used it for grazing or cultivation (interview with Abu Ibrahim, September 2010). The shaikhs accumulated considerable wealth through these leased lands, and there were many cases of corruption in the land leasing process.

The Agriculture Ministry leased land to shaikhs, and part of this land was then leased by the shaikhs to members of tribes. In such cases shaikhs, used to lease land (outside the *siyaj*) to their tribal members and then asked to share a portion of the produce from the cultivation, sometimes expropriating as much as half of the crops (i.e., the shaikh behaved like a landowner). This system continued until 1958, when some Bedouin complained about being exploited by the shaikhs and appealed to the courts for this corruption to stop (*La-merhav*, October 13 1958).

The shaikhs were responsible for the leased land, and they leased it to members of their tribe according to their own preferences. These tribes cultivated about 230,000 *dunams*. However, tribes that had lost their lands were leased tracts of land for seasonal cultivation or grazing only. This land was leased to the Bedouin by the Ministry of Agriculture for annual fees of five *agorot* (Israeli currency = about 11 cents an acre) for cultivable land and three *agorot* per *dunam* (about 7 cents per acre) for grazing land. In total, the Bedouin cultivated some 400,000 *dunams* (about 100,000 acres) (ISA/GL 17093/1). One Bedouin interviewee describes the patron-client relationship in the case of land:

> Shaikhs were leased thousands of land tracts for grazing and planting seeds. Shaikhs used their relations with the state to empower themselves and to help their relatives, though other people in the tribe suffered as a result of this policy and complaints were made against the shaikhs. The shaikhs also exploited the government for the purposes of helping their relatives to get grazing land. There were secrets between the shaikhs and their tribes that no government in the world would know.
>
> (INTERVIEW WITH ABU ʿABDALLAH, SEPTEMBER 2012)

The relationship between the shaikhs and the government created a class typified by an indirect government and patron-client relationship that shaikhs used for their benefit. Shaikhs did not have to supply services to every citizen. This type of indirect government led to discrimination because some clients were issued permits and food and others were not. I came across the case of a Bedouin shaikh who was able to lease thousands of tracts because he had a good relationship with Israel's ruling political party (Mapai). Subsequently, a member of one of the tribes appealed to the court about the evilness of the shaikh, who had benefited from the land and did not distribute it to members of the tribe. The Ministry of Agriculture admitted to the court that the shaikh (an ʿAzazma shaikh) had leased 10,000 *dunams*, which was against the law as well as against the ministry's own regulations (*Al-Hamishamar*, August 2, 1961). This case says a lot about corruption, particularly with regard to leasing land to Bedouin shaikhs and not directly to tribal members. The shaikh's special status as a close friend of the Mapai meant that he had been given special deals by Ministry of Agriculture officials.

The military government's relations with the shaikhs also created conflict among tribes who disobeyed the authority of the shaikhs. Some tribes broke away from the order that had been set up by the authorities between 1948 and 1951. During the late 1950s and early 1960s, there were many cases of tribes who split off from bigger tribes to create their own new subtribes. For instance, in the 1950s, Abu al-Kiyaʾan split from the previous tribal order of al-Huzayil and recognized a new shaikh. In the 1960s, al-Nasasrah of the Maʿaniya tribes split from the tribal order of the Zullam and a new shaikh, Shaikh Sulaiman Mustafa al-Nasasrah of the Maʿaniya, was recognized by the authorities. He became the head of a couple of families who had previously been under a different shaikh. These examples show opposition to the framework constructed by the government up to 1951. The primary reasons were the evil behavior of the recognized shaikhs and the government's eagerness to recognize new shaikhs who were willing to cooperate with the system. Some court cases emphasized that the Bedouin had cultivated their native land without any permits from either the government or the shaikhs. This could have been the result of the government's interest in creating direct conflict between the tribes.

## *Shaikhs as Mediators*

A second tool adopted by the government to control the shaikhs was the system of permits, which was aimed at governing the Bedouin by restricting their daily lives and their mobility. Almost all Arabs were required have permits in order to move between their villages and their jobs. The pass system worked all over the Naqab, the Little Triangle, and the Galilee. In order to obtain a pass, people were obliged to visit the nearest military unit:

> Under the pass system, Arabs are not allowed to travel to Jewish towns and other places far removed from their homes without a special permit . . .

> the authorities maintain that the system is essential to keep a check on the movement of a minority of the Arabs, notably the communists, from whom there is a danger of subversion and spying.
> (PRO, FO 371/128211)

In the Naqab passes were available from the military unit in Beersheba or from the local military unit, where a representative of the military government would be available to issue permits. The trick was that you could not travel to get a pass if you did not have a pass. As a result, the key role in the pass system became that of the shaikhs as clients who were asked to assist their tribes in obtaining permits. Only shaikhs were allowed to travel without holding permits. Tribal members who needed travel permits had to address their requests to their shaikhs. Alternatively, people went to Beersheba and queued all day at the governor's office to obtain permits, though they were sometimes not given them. An interviewee spoke of concerns over getting a permit for a job. He described how it took him almost a day of queuing at a military office in Beersheba to obtain a permit. He then went to take up a construction job and was not allowed to come back before forty days had passed (interview with Shaikh Salih, July 2009).

Cases like this show how difficult it was to get a permit to move around or even to work in a basic job. Amir described how the Bedouin queued from early morning and sometimes waited until dark in order to get a permit. One day around five o'clock in the evening, noticing that some Bedouin were still standing in line and had not yet got permits, he asked Kadori (who was in charge of issuing them) to give the Bedouin permits immediately, saying that no one was going home without getting a pass (interview with Penhas Amir, July 2008).

Such difficulties led many Bedouin to break military rule law and to move around without permits. Another interviewee emphasized that in some cases the shaikhs were useless:

> We needed to go to the military governor to get a travel pass; if you moved around without one you would be arrested or humiliated, it was a really bad policy they employed against us. Everywhere you wanted to go, you needed a permit; if you had a plan to go to Beersheba you'd need a permit. Sometime we needed to bribe someone to get the permit or to pay money to the shaikh. I want to criticize the shaikhs for getting money from some Bedouin in order

> to get permits. The problem was that we were forced to ask for the shaikh's kindness; he was the only one the authorities recognized.
> (INTERVIEW WITH HAJJ SAUD, JUNE 2010)

Bedouin broke the regulations every day to get food and water and to find jobs in order to survive. It was quite normal for the Bedouin to be stopped by the police and arrested. Interviewees confirmed that during the early stages of military rule they struggled to live and to find jobs. In order to find water and food, they had been forced to move about without permits (interview with Abu Ibrahim, September 2013).

The permits system meant that life under the military government was cruel for the Bedouin, especially when it came to finding work, which was one of the main problems confronting them. The jobs available for Bedouin were mostly in agriculture but depended on requests from employers in kibbutzim in the center of Israel. Many Bedouin were employed in road construction, but some started to find jobs in the nearest settlements and managed to work without permits. Marx noted that for limited periods the Bedouin were offered special permits to work outside the military government in seasonal agricultural jobs (in orange groves), building roads, driving tractors (Marx 1967). In order to survive, the Bedouin invented ways of working in Jewish kibbutzim and orchards without holding permits. An Israeli police report in 1955 indicates cases where Bedouin were stopped after a police raid and were found to be doing jobs for kibbutzim and farms without permits (ISA/IP 86/4). One interviewee noted that employment consisted basically of seasonal jobs, and almost all jobs were limited to a few weeks or months. Even if someone wanted to work, for example in Kibbutz Lahav, he had to have a license to do so. Some people got permits to look for jobs. If a Jewish employer wanted to employ some Bedouin he gave them papers to take to the military governor in order to obtain permits to do the work (interview with Dodik Shoshani, July 2009).

## *Shaikhs as Active Agents for Bedouin Rights*

In his most recent paper, Ahmad Saʿdi (2015) has listed a significant number of acts of nonviolent protest by the Palestinians in Israel against the military rule, referring mainly to the protests and demonstrations about military rule in the north and the Galilee. This did not apply only in the north since I found that some leading Bedouin shaikhs had been playing a significant role in protesting against military rule in a variety of nonviolent forms in the Naqab. A number of Shaikhs in the Naqab were active agents in many other matters, especially in resisting military rule instructions, claiming their land, and complaining about many aspects of government policy. In other words, despite the oppressive nature of military rule the Bedouin shaikhs were not submissive. Two cases serve as examples.

The first example shows Bedouin shaikhs not cooperating with military rule and resisting their masters' instructions. In 1955, seventeen Bedouin shaikhs participated in a meeting with the military governor, Verbin, and his senior staff in their Beersheba offices. Opening the meeting, Verbin explained that there were a couple of reasons for the gathering: " . . . one is that we have not had a meeting for long time, and the other is that some instructions are not clear; we have to clarify them." One issue Verbin raised concerned the fact that Bedouin were migrating with their herds without permits and were accused of damaging property such as water pipes and trees. The second related issue concerned the assistance given by Bedouin to *muhajareen* and the continuation of the border economy. The Bedouin were accused of aiding their relatives who were regarded as infiltrators (*muhajareen*) and providing them with food. Verbin also reminded the Bedouin shaikhs to obey the instructions of the military government. Verbin complained that Bedouin shaikhs had failed to bring incidents related to security and order to the attention of the military government. He stressed that Bedouin shaikhs must apply Israeli laws, behave accordingly, and avoid intervening to disrupt law and order.

In return, the Bedouin shaikhs raised a couple of related issues to be addressed by the military government: the Bedouin suffered from a shortage of drinking water and a restricted grazing area, which led them to disobey the military government's instructions, and their rights and needs had to be addressed (ISA/IP 86/4).[2] This case shows that Bedouin shaikhs resisted the military rule's instructions in a variety of ways.

Another case of shaikh resistance against military rule was through the struggle over land. In this regard the Bedouin shaikhs were active agents and had been claiming ownership of land since the early days of military rule. Their most effective form of behavior was to resist the military government's policies of expropriating their land.

In the second example, a Bedouin shaikh was sacked from his position because he campaigned for Bedouin rights and resisted military rule regulations. This was Shaikh Musa al-ʿAtawna, who was known to be active in calling for rights for Bedouin and for recognizing Bedouin land ownership. Some archival reports stress that he had even established a relationship with the Communist Party (IDFA/ 590/1961–60). This leading Bedouin shaikh resisted the military government's policies and disobeyed its instructions. As a result, he was sacked from his leadership position. Shaikh Musa represents a classic case of opposition to military rule instructions.

These cases highlight how the Bedouin shaikhs found different channels through which to challenge the military rule regulations. They were not puppets but instead active agents, defending their rights, opposing the military governors, and struggling against the system. The situation changed after the era of military rule with the emergence of a new form of Bedouin leadership, mostly among Bedouin shaikhs who had campaigned for gaining their historical rights.

## The Hidden Border Economy

Bedouin cross-border relations were often about the border economy (smuggling). During the 1950s the Bedouin adopted smuggling goods as a major tool of economic survival and nonviolent resistance. During this period the U.S. Department of State reported in detail about smuggling:

> Smuggling [border economy], the age-old pastime of the Near East, is another bothersome feature. Many of the ancient smuggling highways from Lebanon and Syria to Egypt run through territory now under Israel's control. Constant vigilance is required on the part of Israel's army and police to make certain that smuggling is kept to a minimum . . . the main articles which [are] smuggled into or through Israel are Lebanese arak, cloth from Damascus, coffee and sweets of all kinds. In most of these cases, smugglers operate at night and consequently the smugglers, if not killed, are able to escape to the hills only to try once again.
>
> (FOREIGN SERVICE OF THE USA, DEPARTMENT OF STATE, TEL AVIV, JUNE 20, 1950, PRO, FO 371/82512)

In the Naqab, the border economy was very attractive and the routes were difficult to control. The Bedouin had inhabited the area for generations and knew all the feasible trade routes. The hidden economy represented the strongest form of Bedouin subsistence since it helped the Bedouin to survive under harsh conditions. Benny Morris refers to their economic and smuggling activities during the 1950s:

> Along the Egyptian border the smuggling was usually conducted between Bedouin tribes on both sides of the line. Occasionally, these tribes, when angered by IDF interception or expulsion, would take revenge by mining IDF patrol roads. Some arms smuggling—specifically by Muslim Brotherhood members in Gaza and Sinai to their brethren in the West Bank—seems to have taken place in the mid-1950s.
> (MORRIS 1993, 45)

Some Bedouin tribal subsections remained in Israeli territory. Other sections were on the other side of the border under the control of one of the neighboring Arab countries. Bedouin used their connections with their relatives across the borders wisely, and with them smuggled everything they possibly could. Amir describes the difficulties of curbing the hidden economy of the Bedouin during the early 1950s:

> The area was open all the time, we had no possibility of restricting or stopping Bedouin movement, especially if they smuggled cows, and slaughtered them immediately. This happened through collaboration between them on both sides of the borders, and no one could stop them. You can catch people while they smuggle, but not afterwards; it did not work because all the Bedouin use to hide everything.
> (INTERVIEW WITH PENHAS AMIR, AUGUST 2008)

Some of the smuggled food was sold to Jewish settlers. Some was used for Bedouin subsistence. Items smuggled by the Bedouin included food and other goods such as razor blades, coffee, transistors, eggs, cigarettes, tobacco, and headscarves, women's clothing, cows, camels, and donkeys (interview with Sultan, August 2012).

Morris reports on the smuggling of Bedouin women's clothing from the West Bank in 1954 as well as large scale smuggling of animals due to meat shortages in Israel:

> In 1954 a senior Israeli officer reported "large scale" smuggling by infiltrators of sheep—for food and/or wool—from Jordan to Israel. Some of the smuggling, according to Glubb, involved traditional Arab clothing, unavailable in Israel: no clothes for Muslim women could be bought or sold in Israel. The Bedouin men of the Beersheba area, sooner than unveil their women and dress them in short skirts, were obliged to "infiltrate" into Hebron to shop for their wives.
>
> (MORRIS 1993, 45)

Sugar and coffee were always in short supply, and the Bedouin smuggled them from Egypt without any intervention from the government. *Manadil* (headscarves) and *qmash* were smuggled from Jordan. *Qmash maʾraq* (clothes for women) were smuggled from both Egypt and Jordan (interview with ʿAbdallah, July 2009).

In 1955, Verbin mentioned in a letter to his superiors that some Bedouin had been sent to court because of their illegal ownership of radios. Over fifty radios had been found with no permits after a check by Israeli police of radio sets among the Naqab Bedouin (letter from Verbin to the Israeli police in Beersheba, October 18, 1955, ISA/IP 86/4). Ten days later Verbin wrote, "We see this as severe and we request suitable legal action in this case" (letter from Verbin, October 29 1955, IDFA 590/1961–60). Another report from the Israeli Defense Force Archive dated March 28, 1956, named forty Bedouin who held radios. They were from a number of tribes and were mostly shaikhs (IDFA 590/1961–45). Military government restrictions failed to deter the Bedouin from smuggling or owning radios. Shaikhs in particular had radios and, in the interests of their tribe, used them to stay connected. ISA reports confirm that smuggling was one of the main hidden economic resources for the Bedouin:

> It is estimated that some 55,000 camels and similar numbers of sheep and goats have been smuggled and sold by the Bedouin during the last ten years. This occupation is not considered by them as illegal, but rather as most honorable and "fit for a man". Moreover, it is not based on livestock alone.

> Their traditional dress, for local use, is smuggled from the Mount Hebron area. Owing to their topographical position, between Jordan and Egypt, they conduct a transit economy . . . coffee, and a wide range of manufactured articles, from transistor radios and fountain pens to shaving blades and other small or portable objects.
>
> (REPORT BY THE STATE OF ISRAEL, GOVERNMENT PRESS OFFICE, ISA/GL 7093/1)

The Bedouin were familiar with desert routes and knew the secret ways to Hebron, Jordan, and Egypt. Tal ʿArad was another economic route on the border with the West Bank. In grazing years Bedouin sometimes built their tents near the border routes:

> The way into Jordan was very close by and was open for cross-border relations. Some of the smuggled goods went to the Jewish settlers. There were Jews from Tel Aviv and Pitach Tiqva who came to buy the smuggled food. We did not harm the state by smuggling; until the 1960s this was the way people survived.
>
> (INTERVIEW WITH MUSTAFA, JUNE 2009)

Another even more attractive smuggling route was through the Egyptian border region. The ʿAzazma tribes were settled in this area on both the Israeli and the Egyptian sides of the border, where a lack of Israeli IDs meant the ʿAzazma enjoyed freedom of movement because nobody knew to which tribe they belonged. Amir described the ʿAzazma situation:

> The big problem of the military government in dealing with smuggling was throughout the Egyptian border area, where the ʿAzazma properties are found until today. Many of the ʿAzazma used to live between the Israel and Egypt borders, and between the Israel and Jordan borders; they lived and migrated between two borders as a very normal way of life without any problem. That area was totally open, apart from Sde Boker, and there were no Jewish settlements there. So the ʿAzazma benefited from that by moving freely between the borders of three countries. They also made use of the fact that they did not have Israeli IDs, especially the ʿAzazma (Sarahin) who lived in the Naqab Mountain (Har Ha-Negev).
>
> (INTERVIEW WITH PENHAS AMIR, JULY 2008)

It was quite natural for a tribe that lived on both sides of the borders to visit other family members and even to share food:

> The resistance of the ʿAzazma Bedouin was invisible to us as a government; they did things secretly without our knowledge. Even though it was a military rule and an enclosed zone, the ʿAzazma Bedouin and other Bedouin lived wherever they wanted; today you'd find them living in one place, and tomorrow in a different place. It was almost impossible to catch the Bedouin while they were smuggling. They knew the area better than we did, and they did not recognize the border—there are no borders in Bedouin life. The government did not tighten its control of the borders.
> (INTERVIEW WITH YITZHAK TSAMAH, AUGUST 2009)

The ʿAzazma Bedouin crossed borders without seeking permission from Israeli officials. In their view, they did not have to think about breaking the law because this was their life and the way they lived.

### *Hosting Muhajareen and the Desire for Reunification*

A second important component of Bedouin cross-border relations was aiding and hosting the natives who were considered *muhajareen* (the term for "infiltrators" used by the Israeli military) by the military rule authorities. Those Bedouin who tried to return to their land practiced their right of return without even thinking about new state regulations and new borders. The Bedouin in the Naqab maintained dealings with their relatives beyond the border in several specific forms: through the hidden economy, by secretly visiting each other in Israel and in Jordan, by maintaining marriage connections across borders, and by hosting visits from relatives. The Israeli army and police worked very hard to reduce the influx of what they categorized as "infiltrators." A report titled "The Present Status of Arabs Resident in Israel, and Plans for their Future," sent by the U.S. Embassy in Tel Aviv to the State Department in Washington, DC, and dated June 20, 1950, stated:

> In an attempt to keep infiltration to a minimum, the police now make periodic raids upon towns and villages in Israel, filter out illegal visitors,

> and eventually return them to the country from which they came. There has already been evidence of a certain amount of cruelty in dealing with infiltrators. And, as the situation grows worse, and the patience of Israel border patrols more strained, the measures taken to discourage infiltration and raids will probably become more drastic.
> (PRO, FO 371/82512)

As Cohen points out, "infiltration was one of the most acute challenges faced by the young state of Israel" (2010, 67). The Bedouin were extremely effective in hosting their "infiltrator" relatives. They found ways to support the *muhajareen* by offering them secure places to stay and supplying them with food and shelter. Maintaining connections with their relatives across the Israeli borders was critical for the Bedouin in the enclosed zone. For the Bedouin *muhajareen*, the clear aim was to be reunited with their relatives who had been separated from them by the borders. The majority of the Bedouin who filtered back into their land were parts of the Bedouin tribes who had been exiled during and after the war. Chanina Porat (1998) notes that Bedouin infiltration continued during the period 1950 to 1953.

The Bedouin regarded their relatives who filtered back as "guests" Those who came at night were considered *dyof al-layil* (guests of the night), which was not how the state perceived them. The Bedouin offered their relatives warmth and security, hid them from the Israeli police, and failed to report them. Cohen reaffirms this when he says that "[the] 20,500 infiltrators who entered Israel between the end of 1948 and October 1953 were allowed to remain and were granted citizenship" (2009, 95). This may also be true for the Bedouin in the Naqab since some Bedouin who filtered back were granted citizenship. Some refugees came to hide with the Bedouin and managed to stay for a long time. Others were captured by the army. In a letter to the Israeli police dated May 9, 1954, Sasson Bar Zvi (Naqab military governor in the 1960s) reported that "a group of infiltrators was arrested at the tent of a Tarabin shaikh ten days ago; they appeared to be family members of this shaikh but were living across the border. The group was captured before crossing the border to Jordan" (ISA/IP 85/33). A letter dated July 14, 1954, from the Israeli police identified Tarabin al-Sanne as challenging order:[3] "Almost all the offenses against this tribe are: leaving the closed zone, moving without permits, and hosting infiltrators . . . one of the family members accused of smuggling rice was imprisoned for two years, and another one escaped to Jordan" (letter from Negev district officer to the military governor of the Negev, ISA/IP 85/33).

Bedouin shaikhs were responsible for reporting cases of *muhajareen* to the military authorities. In some cases shaikhs did report them, though in a great many other cases they secured and protected their tribal members. For example, in 1956 a Bedouin shaikh reported to the military governor that a member of his tribe had left to visit his family in Jordan. In this case, the families wanted to unite (ISA/IP 86/5). Cohen (2010, 73–75) also reports cases of Bedouin shaikhs fighting against infiltrators. However, my findings show that many Bedouin shaikhs offered secure places for the *muhajareen* and helped them to stay, often over long periods.

Such cases overwhelmingly indicate that the Bedouin managed to maintain their tribal relations well into the 1950s. However, it became harder to maintain cross-border relations after 1954, when the Israelis issued ID cards.

Our shaikh who fled in 1948 used to come to see his tribe every day, staying hidden with his family all night. At dawn he would go back to Jordan. He was able to do this until 1956; normal relations existed between the Bedouin from the Naqab and their relatives in Jordan until that year (interview with Shaikh Hassan, June 2010).

Israeli restrictions and military regulations laws could not stop the Bedouin from communicating with their relatives across borders. The Bedouin responded by disobeying the military rule restrictions and maintaining relations with their relatives across the borders.

## *Bedouin Women and Cultural Resistance*

Bedouin nonviolent resistance to the military rule was not addressed or researched by scholars. Only recently has Ahmad Saʿdi (2015) shed some light on nonviolent protest against military rule in the north and the Galilee, though not in the Naqab. A close investigation of the role of women during the military rule reveals interesting new findings. Women played a critical role in cross-border relations as a form of resisting the regulations formulated under military rule. Women participated in different ways such as concealing knowledge from government officials or crossing borders for marriage purposes. Lila Abu-Lughod (1990, 43) argues that Bedouin women "use secrets and silence to their advantage. They often collude to hide knowledge from men; they cover for each other in minor matters." Abu-Lughod's excellent term "hidden knowledge" can be borrowed and will be helpful when looking for how Bedouin women applied it. She also notes folk tales, songs, jokes, and oral lyric poetry as another form of Bedouin resistance (46).

In the Naqab, for example, marriage connections within the same tribe had been affected after the Nakba and during the 1950s when tribes found themselves divided by the borders between Israel and the Arab countries.

During the military government period cases of marriage relations existed between Bedouin in Israel and Bedouin in Egypt and Jordan because at one time, all the tribes across borders were one tribe. They split between the borders after the war. Despite the new borders, marriage relations continued until the 1950s (interview with Hajja Suad, July 2012).

The Israeli State Archives contain many reports concerning marriage relations between Jordanians and the Naqab Bedouin. For example, in 1956 Sasson Bar Zvi reported a case of marriage between a man from the Naqab and a Jordanian woman who managed to visit her relatives in Jordan a couple of times a year before returning to her family near Tal al-Malah (ISA/IP 86/5). In October 1956, Major Penhas Amir reported a case in which a Bedouin from the Tarabin tribe married a Jordanian woman who now lived with him. Both attended the marriage ceremony in Jordan (ISA/IP 86/5).

Military government officials faced significant difficulties due to the sensitivity of certain issues for Bedouin women. The shaikhs refused to report on matters related to women, especially the requirement for them to be photographed for citizenship purposes. One woman commented in an interview that her father told the military governor it was forbidden to take photos of Bedouin women (*Sidreh* newsletter, Issue 5, 2010). Jewish officials were even banned from speaking to Bedouin women—a strong factor in encouraging the Bedouin to continue marrying women from wherever they could. The Bedouin insisted constantly that "our women are not part of the business of the government and its officials" (interview with ʿAbdallah, September 2012). Their reactions to official decisions meant that many things became invisible to the government's eyes. A further form of women's opposition was their own noncooperation with military officials. I encountered instances of such activism in which the women resisted giving information to officials and refused to report anything about their families, especially their husbands.

Bedouin women were also instrumental in helping the Bedouin affirm their *wataniya*. My interviews revealed that one form of opposition and *wataniya* directed toward military government officials was the singing of national songs. During the 1950s and 1960s the women reportedly sang *aghani wataniya* (nationalist songs) and recited poetry in support of the refugees and the *muhajareen*:

> In the late 1950s–60s we lived in Tal ʿArad, along an attractive border economy route close to the Jordanian border. In fact, we saw many border incidents, such as refugees who were injured or shot, others who were trying to return home to their land. As a result we, the women of the tribe, started to sing *aghani* watanya in weddings in support of the Bedouin refugees.[4]
> (INTERVIEW, HAJJA SARAH, SEPTEMBER 2011)

As categorized by Gene Sharp (1973, 149), singing national songs at communal weddings was certainly a form of nonviolent protest. Similarly, the silence and noncooperation of Bedouin women toward Israeli officials was a mechanism for expressing moral condemnation.

Two clear examples of the central roles played by Bedouin women were their feeding of infiltrators and their misdirecting of soldiers when they entered Bedouin encampments to undertake searches. In refusing to provide information about hidden infiltrators the women were employing silence as a useful strategy, thereby targeting a particular policy of the Israeli authorities.

## Continuing Conflict Resolution: Tribal Judges and Hidden Cross-Border Meetings

> My law as a Bedouin is my law, and your law as a state representative is your law. We, the Bedouin, do not take account of state laws, and we live, and wish to live, according to our laws.
>
> —INTERVIEW WITH YITZHAK TSAMAH, JULY 2008

Bedouin intertribal relations were maintained in all their key forms despite the rules of the military government. Shaikhs who fled or were exiled to Jordan or Egypt kept up relations with their subtribes who remained in the newly established state. Daily visits across the borders were sustained without significant control by the government. Subtribes living in Israel hosted their exiled relatives when they came to visit, sometimes for long periods.

The most important form of cross-border relations was through meetings between tribal judges for purposes of conflict resolution. Bedouin shaikhs met each other secretly, either in Israel or across the borders, in order to solve problems arising from tribal matters.

The headquarters of all tribal groups whose members live in Israel remain in Egyptian or Jordanian territory, a fact that, considering Bedouin blood-relationship loyalties and solidarity, has encouraged them over and over again to cross the borders. Very often they take their orders from their chiefs in countries that proclaim their constant enmity toward Israel (ISA/GL 17093/1).

Since most Bedouin leaders had fled or been exiled, and since some were tribal judges, the Bedouin tribal court system was severely affected. In many cases, it was impossible to deal with blood feuds when a qualified judge was absent. Official reports in the Israeli archives from the early 1950s comment on the problems that arose out of this lack of specialist tribal judges.

The most important situation in which the Bedouin lacked qualified judges was in the use of the "ordeal by fire" (*bisha*ʾ) when dealing with tribal disputes. This ritual existed only in the Bedouin court system and was used to decide whether an accused person was guilty. The accused was asked to prove his innocence by licking a hot metal object three times. He was then inspected by the presiding official and designated witnesses. If his tongue was scarred or burned by this "lapping of fire" he was assumed to be lying. After the Nakba, the Bedouin were forced in cases that required *bisha*ʾ to go to Egypt or Jordan in order to find a tribal judge able to conduct such a trial:

> This secret relationship existed between Bedouin of the Naqab and Bedouin of Egypt. Only in Egypt it was possible to find a tribal judge who would be able to decide on blood cases. Sometime Bedouin took the guilty person to Egypt in order to do the *bisha*ʾ and in other cases, they brought the tribal judge from Egypt to the border with Israel in order to apply the *bisha*ʾ process.
> (INTERVIEW WITH ʿABDALLAH, JULY 2013).

Continuation of the *bisha*ʾ demonstrates that the Bedouin continued to practice their tribal court system, disregarding Israeli laws that were contrary to their own legal system. Bedouin blood relations and loyalty to their tribal shaikhs encouraged some Bedouin shaikhs living in exile to return to visit their tribes and inspired some members of the tribes to go to visit them in their "new" countries.

The military rule restrictions and laws failed to stop the Bedouin from communicating with their relatives across borders. They countered the rules by using techniques of resistance and disobeying the military rules and regulations. The controls imposed by the Israeli authorities on Bedouin cross-border relations during this period were insignificant.

### *Border Cases and Bedouin as the Usual Suspects*

Until 1956, the Bedouin were treated as "usual suspects" following any border incidents with Egypt and Jordan. This bias arose from the fact that Bedouin tribes lived only a few miles from the borders in question.

A bus coming from Wadi ʿAraba via Beersheba was attacked in an incident in 1954. According to reports from both Glubb Pasha and the Israeli media, the attackers, who consisted of Bedouin from Beersheba, Sinai, and Gaza, had probably been expelled from their land and had sworn revenge for their eviction (PRO, FO 371/ 111099). Glubb Pasha reported, "The attackers consist of mixed tribesman from Beersheba area driven from their land various times by Jews. Vowed revenge against Jews and Arabs co-operating with them. All planned and carried out from Sinai" (Royal Jordan Embassy, London, from Qiada to T.J.L., March 29, 1954. PRO: FO 371/111099). After this attack, some Bedouin were arrested and beaten or harassed by the army (Morris 1993; Hutchison 1956). Glubb Pasha also reported on Israeli treatment of its Bedouin following the bus incident:

> Arabs from Beersheba report Israeli army taking severe actions against Arab tribes in the area. Camps cordoned and searched. Arrests made. This seems indicate Jews in reality do not know who was guilty of the bus incident. In spite their attempts [to] put blame on Jordan they still seem to suspect their own tribes.
>
> (ROYAL HASHEMITE JORDAN LEGATION, LONDON, FROM QIADA TO T.J.L., MARCH 26, 1954. PRO, FO 371/111099)

The Bedouin were the usual suspects in many other border incidents and in many cases were arrested and badly treated. Another example of the Bedouin as usual suspects is mentioned in a report from the Levant Department to the Foreign Office via the British Embassy in Tel Aviv, on September 30, 1956, which describes how Israel treated its Bedouin:

> A police patrol was fired on by marauders. Shots were exchanged but there were no Israeli casualties. The infiltrators left three donkeys behind. Six Bedouin were arrested by Israeli security forces on 1 October. They were suspected of actively helping infiltrators from Jordan and taking part in the previous night's shooting.
> (PRO, FO 371/121777).

The Bedouin also suffered from border incidents through injury or by losing their herds and properties:

> A group of five armed infiltrators robbed Bedouin Arabs of five Camels valued at IL3000. The infiltrators attacked the Bedouin who were grazing their herds near the Kibbutz, and later escaped across the Egyptian border. In the same area on 16 September, members of another Arab tribe reported being attacked by unidentified Bedouin who made away with two camels and injured a third. Damage is estimated at IL1400.
> (REPORT ON THE BEDOUIN FROM AMMAN TO FOREIGN OFFICE, DECEMBER 17, 1956, REVIVIM, NEGEV. PRO, FO 371/121777)

Other border incidents damaged Bedouin property and killed their flocks. Another report from Amman to Foreign Office noted:

> An exchange of fire took place between an Israeli Bedouin and three suspected infiltrators. The Israeli Arab reported to the police that he had opened fire on three Arabs who had aroused his suspicious. They returned fire, killing one of his goats and wounding another. Tracks of three persons led toward the Egyptian border.
> (REPORT ON THE BEDOUIN FROM AMMAN TO FOREIGN OFFICE, NEGEV AUGUST 17, 1956. PRO, FO 371/121777)

These examples demonstrate how the Bedouin were harmed by border incidents and how military rule policies were consistent in treating the Bedouin as usual suspects when such incidents were spoken about. The Bedouin were arrested, their flocks were confiscated, and sometimes they were pushed into leaving the area altogether.

EIGHT

# The Second Phase of Military Rule, 1956–1963

THE YEAR 1956 MARKED another crucial phase of military governance in Israel. The massacre at Kafr Qassem opened a debate about the future of the military government and the fragile relations between Israel and its Arab minority (Ghanem 2001; Saʿdi 2001). According to Lazar and Bauml (2002), 1956 denoted a new phase of military rule. On the one hand, Israel offered the Arab minority some relaxing of regulations; on the other, Kafr Qassem led to a real discussion about the future of military rule. During 1956 the Israeli authorities continued to exercise the same fundamental set of policies toward the Bedouin and the Arab minority (land expropriation, curfews, expulsion, marginalization, detention orders, limitation of movement, deportation, and continuing application of defense emergency regulations), albeit with some interesting modifications and a new framework. I argue that there was only a limited easing of the restrictions on the Palestinian minority and the Naqab Bedouin during this period and that the military government continued along the same trajectory.

## From the Ratner Committee (1956) to the Rosen Committee (1959)

Oppression and surveillance of the indigenous Bedouin community continued as a core policy of military rule after the Suez crisis. Gathering data about the Bedouin was deemed critical. Prime Minister David Ben Gurion continued to regard the Naqab as vitally important for Israel's security and economy and believed that massive Jewish immigration into the Naqab was critical for creating new settlements: "In the course of the next few years we must transfer at least half a million people to the Negev." His pragmatic view was that the Naqab would be secured "not by arms only," but also through settlement activity (*Jewish Observer and Middle East Review*, May 10 1957, 2).

Thus the policy of settlement expansion continued in the Naqab. Approval was given to continue military rule, and the Bedouin tribes in the *siyaj* continued to live under restrictive laws that prevented them from leaving the zone. While fundamental policies had not changed during the first decade of military rule, two separate ministerial committees were appointed between 1956 and 1958 to review the overall military government framework and to see whether the system of military rule should be continued. Predictably, one committee recommended continuation while the other suggested abolition. These appraisals were the direct result of the debate among Israeli politicians about abolishing military rule because it contradicted the paradigm of a democratic state.

The first Ministerial Committee, the Ratner Committee, was appointed in December 1955 with a sufficiently broad mandate to allow it to evaluate whether military rule should be continued, reduced, or abolished. Meetings were organized with community representatives, and the committee toured the three areas under military rule in order to make an informed decision. The Ratner Committee concluded that the existence of the military government was "essential to maintain state security" and recommended in February 1956 that military rule should continue (ISA/GL 7128/7). Despite the Kafr Qassem and growing opposition among Arabs and Jews, military rule was not abolished (Saʿdi 2001). However, the Ratner Committee did suggest relaxing some rules.

In 1957, after the Ratner Ministerial Committee recommended continuation of military rule, Prime Minster Ben Gurion proposed easing some restrictions. At the same time, he met several Arab leaders in early July 1957, including Shaikh Salah Khneifes, Salah Salim Suliman, Masʿad Kassis, Shaikh Jaber Muʿadi, and Faris Hamdan, none of whom were from the Naqab. Following this meeting, he announced the relaxation of certain restraints on the Druze and Arab communities (*Haaretz*, July 7, 1957).

The *Jerusalem Post* noted that Ben Gurion promised twelve concessions in response to points that had arisen at the meeting, including

> abolition of the need for permits for the Arabs in the Galilee to travel to Acre, Nazareth and ʿAfula; easing the night curfew in the Triangle; opening the Tira-Ramat Hakovesh-Tel Aviv Road; granting of long term agricultural loans; the provision of drinking water to villages; aid in paving roads to villages; improvement of plantations including olives and fruit trees; expansion of agricultural and technical education; and improvement in tobacco growing and marketing. (*JERUSALEM POST*, JULY 7, 1957)

It seems that the loosening of restrictions announced by Ben Gurion in July 1957 did not apply to the Bedouin in the Naqab. They had not been represented, and their issues were not even mentioned. *Al-Hamishmar* noted in October 1958 that the only easing of restrictions offered to Bedouin was that in 1958 they were granted the right to enter Beersheba twice a week for the Bedouin market. Before 1958 the Bedouin market had been open only on Thursdays so they could only go into Beersheba once a week, which restricted their economic activities. After October 1958 they were also allowed to travel on Mondays to Beersheba for the market without holding a permit (*Al-Hamishmar*, October 1, 1958).

These relaxations granted to the Arab minority as a result of the Ratner Committee were limited modifications and in practice did not dramatically change the living conditions or status of the Arab community. The Bedouin in the Naqab continued to live under severe restrictions and continued to resist them. After the Ratner Committee the hosting of infiltrators/*muhajareen* and the invisible border economy continued.

The slogan "abolish military rule" was heard increasingly among Jewish and Arab activists across the new state in 1958. In response, another committee was appointed to evaluate the need for a military government. Named for its chairman, Minister of Justice P. Rosen, the Rosen Ministerial Committee was set up late in 1958 to advise the Israeli cabinet on the future of military rule. Its deliberations continued until June 1959. Composed of eminent ministers, the committee included P. Rosen (minister of justice),

K. Luz (minister of agriculture), B. Shitrit (minister of police), I. Bar-Yehuda (minister of the interior), M. Bentov (minister of development), and Dr. Y. Burg (former minister of posts).

The committee took fifteen months to produce its report and recommendations to the cabinet regarding the future of military rule (PRO, FO 371/142401). It released two reports, one by the committee's Mapai ministers and the other by the remaining members. The members of Mapai (Ben Gurion's party) recommended a general easing of travel restrictions on Arabs and also advised that the re-settlement and compensation of displaced Arabs should be regularly examined with a view to its progressive relaxation. The Cabinet also adopted the proposal by Mapai members that although military government restrictions should be loosened, military rule should not be totally abolished (PRO, FO 371/142401; see also Bauml 2002; Korn 1996).

Further concessions granted to Arab citizens in August 1959 followed the cabinet's loosening of military government restrictions:

> This should allow free movement during daylight between the Arab villages in the Galilee and the Triangle on the one hand, and the neighboring towns, including Acre, Haifa, and Tel Aviv, on the other. It would also allow the Bedouin in the Negev a third day of free travel to Beersheba, but it would not apply at all to the areas immediately adjacent to the border.
> (PRO, FO 371/142401)

It seems that representatives of the Mapai Party on the Rosen Committee had decided that the military government would remain, which represented Ben Gurion's wish not to abolish it (Bauml 2002). In fact, the Rosen report did not dramatically change the future of the Arab minority. While it allowed increased mobility and extended the list of towns available for free movement, it did not totally exempt Arabs from restrictions. As a result, the military government continued to work normally and the Arabs continued to be viewed as a threat to state security.

The key result achieved by the Rosen Committee was that opposition to and criticism of the military rule system began to increase rapidly and to be more frequently discussed in the Knesset during the early 1960s (Bauml 2002). The struggle to abolish the military government is considered in the next chapter.

## Land Struggle: Counter claims and Ideology for Indigenous Memories

The Bedouin became increasingly aware as they engaged in the battle of *sumud* and laid claim to their lands. Land represented the core issue for the Bedouin during the early years of the new state, and their struggle over land continued during the second phase of the military government from 1956 to 1963.

In the Naqab land continued to be the crux of the conflict between the Israeli authorities and the Bedouin. During the first decade of military rule, the Bedouin lost the majority of their lands primarily through Israeli laws in the 1950s (the Land Seizure Law of 1950, the Absentee Properties Law of 1953, and the Land Acquisition Law of 1953) (Abu Hussein and McKay 2003). After 1956, the Bedouin started to claim ownership of their land and took an active role in shaping their situation by developing a new form of agency. They filed their land ownership claims via the Israeli Supreme Court, employed Jewish lawyers, and wrote letters to the government calling for their right to return to their land and to end their status as internally displaced peoples (IDPs) (interview with Abu ʿAmmer, June 2009).

Why did this change come about? What brought about this mobilization of the Bedouin? A key factor was recognition by the Bedouin shaikhs that they were going to stay longer as refugees in the *siyaj* and that they would remain uprooted from their land. They started to grasp hidden Israeli aims, came to understand their policies, and began to react in an organized way. During the first years after the war, the Bedouin believed that their life in the *siyaj* would be temporary and that they would soon return to their own land. Many also believed the Israeli army's story that they were only being evicted for a short time. As soon as they recognized that Israel actually intended to leave them in the *siyaj* forever, the Bedouin shaikhs started to behave as active agents.

The military administration started to receive information about Bedouin agency and their efforts regarding the loss of their land. Major Penhas Amir, military governor of the Naqab in 1957, reported Bedouin activity to the government over the land issue. He confirmed that he had received intelligence from the field that a number of shaikhs had organized a committee to deal with land claims. He noted that the activists included Shaikh Musa al-ʿAtawna (the primary organizer), and Shaikhs ʿAli Abu Qrinat, Hammad

Abu Rabia, Salim al-Oqbi, Hassan Abu ʿAbdon, and Salman Abu Bilal (IDFA 490/1956–47).

The Bedouin shaikhs did not wait long to take action. In a clear demonstration of agency, eleven shaikhs wrote a letter to the minister of justice in April 1958 asking the government to recognize their land ownership. They argued that they had been waiting ten years to solve their land disputes without satisfaction or response from the government:

> For nearly ten years we have been expecting to hear from the government to settle our land problems and ownership. After the war of 1948, the government moved us from our native land and settled us in a land which was not ours. We had been moved to a land which was possessed by other tribes for generations, and it was cultivated by them. Our native land was left without cultivation, and in some cases, no one benefited from it. We do not live in our land, we live on other Bedouin land. Living on other Bedouin land does not permit us any rights, because it is not our land. This is because the government leases us the land every year and we have to pay money for this leased land. This temporary status of our Bedouin tribes in the *siyaj* has not allowed us to develop the current land or to cultivate it.[1]
> (ISA/G 5742/1)

The shaikhs went on to stress that they saw no redress for their complaints and that no government office took any responsibility for dealing with their land disputes. If they did get a hearing, they complained that they were given the stock answer that Bedouin land issues were complicated. They ended their letter by saying defiantly that there was no way to marginalize them and their land ownership, no matter how long it took, and therefore called on the government to deal with their land ownership as soon as possible (ISA/G 5742/1). This first action by the Bedouin is a clear example of nonviolent action and what Gene Sharp calls "group lobbying" (Sharp 1973, 132).

The state reacted to this Bedouin agency on land issues by asking the minister of justice to appoint a special temporary committee to deal with ongoing Bedouin claims. Its brief was to solve land issues arising in both the Galilee and the Naqab. At committee meetings, ideas were proposed for dealing with Bedouin land issues. Consideration was given to how the land ownership claims of internally displaced Bedouin who had been moved from the western Naqab were to be dealt with. It was agreed that solving Bedouin land issues in the Naqab was not an easy task. It was claimed at one point in the discussion that no villages existed in the Naqab. Members suggested that the Bedouin be paid compensation for the land from which they had been evicted (west Naqab) or that every Bedouin family be offered a piece of land similar to that offered to members of a kibbutz. They also discussed ending the practice of leasing land to the Bedouin at some sites (such as Tal ʿArad) so that Jewish kibbutzim could be built on what they considered to be state land (ISA/ G 5742/1).

One proposal that attracted much discussion was how to put an end to the Bedouins' acting as a bridge between Jordan and Egypt across the new state of Israel. The committee discussed methods of wrecking this dynamic. One method suggested was to split the Bedouin into small pockets while enhancing the Jewish kibbutzim that were already interspersed among them. Since many Bedouin had not yet moved from land claimed by the state, the committee argued that the army should be used to build Jewish settlements between the Bedouin and the borders with Egypt and Jordan and to construct Jewish settlements within areas of Bedouin concentration (ISA/ G 5742/1). Later, many of these ideas became official state policy.

One key form of activism by Bedouin shaikhs during this period was using avenues of complaint to lay claim to their land. One technique was to keep their indigenous memory alive and public by visiting their land and informing the Israelis who were occupying it that the land actually belonged to the Bedouin. Physical signs of Bedouin identity remained on the land, so the Bedouin took to visiting these sites. For example, one Bedouin interviewee listed the evidence of land ownership that remained: "the wells we left behind us, the cemetery, the spacious clay houses, and the memories" (interview, al-Tori, July 2009). Such visits are what Duane Champagne (2003) calls the "counter claims" of indigenous peoples, which they did not submit to the government but still made on the land. Oren Yiftachel also notes that the Bedouin developed a counter ideology in claiming their land (Yiftachel 2003; 2008).

The Bedouin acceptance that their banishment to the closed zone would never end is what pushed them to enter into a range of legal actions. This, combined with their growing understanding of Israeli laws, was the main reason they hired Jewish lawyers. As one interviewee pointed out, "It is very difficult for us as Bedouin to live on other people's land, and not to be able to live in our original land. The Israel authorities enacted more laws to seize our land. However, we the Bedouin continued to tell them where our land is located; we did not surrender" (interview with Abu Yousef, May 2010). As the years of military government went by, increasing numbers of Bedouin presented claims to their land by sending letters to the government or hiring Jewish lawyers to act for them. In 1960, for example, the al-Oqbi tribe wrote to the prime minister, the military governor, and the ministers of agriculture and development requesting to be allowed to return to their land. In their formal letter dated July 10, 1960, they stated that they had been evicted from their land by the army in 1951. They claimed that they had been settled on their land both before and after 1948, that there were still no settlements or kibbutzim existing on their land, and that the land was being used by other tribes. Thus the argument being made was that the alienation of the al-Oqbi tribe from their land was arbitrary and had no basis in any of the reasons that the government might usually have put forward (i.e., no presence prior to 1951; the land was needed for Jewish settlement; the land could not be used by Bedouin). Therefore, they petitioned the government to allow them to return to their land. The letter was signed by representatives of the tribe of al-Oqbi, who wished to go back to their land (Kibbutz Lahav Papers, KLA).

Bedouin voices were consistent and persistent in claiming their land and in calling for the right of return. In another example, a letter was sent on August 30, 1960, to the Israeli prime minister, the minister of agriculture, the military governor of the Naqab, and other government officials asking to allow the tribe of al-Afenish to return to their land. Al-Afenish stated in their letter that the army had expelled them from their land in 1951 even though they had lived on that land for generations. They requested to be allowed to return, especially since nobody now lived on their land (Kibbutz Lahav Papers, KLA).

During the late 1950s and early 1960s, the Bedouin raised their land claims in new ways, with greater frequency, and in a more formal and vehement fashion. These more organized forms of resistance and agency challenged the Israeli authorities and demonstrated continued Bedouin commitment to securing their own rights. This was in addition to the continued refusal by many Bedouin to submit any claims for compensation. This fits well into what Gurr and Harf (2004, 165) observe regarding the way indigenous people try to protect what still survives from their traditional land, culture, and resources, and to secure autonomy.

## Education as a Tool for Controlling the Bedouin

Another important Israeli policy during the 1956–1963 period was marginalizing the right of indigenous Bedouin to education. Under military rule education was sidelined, and the Israeli authorities made little effort to improve it. The Bedouin began to be active on this front as well. Their resistance, agency, and voice for protecting their educational rights first appeared during the late 1950s.

After the Nakba, the majority of Bedouin educated elite ended up in neighboring Arab countries. The result was that the remnant Bedouin community lost most of their educated leaders as well as most of those trained to educate. This did not prevent those who remained in the Naqab from placing a high value on education or from agitating for the Israeli state to provide them with a right to education. Several leading Bedouin shaikhs took the initiative and sent some of their children away to obtain primary and secondary education and began to dispatch their older children to the north (Galilee, Nazareth, and the Triangle area) to study in Arab and Christian schools especially for post-primary education (Abu Rabia 2001). Since no high schools existed among Bedouin tribes in the Naqab, the north offered better options. The demand for education drove Bedouin parents to act in a manner similar to those Bedouin who had sent their children to gain high school education in Gaza during the British Mandate (interview with Lord Oxford, July 2009).

For the first few years of its existence, the new state did not invest in Bedouin schooling. This was partly the result of state policies that evicted and shifted the Bedouin from one place to another. Abu Rabia counted nine schools among the remnant Bedouin tribes in 1951, all of which had existed before the expulsion of the tribes and none of which were high schools (Abu Rabia 2001, 94). Only through the personal initiatives of educated Bedouin leaders did the government decide to invest some money to deal with the school system, including obtaining aid from international donors (interview with Daham al-ʿAtawna, June 2014).

The first suggestions for opening schools in Bedouin encampments were put forward in 1951 and 1952. A 1952 IDFA report stated that the military government of the Naqab proposed to open six schools for the Bedouin named after the tribes (Abu Qrinat, Abu Rabia, al-ʿAssam, Abu Irqaiq, al-ʿAzazma, and al-Huzayil). The report recommended that this proposal should be approved by the Education Council as a step toward implementing the new state's compulsory education law (passed in 1949), which required primary education for all children among the tribes (IDFA 405/1954–101). Schools were called after tribal names, which is fairly similar to the Bedouin schooling system today.

Penhas Amir states that education was a crucial question for the Bedouin at the time:

> The educational problem was amongst the most critical issues in dealing with the Bedouin in the Naqab since the situation of the tribes was fragile. Some shaikhs were impressively devoting their efforts to get education for their children, particularly among the ʿAtawna and Abu Rabia tribes, amongst other families. A critical problem was qualified teachers, which we started to bring from the north.
>
> (INTERVIEW WITH PENHAS AMIR, JULY 2008)

The Israeli move toward the provision of schools was disrupted after 1951 and the eviction of several Bedouin tribes from their land. The Bedouin did not wait passively for the government to implement the compulsory education law. As early as April 1952, a group of Bedouin shaikhs demanded that the military authorities open a school in the village of Laqiya. On behalf of their tribes, they requested the assistance of military rule officials in setting up a school for their sons. They had already identified a teacher who was willing to teach, and they were refurbishing a house to be used as the school (letter to the military governor of the Naqab from Shaikhs Saqir Al al-Huzayil, Faraj al-Assad, Hassan Abu ʿAbdon, and Haj Ibrahim al-Sanne, April 21 1952, IDFA 405/1954–101).

Bedouin children were sent away to Arab schools in the north because of the lack of high schools in the Naqab. This had a significant effect on the community. The first group of Bedouin students that was dispatched to the north left in 1952 and 1953 and attended Terra-Santa College in Nazareth. They were followed the next year by other Bedouin students. All these students had to obtain permission from the military governor to live in Nazareth (IDFA 490/1956–33).[2] The numbers continued to grow and the process continued on throughout the 1960s and into the 1970s.

The ability of the Bedouin to achieve education in the north for some of their elites depended on the close relationship that existed between some of the Bedouin shaikhs and the northern Arabs. This relationship had existed throughout both the Ottoman and the British occupation periods. It was not surprising that this relationship continued under the Israelis. One family from Laqiya, for example, had very strong ties with those living in the Little Triangle in the north. These ties had existed during the British Mandate. Under Israeli military rule, the relationship facilitated the sending of Bedouin students from the Naqab to be hosted by northern Arab families. By the late 1950s, this had become a regular process for many students from the Naqab (interview with Hajj Hassan Abu Bader, Lakiya, August 2013).

This north-south relationship also helped with sending Bedouin students to the town of Kafr Qassem. Different shaikhs gathered to discuss this idea, and children were recruited to be sent for advanced education in Kafr Qassem. The mayor of Kafr Qassem, Wadeaᶜ Sarsor, volunteered to host the first group of students in his home. His actions made it easier for students in subsequent years. This revolutionary dynamic had a profound impact on those who moved to the north. One interviewee remembered the journey in 1956 and felt as though he was traveling to another country:

> We stayed in the north for the whole term, waiting a long time until the holidays to go back home to the Naqab. It was very difficult for us as children to leave our homes for a whole term in order to study; we felt at some point that we were in another country. We lived for two weeks in the *Mukhtar's* house until they found us a house; it was such an amazing experience. We were issued a permit for one term from the military governor. My grandfather used to visit us once a month, and we survived and studied in a difficult conditions
> (INTERVIEW WITH ᶜALIYAN AL-SANNE, LAKIYA, AUGUST 2013)

Efforts to obtain education did not stop with sending Bedouin children to study in the north. The whole community was affected and began to look for local alternatives to the lack of education. Tribes began to voluntarily recruit teachers to come to the Naqab. Some of the activists within the tribes became ambassadors for education and organized local parents' committees to search for educational solutions. For example, a group of parents in Tal ᶜArad took up the idea and collected money from members of the tribes to build a school and recruit local teachers. Such agency immediately put pressure on the government to start building schools in the Naqab, especially schools focused on secondary education.

Since there was no secondary school in the Naqab during the 1950s, the goal of getting one built became a campaign for some Bedouin shaikhs. These shaikhs sent letters to the government calling for a secondary school for both male and female Bedouin students. One of the active shaikhs was Shaikh Musa al-ʿAtawna. He consistently wrote letters to the government signed and supported by other shaikhs in order to gain their right to education. In one example, Shaikh Musa petitioned the minister of labor, who was visiting the Bedouin tribes in the Naqab in 1958, about establishing a secondary school in the region (*La-merhav*, June 12, 1958). Other Bedouin leaders involved in this issue included Shaikh Hassan al-Sanne and Shaikh Hammad Abu Rabiaʾ. They were very active in pressing for education. Other shaikhs included Shaikh Oda Abu Maʿamar, who pressed the military government to build schools in his area; and Jadoaʾ al-Huzayil, who also petitioned the government over education (interview with Dodik Shoshani, May 2008).

The head of Bne Shimon Regional Council in northern Negev sent a report from the IDF archive to two government ministries (including the Education Ministry) and the Naqab military governor. The report dealt with the subject of education among the tribes in the council's area of responsibility. It stated that in 1957 only two schools existed among the Bedouin tribes in military zones. One school served al-Huzayil tribe, and the other (in poor condition) was in Beir al-Hamam. Clearly, the compulsory education law was not being implemented among the tribes. The report recommended establishing one school in Laqiya for the tribes distributed in the area (numbering 688 people) and another in Umm Batin (numbering 488 people). It advised refurbishment of the school in Beir al-Hamam and sending it more teachers. It also recommended implementing the compulsory education law (which applied to every child in Israel from the age of five) among the Bedouin tribes. The report estimated that 2,500 Bedouin lived in the region administered by the Regional Council and only two schools existed there (IDFA 72/40–263).

There were many ideas on how to improve the options available to the Bedouin in the Naqab. One proposal circulated was to allocate one of the existing classrooms in a Jewish school in Beersheba for use by Bedouin students. A number of local Jewish activists took up the argument in support of Bedouin education. On May 9, 1961, Dodik Shoshani, a member of Kibbutz Lahav (established in 1952), wrote to Minister of Education Aba Eivan, outlining his concerns about the lack of Bedouin education. He pointed out that since the Bedouin did not have schools for their children, they were forced to send them to the north where around thirty Bedouin young people were studying in Arab schools. Shoshani also mentioned that there were suggestions for how Bedouin educational needs could be met locally, but that nothing been done yet to open up Beersheba High School to Bedouin students. Shoshani's letter criticized the Beersheba mayor and the head teacher of the school for having failed to follow through with integration despite initially agreeing to the initiative (Kibbutz Lahav Archival papers, KLA). I found that a few Bedouin students were enrolled in the Beersheba Jewish high school. Unfortunately, most quickly dropped out because the curricula did not suit them (interview with Daham al ʿAtawna, July 2013).

Similar arguments began to circulate in the Jewish community, especially among Jewish officials who worked with the Bedouin during this period. They began to make claims that local secondary education for the Bedouin should be supported simply because of the radicalizing effect that studying in the north was having on the Bedouin who traveled there for schooling. The need for building schools in the Naqab and the need to prevent Bedouin children from going north for education became linked. As the shaikhs put more pressure on the government to open schools for Bedouin in the Naqab, the military authorities joined in supporting the idea, fearing the radicalization that occurred when Bedouin youth moved outside the closed zone. The military authorities seem to have recognized that the Bedouin students who studied in the north returned politically motivated.

As a result, there are indications that the military rule started to scrutinize Bedouin youth who had spent time in the north and to discourage them from traveling there for education. In effect, they were monitoring nationalism among the Bedouin. One Bedouin student who had studied in the north was arrested because of a nationalist letter he had written after his northern study period:

> The policy of the police and the military government was to try to prevent the students who had studied in the north from developing a Palestinian narrative. However, because we used to read newspapers, watch television, and meet people from the north who were activists, their ideas helped us to get organized and to be motivated and bring change to our communities back in the Naqab. (INTERVIEW WITH ABU JABER, JULY 2010)

The marginalization of indigenous Bedouin education led some pioneer students who studied in the north to develop a variety of skills. They devised ways to resist the restrictions imposed on the Bedouin, using poetry and writing as forms of cultural resistance to express their criticism of military rule.

Little progress was achieved despite efforts by Bedouin shaikhs and their Jewish neighbors to persuade the military authorities to expand primary and secondary education. A report in *Davar* stated that by August 1961 only 50 percent of Bedouin children were enrolled in school, mainly at primary level. Seven schools had been built in the Naqab during the two previous years, and some 700 Bedouin children studied in them. *Davar*'s report was based on a visit by Deputy Minister of Education Asaf and Military Governor Penhas Amir to the Bedouin encampments of Abu Rabia', Abu Rqaiq, and al-Afenish. According to the report, Asaf promised that six additional schools would be added in 1962 (*Davar*, August 4, 1961).

There had been little improvement in the provision of educational services by the time military rule ended. In an interview with *Ha'olam Hazeh* newspaper in 1966, Shaikh Hassan Abu Rabia' reported that only fourteen schools existed in the Naqab. Between these schools were thirty teachers employed in miserable conditions. Abu Rabia' suggested that a key factor for this slow progress was the failure of military rule to apply the Compulsory Education Law to the Bedouin. Other factors included the long distances from the Bedouin encampments to the few schools, the general lack of education facilities, and the critical shortage of teachers (*Ha'olam Hazeh*, June 16, 1966).

The Bedouin struggle for education was a daily battle to gain their rights and to improve the welfare of their families. This struggle required consistency, innovation, and perseverance against the unbalanced policies of military rule. In response to the lack of educational facilities, the Bedouin developed their own options for their children through connections in the north, called consistently for equal treatment under the law, and never ceased to suggest alternatives to the authorities.

## Citizens with No Citizenship: The ʿAzazma and the Borders Issue

Another policy that was applied consistently for over a decade was the continued relocation of the Bedouin. In the late 1950s, such policies were once again directed against the ʿAzazma tribes, who lived on both sides of the Egypt/Israel border. Lieutenant General Burns, chief of staff of the UN Truce Supervision Organization, reminds us that the ʿAzazma Bedouin were the indigenous inhabitants of what became the al-ʿAuja demilitarized zone. They were not permitted to return to their land after they had been forced to leave in 1949 and 1950 (Burns 1962, 93).

During the British Mandate, the ʿAzazma consisted of a coalition of twelve tribes (al-Aref 1999). Most of these tribes had fled or been expelled by 1950, with only one tribe remaining into the 1950s. This one tribe was actually an amalgamation under a recognized shaikh of the remnants of several different ʿAzazma tribes. Various groupings of the ʿAzazma attempted to return to their land after 1950 (Kanaaneh 2009). Some of them were categorized as "tolerable infiltrators/*muhajareen*" and were not driven out of the border areas. However, they did not hold permanent IDs and had no status within the state.

In the 1950s, the military government faced a number of issues with the ʿAzazma Bedouin. The first was that they lived along the borders of Israel, Egypt, and Jordan and kept moving back and forth in order to maintain their territorial claims. In the decade after 1949, they lived and migrated across these borders and carved out some semblance of an existence in the border zones. A second issue was that the ʿAzazma pursued border economy activities in conjunction with their relatives on the other side of the border. A third element that challenged the military rule was the question of IDs. Some ʿAzazma held military IDs while others had no IDs at all. This made it impossible to identity where each tribe belonged and whether an individual was an infiltrator. A fourth problem was the lack of soldiers to secure every part of the state's borders. According to Penhas Amir, the border region was totally open. Apart from Sde Boker, there was no Jewish settlement close to the border. The ʿAzazma benefited from this permeability and lack of resources by moving freely between the three countries (interview with Penhas Amir, August 2008). Until 1959, the ʿAzazma tribes laid indigenous people claims to their historical land (Falk 1988).

The reality was that the Israeli military rule was weak in dealing with the ʿAzazma Bedouin. They failed to secure the borders; they did not know who was from Jordan, Egypt or Israel; and they could not prevent the ongoing border economy activities. For example, an Israeli officer who worked with the ʿAzazma during the 1950s admitted that the army was not able to stop

ʿAzazma movements across the borders. He claimed that those supposedly in control actually suffered from a shortage of soldiers to secure the new state's borders. He said if they had wanted to stop the ʿAzazma and other Bedouin transborder movement they would have needed a whole battalion of soldiers:

> They were very smart people. Those Bedouin knew exactly what happened on both sides of the border; they used to tell each other and maintained excellent relations with their relatives across the borders—they used to get news before we did, even before we heard it on our wireless. The Bedouin collaborated with each other and made the case invisible from the government, no one complained or told the government about what was going on.
> (INTERVIEW WITH YITZHAK TSAMAH, JUNE 2009)

This weakness was to the benefit of the ʿAzazma. For a decade the army was unsuccessful in controlling them. The ʿAzazma could not return permanently as a community to their historical lands and their status was fragile, but in practice they were able to act as if the new Israeli claim to the land was baseless.

Some of the ʿAzazma Bedouin remnants were settled in Jabal al-Naqab (Har Ha-negev in Hebrew; in Southern Naqab) outside the enclosed zone. They included members of the Sarahin Ibn Saʿid tribe and individuals from the al-Janabib and Abu ʿAssa tribes. One report from the IDF in October 1959 states that the Abu ʿAssa remnant tribe consisted of 300 people, of whom forty-five were labeled as infiltrators/*muhajreen*. The same report gave the Sarahin Ibn Saʿid numbers as 400 with another 200 Bedouin settled nearby at Jabal Lutsan (Mount Lutz in Hebrew). They too were regarded as infiltrators (IDFA 22/2009/12). Despite the Israeli relocation activities of the early 1950s, these tribes and subtribes had managed to stay. Many still did not hold Israeli IDs.

A dramatic shift in army policy occurred toward these tribes in 1959 when most of them were expelled to Egypt, with a few fleeing to Jordan. The decision to act against the ʿAzazma followed the killing of a Jewish army officer, Yair Peled, and after some local Bedouin had been sent across the border on an unsuccessful mission to find the perpetrators. As a consequence of the noncooperation of the local Bedouin with those investigating Peled's murder the frustrated army applied collective punishment against all the ʿAzazma.

In a series of actions known as Operation Hagar, the army moved against the Bedouin living close to the Egyptian border and the majority of them were expelled and relocated. Peled had been killed on September 7; Operation Hagar began on September 18 and continued until September 24, 1959.

The zone of operations included the tribes of Abu ʿAssa, Ibn Saʿid, and some other Bedouin labeled as infiltrators/*muhajareen* (IDFA 22/2009–12). Army documents compiled after the operation reported that although the Abu ʿAsa tribe remained in Israel, forty-five infiltrators, as well as the 200 Bedouin who were in Jabal Lutsan, were pushed into Sinai. The situation with the Ibn Saʿid tribe was that some 200 to 250 fled to Har Areef and Har Ardwan, near the Ramon crater. Between fifty and 150 ʿAzazma Bedouin were living here. Another 150 to200 individuals from the Ibn Saʿid tribe were exiled into Sinai. The report estimates that altogether 400 to 450 Bedouin were pushed into Sinai and settled in Qusseima while another 200 to 250 Bedouin from the Ibn Saʿid tribe fled into Jordan. Jordan actually lodged a complaint against this operation with the United Nations (IDFA 22/2009–12).

Facts after the operations show that as a result of the army's actions, between 700 and 750 Bedouin were transferred by the IDF from Jabal al-Naqab to the enclosed zone (ʿAbdah area). They were photographed and registered in October 1959. They were not issued with Israeli IDs, which made it difficult for the authorities to observe their movements or to identify whether they were residents of the area or infiltrators. As a result, the situation of the Sarahin Bedouin was particularly difficult, as they were not officially recognized and did not receive any services from government authorities. A secret report on the Hagar operation shows that after the murder of the Jewish officer Peled, the area of Har Ha-negev was patrolled by the army (IDFA 22/2009–12).

In November 1960, a year after Operation Hagar, the authorities in the Naqab met to decide how to deal with the Sarahin Bedouin who did not hold Israeli IDs. The meeting included the Southern District Command; the head of the Israeli Operations Directorate; the Naqab military governor, Major Sasson Bar Zvi; and Major Benjamin Lovitkin. The committee recommended issuing a temporary confirmation from the military governor approving the transfer of the Sarahin Bedouin into their new reservation in ʿAbdah. Another recommendation was that the case of these Bedouin should be referred to the Interministerial Advisory Committee where the IDF could argue that they should be deported since they were not included in the 1949 population register (letter by Yousef Frisman to the head of Agam November 22, 1960: IDFA 22/2009–12).

Operation Hagar marked a turning point in the new Israeli border policies. After the remaining ʿAzazma and other Bedouin had been expelled and relocated in 1959, Israeli control over its borders with Egypt was much more regulated. Even so, the remnants of the ʿAzazma succeeded in maintaining relations with their relatives in both Jordan and Egypt as a result of not having permanent Israeli IDs (interview with Mohammed of the ʿAzazma tribe, May 2014).

## Bedouin Voting Habits and Political Fragmentation

Obstruction of the development of indigenous political parties was particularly evident in the Naqab. As a result of the Nakba, the Bedouin had lost most of their political and intellectual leadership after 1948. However, the government recognized a number of Bedouin shaikhs, regarding them as the political leaders of the community.

During the period of military rule, the politics of the Bedouin were shaped by the politics of shaikhdoms that received support mainly from the Labor party since it was acknowledged that the Naqab Bedouin represented a potential political force that they might mobilize for their own benefit. As Jakubowska (1992) points out, creating an ethnic identity for the Bedouin was one way of separating them from the rest of the Arab population in Israel. Splitting up the Bedouin politically became another way to control them. Smooha (1980) notes that early Israeli policy regarding the remnant Arabs was one of divide and rule with the aim of dividing the Arab population into disparate ethnic groups based on their geographic distribution.

Israel attempted to implement this divide-and-rule strategy by fragmenting the Bedouin politically and encouraging them to vote for Jewish parties. At about the same time, Bedouin shaikhs began to find their political voices. The pattern of Bedouin votes in Israel in general (including the northern Bedouin) in the 1955 elections indicates that 59 percent of direct Bedouin votes were given to the ruling Jewish parties (Soen and Shmuel 1987, 337).

One policy adopted by the military government toward the Bedouin was to push them to vote for the Jewish Mapai and Mapam political parties.[3] Convincing the Bedouin to vote between Mapai and Mapam was a strategy used by the Labor Party to strengthen its control over Bedouin voting habits

(Sa'di 2014). In this way, these two leading parties obtained most of the Bedouin vote, thereby crushing Bedouin political power. As Zureik notes, "It is among voters in small villages and Bedouin tribes that the Zionist parties obtain the largest portion of Arab votes" (1979, 169).

The Mapai party succeeded in recruiting Bedouin in the Beersheba area as party members and used them for its political ends. One shaikh who joined the Mapam Party in the late 1950s was Shaikh Musa al-ʿAtawna. He took advantage of his position to obtain more rights for the Bedouin, particularly land rights (interview, Daham al ʿAtawna, May 2014). In 1958, when Mapam held a study day in Beersheba to begin organizing Bedouin into the party, he used his influence to push them to attend. The result was that Bedouin from across the Naqab participated in the seminar, and membership cards were distributed to them by Shaikh Musa (*Al-Hamishmar*, November 10, 1958).

Joining Jewish parties was not the most dramatic form of Bedouin political activism. Bedouin shaikhs worked to establish their own political structure. For example, a conference of Bedouin shaikhs was organized in 1959 with the explicit intention of putting political pressure on the Israeli leadership to make them stop their fragmentation policies. On May 9, 1959, eleven Bedouin shaikhs[4] met at the house of Shaikh ʿAli Abu Qrinat to discuss their political future. The aim of the initiators, Shaikhs Musa al-ʿAtawna and ʿAli Abu Qrinat, was to organize a political movement that would be able to elect one of the shaikhs to represent the Bedouin in the Knesset. They wished to unify the Bedouin vote so that a Bedouin could win a Knesset seat. A smaller committee of six shaikhs was elected to represent the other shaikhs in discussions concerning the Bedouin block vote being given to Jewish parties such as Mapai, Mapam, and Ahdut Ha-Torah (IDFA 611/1960–22). This was an example of what Gene Sharp (1973, 132) termed "group lobbying" as a form of nonviolent action to support Bedouin interests in the Naqab.

Bedouin anger about the military government and the Mapai party that ran it was evident in winter 1959 at the elections for the fourth Knesset. Since the Bedouin were organized politically by this time their votes made a difference in that election. According to Chanina Porat, over half of the Bedouin who were connected to Mapai voted for Mapai. Interestingly, Mapam received 30 percent of the Bedouin vote, which could be seen as a significant Bedouin protest against both Mapai and the military rule (Porat 2007, 143).

Having around 30 percent of votes against them was worrying for the Mapai party. A campaign was launched to keep Bedouin tribes loyal and under Mapai control. Some Bedouin shaikhs duly traded on this desire for Bedouin support as a way to gain more rights and worked to persuade more Bedouin tribes to vote for Mapai. This struggle for the Bedouin vote divided the community. Shaikh Musa al-ʿAtwana in particular, who had tried for many years to strengthen the Bedouin voice in government, actually worked for Mapam. Yet the majority of Bedouin did vote for Mapai. A *Jerusalem Post* article in 1961 titled "The Negev Remains Loyal to Mapai" stated:

> The Negev in general remained faithful to Mapai, with an increase in several areas. . . . Mapai also showed surprising gains among the Bedouin tribes. In the Mapam stronghold of Musa Al ʿAtawna, Mapai received nearly half the votes. However, in the el Huzayil tribe, which rival parties charged Mapai had bought with the release from jail of the shaikh's son, Mapai also received just about half of the votes.
> (*JERUSALEM POST*, AUGUST 17, 1961)

Such tactics occurred frequently. Mapai, for example, succeeded in splitting the Bedouin shaikhs by assisting them in cases that involved personal issues. Other parties often accused Mapai of assisting particular Bedouin shaikhs in order to gain more votes. There were also numerous reports of such activities by Mapai. *Haʾolam Hazeh* newspaper wrote a full report in 1961 about a prominent Bedouin shaikh who had recruited other tribes to vote for Mapai so that his son would be freed from prison. The shaikh's son had been charged with sensitive infractions and received a lengthy sentence. He was released before his sentence was up because of his father's activities in supporting Mapai (*Haʾolam Hazeh*, August 2, 1961).

During the 1960s, there was a noticeable decline in the percentages of Bedouin voting for the ruling parties (Soen and Shmuel 1987, 337). As Landau (1969) discusses, some Bedouin in the Naqab resisted participation in the elections in the mid-1960s. This was perceived as another form of resistance to Israel's divide-and-rule policies toward the Bedouin. Landau notes that

> during the elections to the sixth Knesset in November 1965, ballot polls were placed in several Bedouin tribes. The Huzayil tribe considered some of these socially inferior Bedouin. As a result the elders of this tribe refused to vote, and only 40 percent of the registered electors cast their votes.
> (LANDAU 1969, 27)

Here there was an element of pragmatism in the patron-client dynamics set up by the Jewish political parties with the shaikhs. Both sides benefited. However, it should be understood that the shaikhs were able to use the needs of both Mapai and Mapam for their own purposes. By putting more pressure on the two parties, the shaikhs were able to achieve some of their goals and rights. This tactic represents a form of manipulation and agency.

Despite the significant efforts made by a number of active Bedouin leaders to develop new forms of politics, the Mapai was dominant among the Bedouin and received more of their votes. Only in 1977 did the Bedouin secure their first Knesset Member, MK Hammad Abu Rabia. Later, in 1992, MK Talab al-Sanne entered the Knesset as a member of the Democratic Arab Party.

Former MK Abd al-Wahab Darawsha has argued that since the early 1990s, the Naqab was witnessing a political and an Arab awakening among the youth. Part of this movement was against voting for the Mapai party and the shaikh's fragmented politics (interview with Abd al-Wahab Darawsha, October 25, 2014, Iksal). At the same time, different community conferences were being organized in an attempt to establish a unified party that would speak on behalf of the Bedouin (Kul al-ʾArab, 1996). The local MK from Lakiya, Talab al-Sanne, claimed that since Oslo, political awareness among the Naqab Bedouin had increased. He said that this could be attributed to the ongoing marginalization of the Bedouin cause (interview with Talab al-Sanne, Kul al-ʾArab, February 16, 1996).

## Drought Years and Economic Restrictions, 1958–1960

The economic situation of the Bedouin in the *siyaj* remained fragile following the Suez crisis and up to the early 1960s. The economic policies of the Israeli military authorities restricted the welfare of the Bedouin and significantly eroded their indigenous economy. The military government did not provide the Bedouin with sufficient jobs and economic possibilities, with the result that they were forced to find other opportunities for survival.

The drought years of the late 1950s had added to the harsh economic regulations imposed by the military government. This combination hit the Bedouin particularly badly. Epidemic diseases also swept the Bedouin in the late 1950s, adding to their misery. According to Porat (2007), the Naqab was hit by drought in 1955, 1956, 1958, and 1960. Herds in drought conditions suffered from dried out grazing and water shortages.

The three years of intense drought exacerbated an already critical economic situation in the late 1950s. The terrible drought plus the repressive military government meant that this period became seared into Bedouin memory. The Bedouin remember that era as *sanat al-limona* or "year of lemons" because of its particular intensity and the death of so much of their livestock: "People mostly were not allowed to migrate with their flocks to the northern part of the country as they had done in the past. Flocks died in the places where we were able to forage because of the drought, or because of the military police activities that were undertaken in order to scare us" (interview with Sultan, July 2011). The Bedouin lost more than 30 percent of their flocks during these bitter years of drought. In some cases, the military government allowed certain Bedouin to roam outside the *siyaj* zone. In other cases, it restricted any free movement. A review of the archives of this period suggests that the military government had no clear policy for dealing with Bedouin affected by drought. Sometimes decisions were taken to allow Bedouin to graze outside the military zone. Other times Bedouin permits to leave the closed zone were cancelled. A letter to the Israeli Operations Directorate (Agam) reported that starting on January 27, 1955, permits that had been issued to Bedouin to graze east of the enclosed zone would be cancelled (IDFA 584/1958-4). In practice, the Bedouin were not allowed to graze their animals at random since many areas were closed to them. Although the land issued to the Bedouin for grazing was insufficient for their needs, they were not permitted to enter the closed zones with their livestock (interview with Abu Ahmad, June 2009).

The military government did consider alternatives for allowing the Bedouin to migrate outside the *siyaj*. One solution was to move them to the Galilee in the north for grazing purposes, a scheme that was reportedly approved and actually appeared to offer some respite. However, it was cancelled at the last minute (*La-Merhav*, February 17, 1959). In 1959, after some Bedouin had been allowed to travel north for grazing, but military governor Penhas Amir suddenly asked the Bedouin to migrate back to the Naqab to their encampments in the *siyaj*. The Bedouin were not happy and complained about this policy on the grounds that they had paid money to lease land from kibbutz and Jewish landowners. They were unhappy about having to return their herds to the *siyaj* and complained that their livestock would suffer and die from the harsh drought conditions (*Al-Hamishmar*, March 17, 1959).

Another response to the desperate situation of the Bedouin in the late 1950s was through monetary grants or compensation. The military government would pay compensation for what had been lost during the drought. One way in which the money was distributed was through Bank Hapoalim in Beersheba. *Davar* mentions that the military governor of the Naqab, Bedouin shaikhs, and representatives of the Ministry of Agriculture took part in one such distribution. Shaikh Musa al-ʿAtwana duly expressed his appreciation of the government's compensation policy (*Davar*, January 1, 1959). Another report stated that the government also opened up more land for Bedouin grazing in order to help them. They even distributed food and water supplies and job opportunities. However, these measures were not intended to solve Bedouin economic problems for the future. According to this report, they were to be regarded as temporary (ISA/ GL 17019/6).

The Bedouin leadership used these desperate circumstances to advance Bedouin interests. The shaikhs increased their complaints to the military government about the shortage of grazing land and insisted that more land be opened for their herds. Following these complaints the military government decided to open other areas for Bedouin grazing (*Haaretz*, September 22, 1958). The Bedouin demonstrated other tactics of agency. One was to establish themselves near Jewish settlements in the Naqab and graze their herds even when this was opposed by some kibbutz members. Bedouin elders recounted complaints from kibbutz and Jewish settlements that the Bedouin livestock had sabotaged their orchards (interview, ʿAbdallah, May 2012). The Bedouin used this tactic in order to graze their herds without taking settlement properties into account. Another approach used by the Bedouin was to continue to resist military rule regulations during the drought years by grazing their herds outside the closed zone without any permits. The drought years also drove the Bedouin back into smuggling as a way of keeping their families fed (interview, ʿAbdallah, May 2012).

The Bedouin became more politically vocal as a result of their desperation. For example, in 1959, Mapam organized a conference in Beersheba at which suggestions for helping the Bedouin tribes were mooted.

The Bedouin used the forum to discuss the implications of the drought and to complain about how they were segregated when compared to Jewish farmers (*Al-Hamishamar*, February 27, 1959). The Bedouin used any opportunities created by the drought to raise all their fundamental issues with the government.

Bedouin reactions to military government policies varied. In 1959, they complained that the Ministry of Agriculture had not provided enough land for grazing, resulting in the death of their herds:

> For months the Ministry of Agriculture did not care to supply the Bedouin with grazing land for their flocks. This resulted in the massive death of Bedouin herds, complained representatives of Bedouin shaikhs to *Haaretz*. The shaikhs asked for the creation of a committee of investigation, including members of Knesset, in order to examine who was guilty in not moving Bedouin flocks to the north, which had resulted in severe losses of more than one and a quarter million lira.
> (*HAARETZ*, FEBRUARY 5, 1959).

The Bedouin used their new forum to bring up the issue of corruption in the process of distributing grazing permits during drought years. They blamed the military governor of the Naqab and his officials for not having issued them permits to move with their herds and complained that sometimes the officials offered to let them go to the north for grazing purposes and then stopped them from leaving. They mentioned that the military government and officials had allowed some but not other Bedouin to have permits to take their herds to the Galilee. While some individuals were issued permits, others were prevented from enjoying the same rights, which the Bedouin saw as government corruption (*Al-Hamishmar*, February 13, 1959).

Another tactic mentioned by interviewees was to move nearer to the borders. The Bedouin duly pitched their tents close to the borders with Egypt and Jordan in order to benefit from the cross-border economy. Financial assistance from relatives enhanced economic links were established via infiltrators (interview with Hajja ʿAysha, September 2009). In sum, Bedouin reactions to the drought demonstrate multiple forms of resistance and a creative use of opportunities. The very real conditions they experienced allowed them to bend the rules even further.

## The Appearance of Urbanization Plans

The whole structure of military rule in the Naqab had begun to break down by the early 1960s. It was in this context that the Israeli authorities began to look for new strategies for dealing with the Bedouin. The urbanization plans that emerged marked a fundamental shift in Israel's policies for controlling the indigenous people.

This shift was clearly communicated in 1957 by Mordechai Bentov, the minister of development, who stated in a newspaper article that the Naqab needed to receive greater attention from his ministry so that what he called the "Deep South" of the Naqab could be developed:

> Today, the area of the country south and east of Beersheba, which accounts for about half the total territory of the state, contains altogether 20 settlements or populated points with only 4000 inhabitants . . . we have to usurp the functions of other Government departments. But our task is the supervision and co-ordination of their various activities in Eilat and the Southern Negev, as well as the development of mining and industry in these areas.
>
> (*JEWISH OBSERVER AND MIDDLE EAST REVIEW*, APRIL 19, 1957, 12).

Bentov's statement indicated that he favored greater attention to and investment in the Jewish community in the Naqab, but that he had no regard for the Bedouin.

The urbanization of the Bedouin was officially proposed in 1959 when Prime Minister Ben Gurion announced a multiyear plan to concentrate the Bedouin into permanent urban settlements (Swirski and Hasson 2006). This desire to settle the Bedouin had already been mooted in 1958 by Eliahu Elath, Israel's ambassador to London. Elath had reviewed prospects for settling the Bedouin and turning them from nomadic and seminomadic herders to permanent settlers: "We hope and believe they will come to live by agriculture run on modern lines, like their neighbors in Jewish settlements" (*Jewish Observer and Middle East Review*, January 31, 1958). Within this vision of urbanization for the Bedouin, plans were suggested that often contradicted past policy. One major alternative was forcefully acculturating the

Bedouin and transforming them into a controlled population of cheap labor. This draconian option sought to secure more space for Jewish settlers and remove Bedouin from sensitive locations near borders.

Over the next two years, two options were debated among government ministries and the military authorities. One plan was to settle the Bedouin in the Naqab. The second was to settle them in mixed cities in the center or the north of Israel. Certainly, the period from 1956 to 1963 saw a noticeable increase in the numbers of Jewish settlers moving into the Naqab, which systematically pushed the Bedouin more deeply into the enclosed zone.

It must be remembered that such schemes arose within the context of a suggestion by Moshe Dayan in 1960 that was opposed by Yigal Alon, the minister of labor. Alon had commanded the forces that had conquered the Naqab in 1948 and felt he had a right to comment on Bedouin settlement plans. He wanted them settled in the *siyaj* enclosed zone in urban settings (Swirski and Hasson 2006). These alternatives took more formal shape in 1963 when General Moshe Dayan publicly announced his preference for urbanizing the Bedouin by settling them in mixed cities:

> We should transform the Bedouin into an urban proletariat—in industry, services, construction, and agriculture. Since 88 percent of the Israeli population are not farmers, let the Bedouin be like them. Indeed, this will be a radical move which means that the Bedouin would not live on his land with his herds, but would become an urban person who comes home in the afternoon and puts his slippers on. His children would be accustomed to a father who wears trousers, does not carry a *shabria* [the traditional Bedouin knife] and does not search for vermin in public. The children would go to school with their hair properly combed. This would be a revolution, but it may be fixed within two generations. Without coercion but with governmental direction . . . this phenomenon of the Bedouin will disappear.
>
> (MOSHE DAYAN, *HAARETZ* INTERVIEW, JULY 13, 1963)

The suggestion for settling Bedouin in mixed cities is contained in a document in which the Agriculture Ministry/Department of Land considered General Moshe Dayan's proposal to move 1000 Bedouin families from the Naqab to the Ramle area, Jaffa, and Beersheba. Dayan's idea was supported by the argument that around 1,000 Bedouin were already working outside the *siyaj* at that time. Of those, 700 to 800 worked in Ramle, Ledda, and Rohovot. The other 200 worked in the Beersheba area. The result was a plan whereby the Bedouin who would be moved would be considered evacuated. This would ensure that every family would receive IL2,500 from the government as compensation. The time frame for carrying out the plan indicated that the first 500 families would be moved to the suggested mixed cities by April 1, 1962 (IDFA 22/2009–12).

Moshe Dayan had first addressed this issue in 1960 in a letter in which he suggested settling the Bedouin in mixed cities. According to this letter, the decision of the government dated May 29, 1960, had been passed for discussion to the Committee of Ministers for Economic Affairs. The subsequent proposal, dated July 5, 1960, said that the government encouraged the idea of moving the Naqab Bedouin to mixed cities. The government believed this plan would help to create suitable employment resources and organize housing for the Bedouin. Dayan stated that the funding for this project would be taken from the budget of IL10,500,000 that the government had decided to allocate for the purpose of assisting the Arab minority to move to mixed cities.

Dayan explained that this decision had been reached after a long-term plan for the settling and rehabilitation of the Naqab Bedouin tribes had been submitted. The problem had escalated during the three years of drought. According to Dayan's proposal, the plan represented the first phase of the general plan to settle the Naqab Bedouin (ISA/G 6405/5; also IDFA 22/2009–12). However, the Bedouin strongly rejected Dayan's vision. One well-known Bedouin shaikh criticized the plan publicly:

> The Jewish want to develop the Negev and make efforts to settle it. It is a sign that there is a future for it, so why do we have to leave the "Negev?" If it is good for the Jews in the Negev, it would also be good for the Bedouin. Such a combination of reasons helped derail the plan to move Bedouin families to the north and the plans were frozen.
>
> (*MAARIV*, APRIL 21, 1961)

There was a very powerful Bedouin reaction to these early plans to resettle and urbanize them, a reaction that demonstrated agency and creativity. Although Dayan and Alon had their plans to settle the Bedouin, they failed to notice that the Bedouin had produced their own mechanism for actively demonstrating land ownership:

> Suddenly the Bedouin tried to prove their ownership of the land by building new shacks; this contradicted the state policy of perceiving the Bedouin as seminomadic. So the government immediately reacted to the Bedouin policy of building new permanent shacks, in order to plan villages for them rather than allowing them to build freely in the desert.
> (INTERVIEW WITH ABU AHMAD, JULY 2009)

Archival reports confirm that some Bedouin tribes reacted to Dayan's proposal of sending them to live in northern towns by accelerating illegal building. The reports estimated that 300 hundred extra huts and cement buildings had been constructed by the Bedouin after 1960 (ISA/G/ 6405/9105). The leading Bedouin shaikh, Musa al-ʿAtawna, responded quickly and clearly to these government plans. He pointed out that the only Bedouin who would agree to move to towns in the north were those who did not own land. He reiterated that Bedouin wanted to settle on the land that they had owned for many years (Porat 2007, 139). Moshe Dayan then withdrew his proposal to settle the Bedouin in mixed towns. The result was that Yigal Alon's vision of settling the Bedouin in the Naqab became the more solid and achievable prospect (Swirski and Hasson 2006, 17). Israeli policy sought to encourage the Bedouin to leave the Naqab and to distribute them in more than one location, but this strategy has so far failed.

Interestingly, some Bedouin families asked to leave the Naqab and to live in Ramle or Lydda, where they still live today. They were badly off financially when the drought set in, and thus were tempted by the idea of modernization and better living outside. One such case was the Al-Baz family who wrote to the military governor of the Naqab in 1960 asking to go to Lydda, arguing that the economic situation in the Naqab made it very difficult to survive. They asked the government for a piece of land and a house for the purpose of settling in Lydda. In another letter in the Kibbutz Lahav Archive (KLA), Shaikh Jaber Abu Srihan wrote to General Moshe Dayan, the minister of agriculture, on February 22, 1960, asking to move to Ramle/Lydda. Shaikh Jaber Abu Srihan justified his request by the fact that the Bedouin economy had been badly affected by the three years of drought. He emphasized that his tribe lacked the resources to live and that their situation was very hard.

The land on which he and his family lived was not economically productive, water was in short supply, and his herds had died because of the drought. In addition, the Bedouin were not allowed to work in the Naqab. Allowing them to move to Ramle-Lydda would enable his tribe to live and to work in agriculture and thereby to improve their critical economic situation (Kibbutz Lahav Archival papers).

Although the Bedouin had been subjected to a variety of ongoing draconian state policies aimed at control and quiescence during this period (1956–1963), their continued existence on the land forced the Israeli authorities to rethink their strategy. The military government was desperate to build a wall of Jewish settlements between the Bedouin and the borders. New settlements like 'Arad, established in 1962, were part of this strategy to populate the northeastern Naqab with Jewish immigrants and to create a wall of settlers in sensitive regions close to the borders. This desire to allocate more space to Jewish settlements in the Naqab was obvious in the plans to urbanize the Bedouin by sending them to mixed towns like Ramle and Lydda.

In one way, the appearance of the urbanization policy can be seen as marking a new phase of Israeli policy. This new phase had come about because the indigenous Bedouin remnant had resisted modernization plans and still struggled to continue their traditional lifestyle (Tully 2000). Certainly the indigenous Bedouin had resisted changes that might have demolished their culture (Champagne 2003). Globally, states have long sought to urbanize indigenous populations. In response, indigenous people have struggled to protect what survives of their traditional lands, culture, resources, and autonomy. For the Bedouin, moving away into mixed towns was not an option.

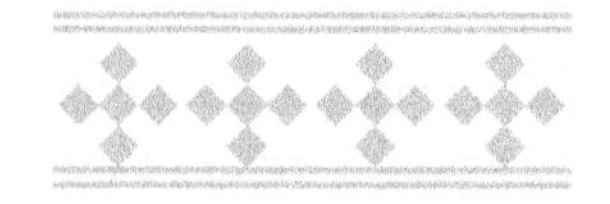

NINE

# The End of Military Rule and Resistance to Urbanization Plans, 1962–1967

> Israel maintains her Defense Forces against the enemy Arab armies and maintains Military Government against internal security dangers. If the very existence of the State of Israel is moral, then Military Government is moral.
>
> —SHIMON PERES, *JERUSALEM POST*, JANUARY 1962

THE MILITARY GOVERNMENT was abolished in 1967 after heated debate within the Israeli Knesset and continued protest activities in the Naqab, the Galilee, and the Triangle. Israel's official policy toward the Bedouin shifted even though the substance of the state's approach to the Naqab Bedouin remained unchanged until the Prawer plan. Recent findings by Ahmad Saʾdi provide new insights into the protest activities of the Palestinians in Israel—mostly nonviolent actions—under military rule (Saʾdi 2015, 463). It is clear that the demonstrations and ongoing complaints by the Palestinian Arab minority played a significant role in bringing military rule to an end.

## The Knesset Debate Over the Military Government

Discussion about the status of the military government began in 1956 with the Ratner Committee, which recommended its continuation. In 1959, the Rosen Committee advised abolishing military rule, but did not succeed. The debate was transferred to the Israeli Knesset where discussion about the future of military rule became a central issue. During the early 1960s, the debate received more or less daily media coverage and almost all Israeli newspapers carried regular reports about the issue.

Like the Prawer discussion, in the Knesset the debate was initially between supporters and opponents of abolition. It took a political form when it started to occur between different parties, coalitions, and oppositions interested in abolishing or continuing military rule. One example was the formation in late 1961 of a Jewish-Arab committee that held rallies, protested, and sought civil support for eliminating the military government (Jiryis 1976, 43). In September 1962, four bills concerning either abolition or reduction were tabled for normal discussion in the Knesset. There were two equal camps between coalition and opposition. Three bills were submitted by Knesset members Moshe Sneh (Communists), I. Bader (Hirut), and I. Kamis (Mapam). A fourth bill was put forward by M. Carmel (Ahdut Ha-ʿAvoda). A background paper to the debate on military government was issued on February 11, 1963, by the Foreign Affairs Ministry of Jerusalem. The core debate was whether to abolish the Military Government or to rescind only the military defense regulations (ISA/GL 7128/7). A proposal by Pinhas Rosen (Liberals) was rejected since it only proposed replacing the existing military emergency regulations with new ones (Bauml 2002).

If the political status of these parties is examined, the underlying agenda behind their positions can be seen. Hirut asked for absolute abolition of the Emergency Regulations. It favored repeal of the emergency regulations of 1945 within one year and the adoption of a law for the security of border areas (*Jerusalem Post*, January 18, 1962). Ahdut Ha-ʿAavoda, on the other hand, was one of the main parties favoring abolition of the military government and regularly raised this bill during the Knesset discussions. It proposed the transfer of authority from the special military branch to the regular military command. It hoped that its bill would abolish the military government machinery at all levels but without totally repealing the military defense regulations, since to do so would abolish the requirement for travel permits, which the party wished to retain (*Jerusalem Post*, January 29, 1962).

The Israeli Communist Party took a third position. It requested the immediate abolition of the military government and sought instead to employ civilian institutions. The Liberals supporting the Rosen Proposal wanted to abolish the military government, having previously suggested this in a private bill. Finally, Mapai, the ruling party, opposed abolition of the military government and supported its continuation. The National Religious Party and the workers' wing of Agudat Israel also argued for this. Interestingly, it could be said that the military government was saved thanks to Arab votes, since on this occasion four Arab members of the Knesset voted for the continuation of the military government because they were controlled by Mapai (Anonymous, *New Outlook* 1963).

Mapai clearly put pressure on its Arab members to vote against the abolition of the military government, even if they personally supported its cancellation. The resulting vote in the Knesset was for retention of the military government. However, this did not end the debate. A ministerial committee was appointed to offer suggestions and to canvas the opinions of various parties as to whether to abolish the military government. Unhelpfully, this committee failed to present any concrete suggestions to which all the parties could agree. As a result, the debate continued in the Knesset without the parties reaching a consensus on the future of the military government (*Haaretz,* January 29, 1962). It should be noted that the Mapai continued to pursue its campaign against abolishing the military government. It favored the government's modification, not its termination. Shimon Peres, deputy defense minister, categorized the Arab population in Israel into three types—the indifferent resigned, the hostile resigned, and the activity hostile. He justified his party's support for retaining the military government on the basis that it was essential to Israel's security. For him, the military government was a moral institution that protected the security of the population in Israel. He opposed its abolition, arguing that it prevented the extremists among the Arabs from becoming dominant.

The Mapai party was accused of using military rule for its own advantage (Bauml 2002). Despite this, Prime Minister David Ben Gurion's commitment continued. He rejected abolition again in a speech in the Knesset in 1963, saying he was determined to maintain his stand (Jiryis 1976, 44). His reaction to the bills proposed by other parties was to offer to modify his own position while supporting the military government despite repeated calls for its termination. He stated on February 20, 1962, in the Knesset that

> if we wish to protect the Arabs who long for peace, not only inside the country, but also between Israel and her neighbors; if we want to deter the destructive forces from listening to such incitement as I have quoted; if we want to prevent bloodshed and vain and foolish attempts to turn Galilee, the Negev and the central parts of the country into dangerous areas of strife, we must maintain Military Administration, with the relaxations I have mentioned, which have been confirmed by the government. I therefore propose,

> in the name of the government, to remove from the order paper all the bills proposed on this subject by Ahdut Ha-ʿAvoda-Poalei Zion, Mapam, the Communists, the Liberals and Hirut.
> (ISA/ GL 7128/7)

Ben Gurion resigned as prime minister in 1963 and was replaced in office by Levi Askhol. Levi announced his intention to follow relaxation policies for the military government. He favored either the immediate abolition of the military government or the abolition of the military emergency regulations. He also declared that as one of the key modifications, there would no longer be any need for permits for Arabs in the Galilee and the Triangle, except for Arabs who were perceived as a security threat. It was a lead-in to his attempts to abolish the military government.

## Forcing Urbanization Plans on the Arab Bedouin Citizens

While heated discussions were taking place in the Knesset over abolishing the military government interministerial committees were developing settlement plans for the Bedouin. These urbanization plans were intended to serve the Jewish state and to preserve more land for Jewish settlers. According to Lithwick the aim of settling the Bedouin was to control their land for the Zionist project (2003, 185). Kellerman notes that one option available to settler societies in dealing with indigenous people is tight control (1993). Israel adopted this policy for controlling its indigenous community by forcing them to settle down. Zureik (1979) says that Israel was practicing internal colonization toward its indigenous Bedouin by developing urbanization plans. This meant that the Israelis wanted to exploit what was left of Bedouin lands and resources for the benefit of the state (Yiftachel 2013).

Such ideas continue to run through Israeli thinking. For example, in 2007 the former prime minister of Israel Ehud Olmert claimed that Bedouin did not have land rights and had to live in settled townships. The 1960s plans to modernize the Bedouin and to expropriate more of their land is alive and well among Israel's top politicians. In a film by Mark Willacy (2005), Olmert says, "You want them to be given an extension of time; but at some point you just have to remove them from a particular piece of land which is not theirs . . . over the years they have spread onto land that isn't theirs" (Ehud Olmert, interviewed in Willacy 2005). Regional planning by settler societies has always been a major instrument for controlling minorities. Yiftachel describes this tactic as similar to the territorial containment used against the Bedouin (2003, 25). He also uses other terms to reflect the government's plan to settle the Bedouin, referring to it as a "top-down Judaization and modernization program" (Yiftachel 2003, 27–35).

The process of urbanization started to take shape in 1962 concurrently with the debate that was taking place in the Knesset over abolishing the military government. This ambition for settlement accelerated the process of searching for possible sites where the Bedouin could be established. On March 25, 1962, the government agreed in Decision No. 363 to set up an interministerial committee headed by Yousef Weitz, head of the ILA. This committee would consider suggestions for finding suitable locations for the Bedouin. Other tasks on its agenda included ascertaining Bedouin land ownership and employment status and checking on illegal construction (ISA/GL 17001/21).

The plans to settle the Bedouin became increasingly fierce as Israel began to claim that the Bedouin had built illegally. Since the Israeli authorities saw illegal Bedouin buildings as invasive (*Hitnahlut*), they tried to make plans for reducing illegal housing. In 1962, Minister of the Interior Yigal Alon reported to the government on illegal Bedouin housing in the area of Tal ʿArad. He insisted that discussion of the report should not be delayed since Bedouin activity needed to be controlled. His report noted that around 10,000 Bedouin lived in the area and had adopted the idea of building illegally in order to prove their land rights. The report also mentioned attempts already undertaken to convince the Bedouin to settle. It stressed the benefits of moving Bedouin to permanent towns where new job possibilities and other facilities would be available to them (ISA/A 7164/7).

In September 1965 the Knesset Finance Committee decided to approve a sample of three sites for Bedouin permanent settlement: one near Beersheba (Tal al-Sabaʿ), a second near Kibbutz Shoval (Rahat), and the third at Tal al-Malah-Kseifa (Swirski and Hasson 2006; Jiryis 1976, 125). It was initially planned that each permanent site would include plots of land for construction. The sites would also include education facilities, clinics, community buildings, roads, running water, electricity, and sewerage systems. These details were included in a secret letter sent by Secretary of the Committee of Ministers for Economic Affairs Shamai Tsavihrick on September 14, 1965,

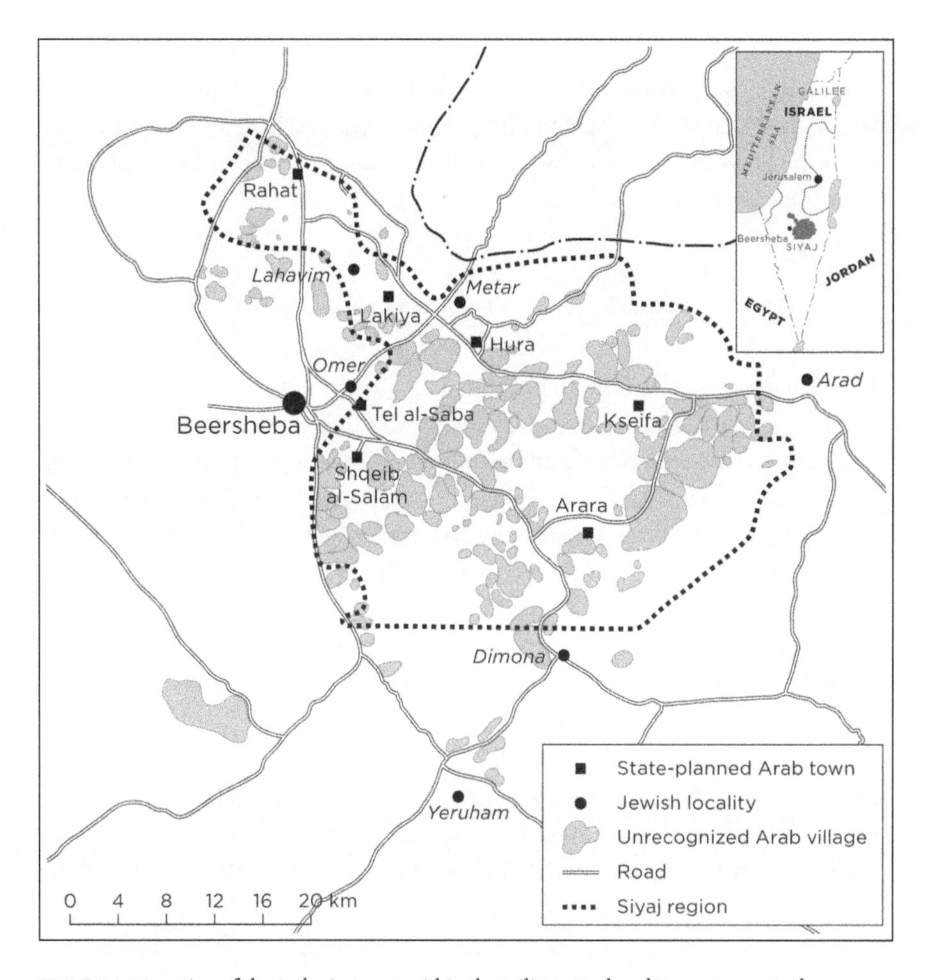


FIGURE 9.1 Location of the Bedouin towns within the Military Enclosed Zone. *Source*: Author.

to the prime minister and the ministers of finance, defense, labor, interior, housing, and tzahal (ISA/G 6405/5). During the first stage, the government approved three areas for the construction of Bedouin towns. These were then followed by another four sites. Seven sites in total were built for the Bedouin—Lakiya, ʿAraʿra, Shqeib al-Salam, Hura, Rahat, Kseifa, and Tal al-Sabaʿ—in what Yiftachel calls an Israeli plan to urbanize the Bedouin.

Adoption of this policy meant the Bedouin were being forced to leave their traditional way of life. The promised modern towns with high living standards appeared later as a government strategy (Law-Yone 2003, 178).

Instead of building agricultural settlements that would have suited the Bedouin, the Israeli authorities planned permanent towns that required less land (Law-Yone 2003). The Bedouin persist in requesting the Israeli government to allow them to establish agricultural villages on their land as is done by neighboring Jewish kibbutzim.

## *Why the Israeli Model of Modernization?*

The Naqab faced Israeli policies aimed at preserving the Jewish character of the state similar to those enforced in the Galilee (Kanaaneh 2002, 50). Relocating the Bedouin into planned settlements was a policy that aimed to secure land for Jewish settlements. It was justified on the basis that it dealt with the growth of Israel's Jewish population by meeting its economic needs (Jakubowska 1992, 91). According to Kanaaneh (2002), the concern of Jewish leaders about the demographic balance in areas such as the Galilee was clearly presented by Ben Gurion. In the Naqab the distribution of the Bedouin tribes in the *siyaj* area pushed Israeli leadership to produce plans for controlling and urbanizing them.

The government's policy was to settle and modernize the Bedouin as they were perceived as backward (Shamir 1996). Law-Yone (2003, 180) notes the Israeli approach contained three spatial strategies: relocation, resettlement, and restructuring. Israel employed aggressive methods to force the Bedouin to move into towns in implementing the 1965 Law of Planning and Construction (Shamir 1996, 246). Falah (2005) uses the term "enclavization" to describe these policies of spatial control. Said policies severely damaged the Bedouin way of life and forced them to live in a shrinking space.

One aim of the government's urbanization plans was to break up Bedouin tribes and extended families and force them to live close to other tribes with whom they never had any previous connections. One segment of a family lived in one town and another segment lived in a different town. It was the same policy that had been adopted by the state of Israel after the Nakba when it recognized only a few tribes; all the others had to join them. This new urban settlement policy conflicted with Bedouin claims for land ownership and historical territory. As Champagne notes, "claim to territory is a fundamental value for most native groups" (Champagne 2003, 250).

The government plan was designed to weaken Bedouin land claims and to reduce their spontaneous settlement activities. Such de-Arabization of the Bedouin was intended to modernize them and to implement Judaization of the land (Abu Saad 2008; Abu Saad, Yonah, Kaplan 2004; Shamir 1996; Yiftachel 2003; Law-Yone 2003; Falah 1989a, 1989b). Bedouin interviewees used the Arabic term *istitan qasri* (forced sedentarization) to refer to this process since they were never consulted about the plans. One of the main tools used by Israel in this sedentarization was manipulating building permits as a way of minimizing Bedouin control of land (Maddrell 1990, 9).

The Israel Land Administration (ILA) employed experts such as anthropologists and sociologists to draw up plans for the Bedouin towns. These experts did not understand the mentality of the Bedouin that were to be settled in them. They had a limited understanding of tribal perceptions of settlement plans.

### *A Wrong Start: The Tal al-Saba*ᶜ *Model*

Approval of the urbanization plans by the interministerial committee required the construction of a sample town. The first town to be built formally by the government to accommodate Bedouin was Tel Sheba, which was established a few miles north east of Beersheba. A number of concrete houses were constructed there in 1965 (Lithwick 2003, 185). In 1968, the Israeli authorities built forty-nine small huts and supplied them with water and electricity (Lewando-Hundt 1979). Each hut had two rooms. This was considered sufficient to accommodate one family (*Sawt al-Bilad*, July 1, 1984). Most of the huts built by the government remained empty, apart from a few that were rented by some northern school teachers who worked in the Naqab but were not citizens of Tal al-Sabaᶜ. Medical services were also available.

The Bedouin resisted living in Tal al-Sabaᶜ primarily because of land claims. Jakubowska described how Tal al-Sabaᶜ was left empty for a number of years (1992, 91). Meir emphasized the fact that Tal al-Sabaᶜ was a failure as a planned government project because only twenty-seven nuclear families moved into the town. The original plan had been to include 1,200 families (Meir 1997, 97). The Bedouin were eager to avoid losing their claims to the land.

The Bedouin response to this poor planning policy was to resist moving into the small houses since the Tal al-Sabaᶜ project did not suit their way of life. Although the government mistakenly thought that the Bedouin would be falling over each other to live in them, the Bedouin avoided living in Tel Sheba on the grounds that no one had consulted them before constructing the buildings. In addition, the buildings were of poor quality and had insufficient space to accommodate large families with children. In other words, the Israeli authorities failed to take into account Bedouin needs and tribal structures and completely ignored their cultural values.

Failing to consult with the Bedouin about the preplanned houses in Tal al-Sabaᶜ led to the failure of the project. This was a direct consequence of Bedouin resistance and led to a policy shift by the authorities. They started to take Bedouin needs into consideration. The failure of the Tal Sabaᶜ plan was a Bedouin way of resisting change that might disturb indigenous life (Champagne 2003, xxxi). The failure of this first urbanization project can be seen as a method of social noncooperation. This also shows how the Bedouin disobeyed laws that they considered immoral in order to marginalize Israeli plans. It was a spontaneous action adopted by the Bedouin.

Settler states need to begin to negotiate with their indigenous populations and to respect their culture. Since Israel had not consulted with Bedouin before making plans to urbanize them, these plans were not respected by the Bedouin. Sharp (1973, 286) highlights this response as a Bedouin form of political noncooperation.

## Bedouin Reaction to the Urbanization Plans

The immediate reaction of the Bedouin to the government's urbanization plans was to adopt a spontaneous strategy that involved building wood and cement houses on their land. Falah calculated that 80 percent of Bedouin settlements before 1970 were spontaneous and unrecognized by the state. Israel claimed that structures of this type were built illegally (Falah 1989, 48). The Bedouin chose *sumud* (steadfastness) as a way of resisting for survival by building on their land without permits. This was their most effective form of resistance to military rule and it alarmed Israeli policy makers.

They feared that the Bedouin would not give up their land claims. During the 1960s, clusters of wooden and concrete shacks suddenly started to appear. There was no effective policy to stop them. These small hamlets that were regarded as illegal by the government began to emerge spontaneously in the Naqab once the military government ended (Jakubowska 1992, 90). Today, half of the Bedouin still refuse to move to permanent settlements (Shamir 1996, 246). As noted by Champagne (2003, xxv), indigenous traditions "uphold claims to land."

The Bedouin had already claimed some of the land on which the planned townships were to be established. This led them to resist moving to these towns until the land issue had been resolved. Many houses in the Naqab were constructed within a short time, often built at night to avoid clashes with government agencies. Such building was not a form of organized community action, but did include extended family members and friends. The Bedouin cooperated in house building and in rebuilding if houses were demolished. The entire family would gather and in one night would build a house, donating money or cement. In many cases, the Islamic movement collected donations in mosques for providing cash to build the houses. Bedouin referred to this act of *sumud* (steadfastness) as applying to the whole Bedouin community, using the concept of *al-Naqab al-samid*. Bedouin use of land for constructing houses prevented the Israeli authorities from taking it away.

The failure of the Tal al-Sabaʿ project forced the government to make hasty changes to its sedentarization and forced urbanization plans. The next village, Rahat, built in 1972, was totally different because Bedouin were permitted to construct their own houses.

Some Bedouin agreed to live in towns, either by reaching an agreement with the state or by being forced into doing so. Some who did not own land found it easier to move to towns since they had nothing to lose. However, even today Bedouin who moved still regret having taken this step as they feel that they were trapped by poorly defined state plans. Even worse, there were cases of Bedouin who agreed to move to towns because the state promised they would gain recognition as a single tribe. In such cases the state only recognized some new shaikhs because they had made the move into towns—the ideal state fragmentation policy.

Many would prefer to go back to their land rather than live as strangers in one of the townships. The testimony of one Bedouin who had moved into

Rahat during its early stages reveals the bleak outcome of Israeli urbanization policies for the Bedouin:

> Relations are not at all good here. It's like a prison. You can't even open a window here to get some air. If you open a window there's always someone looking in at us. It's heartache. Sometimes I go back to see people who live in the desert, to the peaceful, relaxed life, the good wind, even the fresh air. I miss it. We look for it. Here everything is wrong—even the air. It's not clean.
> (INTERVIEW BY MARK WILLACY WITH EHUD OLMERT, 2005)

Many Bedouin expressed their displeasure with the urbanization policy. They referred to it as control of their native land, not modernization.

After the government had formulated its program to settle the Bedouin in three towns they "discovered" that their plans did not suit the Bedouin. This says a lot about the obvious failure of the construction of Tal al-Sabaᶜ. Bedouin resistance to urbanization started with the building of shacks instead of tents in the late 1950s and 1960s as a step toward proving their existence on their land. They used the term *al-Naqab al-samid* as a form of cultural resistance. In other words, after the abolition of the military government Israeli authorities lost control of the demographic spread and movement of the Bedouin. Because the pass system, no longer applied Bedouin mobility started to be more fluid (Belge 2009). Vashitz outlined the Bedouin method of resisting Israeli settlement plans:

> The Bedouins tend to settle by building a house where their tent once stood. . . . But the Bedouin is attached to his land and is opposed to the merging of different tribes. He puts up illegal buildings, the authorities issue orders to remove them, and the Bedouins resist.
> (VASHITZ 1971, 42)

Another Bedouin response to urbanization plans was to push for resolution of their land ownership claims before removal to towns took place. They raised their voices to call for the disputes over their land to be solved before they would move. They asked the government to build villages on sites that the Bedouin themselves proposed. *Davar* reported that several Bedouin shaikhs warned the government that they would appeal to the courts to resolve their land claims before the urbanization plans could start. For example, the al-ʿAtawna tribe turned to the Ministry of Agriculture to settle the tribe's land ownership before there were any plans made to move them into towns (*Davar*, June 29, 1960).

The Bedouin escalated their campaign by summoning a tribal conference to adopt a unified policy in response to the Ministry of Agriculture's plans. Champagne reiterates the point that the Bedouins' counterclaim to their territory antagonized the objectives of the nation state (Champagne 2003, xxv). Yiftachel (2003) emphasizes the fact that the Naqab Bedouin developed a counter ideology to the government's policies.

In a petition letter signed in 1965 by eighteen Bedouin shaikhs, the government was asked to solve the Bedouin land ownership problem before imposing settlement plans. Linda Smith (1999, 109) describes the struggle of other indigenous people to obtain their land rights as direct actions and petitions. The Naqab Bedouin adopted petitioning as a form of resistance to gain recognition of their land ownership. For example, another petition copied to twelve different governmental ministries was sent to Prime Minister Levi Askhol on June 20, 1966. While the 1965 petition had raised other problems faced by the Bedouin, this time the main issue was that of land. In their letter, the shaikhs reminded Israel that in 1948, they had agreed to stay under Israeli rule on the condition that the land issue would be dealt with. They argued that they would live on their land and cultivate it just like the rest of the state's citizens. The letter went on to remind the Israelis that the government had agreed to their request to stay on their land and that this was the reason they agreed to stay within the Israeli border. These promises had not been fulfilled.

Other points raised in the 1965 letter included the fact that the Bedouin were not allowed to cultivate their native land, from which they had been expelled, and that Bedouin tribes had become internally displaced people (IDPs) within Israel. The shaikhs asked the prime minister to consider certain factors when looking at their claims. First, they wanted government recognition of land ownership as it had been during the Ottoman period and under the British Mandate. Second, the government needed to solve the IDP problem by allowing them to return to their land. Third, the government had to resolve Bedouin land ownership claims before initiating any policy of moving them to towns. Fourth, the letter said that the Bedouin would not relinquish their land ownership claims as long as they were alive, even if the government used violence against them. Finally, the Bedouin shaikhs reminded the Israeli government that they had been waiting eighteen years for the government to solve their land ownership claims (ISA/GL 17003/1).[1]

The pressure from the shaikhs produced some immediate successes. A meeting was achieved with Tolidano, the adviser on Arab Affairs, and with Aluf Shlomo Shamir, manager of the ILA (the *Keren Kayemet*). Around sixty shaikhs met Tolidano and Shamir in Beersheba in June 1966. At this meeting, the shaikhs returned to the central issue of land ownership that had been raised in their petition letter. They also raised another important issue concerning new settlements proposals and resolution of Bedouin land claims related to the planned towns (ISA/ GL 17003/1). Importantly, this example demonstrates that Bedouin action was carried out as a group. For Sharp such letters of opposition represent nonviolent protest. The Bedouin tried to influence the authorities' decision on urbanization, and their meeting with Israeli officials was a form of deputation and group lobbying (Sharp 1973, 120–133). For Hollander and Einwohner (2004, 536), these Bedouin actions are resistance, requiring a level of coordination and purposeful acting together.

Other complaints were made directly to the military governor himself. In 1966, Shaikh Hassan Abu Rabiaʾ publicly expressed his views to Sasson Bar Zvi about the Bedouin campaign to get their land recognized: "in our struggle for land rights, we will not flinch from demonstrations, arrests and deportation, we will not give up" (IDFA 72/70–187). Abu Rabiaʾ warned military government officials that the Bedouin would resist in many ways, including through violence.

The Bedouin also expressed their attitude to the urbanization plans by saying "we are not going to live in towns, stuck between walls." However, some were convinced to settle in towns and build permanent houses. Some of these were actually leading shaikhs who had established good relations with the government. In the end only half the Bedouin eventually moved into the planned townships. The rest have continued to live in what are called unrecognized villages and resist any move into towns.[2]

## Abolishing the Military Government: A New Frame for an Old Picture

For almost two decades the military government hung like a millstone around the neck of the Palestinian minority in Israel. The final stages of its modification and abolition were implemented in early January 1966 (Jiryis

1976, 54–55). The result was that Bedouin in the Naqab could enjoy going to Beersheba and the north:

> The new orders take effect in central Galilee and in the Negev and were issued upon instruction by the Prime Minister Eshkol . . . under the new orders more than 20000 Bedouin living in restricted areas of the Negev will now no longer need individual permits to move into any part of Israel. Another 60000 inhabitants of the Triangle will also not need permits for entering closed zones . . . however, Nazareth residents still cannot enter the Triangle without permits. (*JERUSALEM POST*, JANUARY 19, 1966)

The abolition was made public on November 8, 1966, when Prime Minister Levi Ashkol addressed the Knesset and announced the demise of the military government: "The government has decided that, with effect from 1 December this year, the machinery of the Military Government will be abolished, and the functions with which the Military Government was charged will be transferred to the jurisdiction of the relevant civilian authorities" (ISA/ GL 7128/7). The Knesset approved Ashkol's announcement and voted 48–7 for an end to the Military Government:

> The Knesset yesterday approved a statement by the Prime Minister announcing the abolition of the Military Government organization and the transfer of most of its functions to the Police. The vote was 48–7, with Rafi and the New Communists voting against and Mr. Uri Avneri abstaining. Gahal did not vote. (*JERUSALEM POST*, NOVEMBER 9, 1966)

The formal end of the military government came on December 1, 1966, when most of the existing military government stations were closed and their control transferred to the police. The duties of the military government were moved to the civilian authorities, and the permits system ceased to operate (Bauml 2002; Jiryis 1976). The *Ha'aretz* headline read: "The military government is cancelled; official authority is transferred to the police." The police were now responsible for dealing with passes, and Arabs were allowed to obtain permits from any police station—note the contradiction concerning permits (*Ha'aretz,* December 2, 1966). According to Jiryis (1976, 63), the immediate effect of Eshkol's announcement was the closing down of twelve military government offices in the three districts populated by Arab citizens: the Galilee, the Little Triangle, and the Naqab. However, military regulations were not totally abolished until 1967.

On paper, the military government had been abolished. Nevertheless, the Arab community continued to suffer in a variety of ways, albeit now within a civilian context. Instead of the army, the police and civil authorities took command, which indicated that it was still a policing system. *Al-Hamishmar* reported that five months after the abolition of the military government, the Arabs were complaining that although the military government had gone, severe problems remained. The administrative adjustments of December 1966 had not been fulfilled, so Arab hopes of seeing a real change were smashed. The prevailing mood in the testimonies of some Arabs in the north was one of depression, and they were described as being negative and forlorn (*Al-Hamishmar*, April 26, 1967).

The "new" policy was simply a new frame for an old picture. The behavior of the authorities toward the Arab minority was unchanged. Policies were scarcely any different. Attitudes were the same. The abolition of military government in the Naqab did not modify the situation of the Bedouin who were still assumed to be a security risk. My interviewees referred to the abolition as a tactical shift that did not achieve any noticeable change. Some interviewees spoke of the period following the termination of the military government as having, in practice, been much more difficult to deal with. This is because the authorities shifted toward an urbanization policy that made Bedouin life much more restricted.

Sabri Jiryis refers to the abolition of the military government by the Israelis as propaganda. Many areas remained closed. A number of Arab villages that had been demolished continued to be off-limits, preventing former villagers from returning. Emergency regulations were still in effect (Jiryis 1976, 64). Bauml states that in early 1967, nothing significant had changed regarding the status of the Arab citizens of Israel since security areas remained and emergency regulations still applied. The abolition of military government did little for Bedouin in the Naqab (2002).

Space and freedom are the most important aspects in life for Bedouins. As soon as these were gone, life in towns meant a new form of governance. With the abolition of military rule, some people lost hope of claiming their land because it would become territory subject to planning. In response, they refused to live in planned towns, preferring to stay on their land and retain their freedom. Bedouin expectations of land recovery reached high levels of disappointment and frustration. This meant a move toward a more effective form of resistance and *sumud*. Walid Sadik remarked in an article in *New Outlook* that: "The military government was abolished, but the philosophy that nourished it is still alive and flourishing among the formations of policy for the Arab, and among the general Jewish population" (Sadik 1978, 54).

During the 1967 war, military rule was reimposed on Arab citizens. Movement restrictions were not lifted until October 3, 1967, when it was decided that "Arab citizens could move in almost every territory with no need for passes." Enforcement of military defense regulations eased in 1968, but the civil government was strengthened (Bauml 2002, 154–55). During the war, some Arabs had been arrested to prevent them taking any hostile action against the state at that time. After the war, the Israeli government adopted a policy of house arrests as a result of growing nationalism among the Arab minority (Jiryis 1976, 65). This supports the argument that the military government was not totally abolished in 1966 and continued into 1967.

Israeli authorities continued to relocate and expel citizens after the supposed abolition of military rule. The most well-known example was the case of Tal al-Malah in the early 1980s, following the signing of the peace treaty of Camp David with Egypt. The agreement meant peace with Egypt, but expulsion to local Bedouin families. Thousands of Tal al-Malah villagers were expelled (e.g., al-Nasasrah, al-ʿAmor, al-Zabarqa, Abu Jweyaʾd, Abu ʿArar, etc.) from their land and pushed to move to planned towns such as Rahat, Kseifa, ʿAraʿra, and to the the northern towns of Tayibea and Qalansawe as a result.

TEN

# Postmilitary Rule, the Oslo Era, and the Contemporary Prawer Debate

DESPITE THE FORMAL ANNOUNCEMENT of the end of military rule, on November 6, 1966, its dynamics and characteristics continued for a number of years. Other state agencies filled the roles previously occupied by the military government. At this time, new structures and governance bodies started to appear in Bedouin villages. These new state agencies took charge of law enforcement among Bedouin and encouraged plans for urbanization.

In their attempts to control the Bedouin, the Israelis used legislation to establish special government agencies to deal with them. These new state agencies filled the same role as the military government. They followed a similar plan for controlling the Bedouin. If one examines the Naqab after the formal abolition of the military government, it is easy to identify many state agencies that played a role in imposing state laws on the Bedouin. For example, the Bedouin Development Authority (BDA), the Bedouin Education Authority (BEA), and the Israel Land Administration (ILA) all performed functions previously taken on by the military government (Abu Saad and Creamer 2012). Other state agencies such as the Jewish National Fund (JNF) and the Jewish Agency for Israel (JAFI) also played a role in governing the Bedouin (cf. Amara and Miller 2012).

Government bodies such as the Unit for Housing Inspection in the Ministry of the Interior and the Land Settlement Registrar at the Ministry of Justice also participated in imposing state policies on the Bedouin.

These agencies were responsible for acting against illegal Bedouin housing and for land-claim registration (Greenspan 2005). There was also an Implementation Authority. The Rotem was a special police unit for law enforcement among the Bedouin (Yiftachel 2003, 36). From time to time, the ILA disrupted Bedouin who were continuing to live on their land. The ILA would raid the Bedouin in order to try to impose land utilization on them. The ILA excuse was that the Bedouin had built illegally on state land without permission (Jakubowska 1992, 90).

In 1976, Ariel Sharon established a key government unit that contained and amplified these post-military developments intended to enforce restrictions on Bedouin life. Part of the Agriculture Ministry, this special unit was called the Green Patrol. It was set up to guard and protect state land from the Bedouin (Swirski and Hasson 2006). Bedouin women called it the "Black Patrol" (interview with Amneh, July 2013). Members of the unit usually arrived with the intention of fighting so-called Bedouin infiltration and reducing the number of Bedouin flocks to stop overgrazing (Falah 1985; Horowitz and Abu Saad 2007). The Green Patrol confiscated Bedouin flocks and demolished Bedouin tents. It justified its actions against the Bedouin by arguing that they damaged the desert environment with their black goats (Jakubowska 1992, 90–91). It also claimed the Bedouin had been grazing their livestock in a closed military area. Shepherds had to pay high fines to retrieve their herds and sometimes recovered considerably fewer animals than had been taken.

The Green Patrol became the main tool used by the Likud party and the Agriculture Ministry to gather the Bedouin and settle them into specific places. It employed a policy of pulling down and demolishing Bedouin tents and houses. It expropriated, killed, or sold thousands of animals and sometimes required their owners to pay high fines. The Bedouin assumed that these policies intended to terrorize them in order to make them leave their land (*Sawt al-bilad*, July 1, 1984). They therefore resisted such actions. They continued to graze their flocks wherever possible and even took to concealing the tracks of their animals. Sometimes the women spoke to the Green Patrol as a tactic to marginalize the patrol. Testimonies of Bedouin women show that the Green Patrol would raid their encampments and pull down their tents. The patrol would cut the main ropes and then drag the tents behind their jeeps in order to force the Bedouin to leave (interview with Hajja Sarah, May 2014).

Government agencies started to find new tactics to force Bedouin to submit and to follow government policies. Greenspan (2005) describes the authorities' enforcement policies toward the Bedouin. Some of these worked against those who used state land or against those who built illegally. The government used the Green Patrol to enforce these acts. In an interview conducted in al-ʿAraqib (north Rahat) before its demolition in 2010, the shaikhs of the village confirmed that the authorities used tough tactics to force the Bedouin to leave their land. These tactics included assessing and imposing fines, sending shaikhs to court, prosecuting tribal members, issuing demolition orders, bulldozing cultivated fields, and spraying toxic chemicals on crops. Some family members became ill and had to have hospital treatment because they had been poisoned (interview with Haj Ismael al-Tori, August 2010).

The policy of demolishing Bedouin homes begun in the 1960s has continued until the present (well-known cases are al-ʿAraqib and ʿAtir Um al-Hiran). In the wake of the abolition of the military government, agencies such as the ILA and the JNF continued to demolish the lives of the Naqab Bedouin. However, the Bedouin did not submit.[1]

## Memory and the Bedouin Right of Return

Bedouin started to submit more demands for the right to live on their native land after the abolition of the military government and the start of urbanization. Reclaiming the land had not been possible during the military government. In some cases, the Bedouin began to cultivate their land. This linked them to the past and was important in helping them remember their history. This indicates that Bedouin awareness of their native land became stronger after the termination of the military government.

Bedouin adopted the return to their land (*al-ʿawda ila al-diyar*) as a historical reimagining of their past. The act of remembering the past, especially historical lands and names of places, played a crucial role in Bedouin survival tactics. They strengthened their land claims by using memory to tell the authorities that they would never forget their land. Stories of the past narrated by Bedouin emphasized the role of memory as a survival strategy. According to Aburabia (2014), telling stories about the past and visiting their former lands became an integral part of Bedouin rituals. If asked, almost any family in Rahat today has a story to tell of land claims and their willingness to return.

The Bedouin right of return to their ancestral land manifested itself in various ways. Through cultivating their land, bringing their extended families, and telling their children about their past, the Bedouin conveyed a sense of consciousness of their former lives (interview with Hajja Fatmeh, March 2014). They started to return on weekends and holidays to visit their indigenous and historical land. These everyday acts turned into acts of survival and of bringing the past to life. For example, the two religious feasts of ʿEid al-Adha and ʿEid al-Fitr became crucial holidays for returning to the land, remembering the past, and exchanging stories. In this way, Bedouin visits to demolished villages and expropriated land turned into emotional events that recalled happy childhoods and strengthened old memories. Parents were proud to tell their children, "This land was our land, *ardna,* and we shall return to it one day" (interview with Abu Ahmad al-Nasasrah, March 2014). Taking photographs of the land that included their children was an obvious way of laying claim. In some cases, when access to a particular site was barred, the photos were taken from behind a fence. Today, in many Bedouin houses, one sees framed pictures hanging in the sitting room that include scenes of the family on their historical land. In many cases, women's embroidery includes the Palestinian flag, often seen hanging in Bedouin living rooms. Every visitor is told the history behind each picture.

When I conducted interviews in Rahat, I heard stories of how the Bedouin perceived their new life in the towns. Some of these attitudes were shocking. Some interviewees referred to the day they moved to Rahat as a "black day" (*yawm aswad*) in their life. Others said that they were living in a "diaspora" (*al-mahjar*) and never felt loyal to Rahat as a town. For example, a Bedouin who was forced to leave his land east of Beersheba and to live in Rahat said:

> I wish I could go to my tribe's land and to live on it, from where we were evicted and to which we were not allowed to return. Here in Rahat we feel like strangers, we feel that we do not belong to this town at all. I do not see my future in this town, I want to go back to my ancestral land; even living in a tent is much better than this nightmare called Rahat. I am "strange" in Rahat, I have no land, and I live on other Bedouin land, even though we bought it from the government. There is no value in living in this town, as we do not have land of our own here.
>
> (INTERVIEW WITH AHMAD, MARCH 2014)

Other Bedouin reclaim their identity by taking their children to see their ancestral land: "The children must know where we lived before the Nakba, they must memorize the names of the valleys and names of different routes." As one interviewee explained:

> I live in Rahat today, but my land in Tal al-Malah is still empty and we are not allowed to enter it except once or twice a year only, on holidays, such as al-Adha. Every ʿEid I take my children to our land east of Beersheba, we take pictures and I remind my sons that here was my house, here are our dams, wells, olive trees and grape vines. All that remains to us is 'memory,' we will not forget the piece of land. I was born on it, I will say until my last breath that it is my land and I wish to be buried there.
>
> (INTERVIEW WITH MUHAMAD ABU NASSAR, JUNE 2013)

During the last two decades, visits to Bedouin native lands have taken different shapes and have even turned into permanent living arrangements. Many Bedouin families, disillusioned by the empty promises of Israeli authorities, began to employ much more effective forms of resistance by building their tents and wooden shacks on their ancestral land. Sayah al-Tori recounted the story of how his tribe had gone back to their land at al-ʿAraqib after it had become tired of government pledges. This Bedouin shaikh was evicted from his land in the 1950s but had been promised that he could return in a few months. However, the struggle to return continued until the tribe understood that the Israeli authorities would not allow it. When I interviewed the shaikh in 2009, he said that they were fed up with Israeli promises:

> I have been waiting for more than forty years to be allowed to return to my land, but this dream has never come true. The Israeli authorities promised us a couple of times we could return to our land, but it was only on paper. As a consequence, we decided to return into our native land and to build our houses without having the authorities permit. This is our land, and I will live here forever, and I will not wait for the Israeli authorities to defraud us any longer. Now we are cultivating our land and remembering our past, whether the authorities want it or not.
>
> (INTERVIEW WITH SAYAH AL-TORI, JULY 2009)

Al-ʿAraqib village was neither the first nor the last case in which the Bedouin finally started to return to their land.[2] Enforcement tactics did not stop the Bedouin from continuing their lives.

Another village that faced destruction was Twayel Abu Jarwal, near the village of Laqiya. The al-Talalqa tribe lived in the village for generations before the establishment of the state of Israel. They have resisted attempts to make them leave their land and have confronted the destruction of their village more than thirty times. They continue to resist, putting their shacks and tents back together again. Each time they rebuild, the government returns, harassing them, uprooting fences, and demolishing the village yet again. From time to time, government agents come to make sure the work is complete and that there are no Bedouin still living there. This tribe has also been subject to arrest for rebuilding their houses and working on their land. Recently, the police arrested fifteen members of the tribe, claiming they had attacked JNF workers over a land dispute. The police maintained that "the sabotage and violence were perpetrated by an organized, hierarchic group which operated secretly."[3]

In both of these cases, Bedouin rejected state policies by going back to their historical land.[4] They marginalized the state's policies and adopted silent resistance. They claimed their land and visited it with their children. Land claims represented one form of resistance adopted by the Bedouin after the abolition of the military government, and beginning in the 1970s, numerous Bedouin land claims appeared in Israeli courts.[5] But these were not sufficient. The Bedouin had to physically to return to their ancestral land and cultivate it again, arguing that it was their land:

> Everywhere I go with my family and we cultivate our land; this is what remains from our past. In order not to marginalize our historical claims for our land, cultivation is the symbol of our land and past. At least we will not give up, this is the piece of land where we grew up and played together, and I remember every metre of it, the valleys, the dams, the wells, and I could even tell you the number of trees we planted there. These olive trees, vines, and fig trees are the symbol and testimony that it is our land; it does not matter what the Israelis think. (INTERVIEW WITH YOUSEF, MAY 2014)

Memory has taken another shape among the 1948 generation, who still use the historical names of their demolished villages and land. It is immediately recognizable that the past is still alive and remains within their memories. They do not used any of the names Israel has created in order to change the identity of places in the Naqab. Mentioning the original names of valleys, villages, dams, wells, and roads is one form of memory that challenges the Israeli policy of "Hebrew-izing" the historical names of al-Naqab.

The majority of my interviewees negated the "Hebrew-izing" of their villages and land names. When they refer to Beersheba, they always say Biʾr al-Sabaʿ. It is the same for Wadi al-Shalala, Bir al-Mshash, Tal al-Malah, Wadi al-Shariaʾ, Kharbit Zummara, al-Hdeiba, Tal Abu Jaber, and many more.

## The Unrecognized Bedouin Villages

After the abolition of military rule, the Israeli authorities planned and recognized a few Bedouin villages. According to Moshe Arens (2013), "Only a process of Westernization, or in this case Israelization, can bring normality to Bedouin society."[6] However, after the Israeli authorities had created the seven permanent Bedouin towns, the phenomenon of unrecognized villages emerged. Despite being full Israeli citizens, all Bedouins who refused to move into the planned towns were categorized by the authorities as illegal and unrecognized. Most of the unrecognized villages were created before the establishment of the state of Israel. Some came about because of special orders issued by the military governors in the 1950s, as in the case of ʿAtir Um al-Hiran (Nasasra 2012). At that time, the military governors pushed the remaining Bedouin to move to the enclosed zone, and this led to the development of new unrecognized villages.

Today, the thirty-six unrecognized villages accommodate half of the Arab Bedouin citizens of Israel. They are deprived of basic services such as housing, water, electricity, education, and health care directly because of the conflict over land ownership and indigenous rights. Bedouin residents of unrecognized villages resisted moving to the planned towns because doing so meant that they would lose their land rights.

The government took a significant step toward resolution of these challenges in 2000 by beginning the process of recognizing another set of Bedouin villages (Abu Saad and Creamer 2012, 40–41). Recognition (both full and partial) was granted to ten new villages: Elgren, Um Bateen, Um Metnan, Qasser Al Ser, Tlaaʾ Rashid, Abu Tlool, Alforaʾa, ʿAmrah, Beir Haddaj, and Drijat. While the government now legally recognizes these villages, it has made no investment in them even though they accommodate thousands of Bedouin citizens. Essential medical and welfare services are still lacking today in most of these villages.

According to a Human Rights Watch report (2008), the overall umbrella for the proposed new villages was the Abu Basma Regional Council. This council began to operate early in 2004. A Jewish mayor heads the council, and there is no significant administrative role for the Bedouin residents. Even though the official recognition process has begun, the procedures needed for obtaining full recognition, such as having full representation, remain complicated. In some cases, this is because of disputed land ownership. In others, it is because of slow-moving or blocked procedures. For the regional council, legal recognition of the ten villages does not seem likely to settle the conflict over recognition of historical Bedouin villages.

## The Oslo Era and Raising Awareness of the Bedouin Struggle

The rise of indigenous Bedouin politics and efforts to establish a Bedouin political party accelerated following the signing of the Oslo Accords (1993, 1995). Awareness of Bedouin marginalization and the struggle for recognition also increased considerably.

Interviews that I conducted in the Naqab confirmed that the Oslo Accords strongly contributed to the politicization of the Bedouin community. Former MK ʿAbd al-Wahab Darawsha maintained that since the early 1990s, the Naqab has witnessed an Arab political awakening among the youth. According to him, many of these young people were against voting for the Mapai party and the fragmented politics of the shaikhs (interview with ʿAbd al-Wahab Darawsha, October 25, 2014, Iksal). At the same time, the Bedouin organized community conferences in an attempt to establish a unified party that would speak on their behalf (*Kul al-ʿArab*, February 16, 1996). Talab al-Sanne, the local MK from the Bedouin village of Lakiya, believed that political awareness of the Naqab Bedouin had increased since the Oslo Accords. He felt that this new awareness could be attributed to the ongoing marginalization of the Bedouin cause (interview with Talab al-Sanne, *Kul al-ʿArab*, February 16, 1996). According to Darawsha, a number of Palestinian leaders, such as Jibril al-Rjob and Saeb Erikat, arrived in the Naqab after the Oslo Accords were signed. This contributed to awareness among the Palestinian leadership of the marginalized situation in the Naqab (interview with ʿAbd al-Wahab Darawsha, October 25, 2014, Iksal).

After the Oslo Accords, there were significant efforts to establish a political list for all the Naqab Bedouin in 1996. As Darawsha put it, the Naqab had witnessed not only an Islamic awakening but also an educational, Arab, and national awakening (interview with Darawsha, October 25, 2014, Iksal). Activists and local educated leaders began to establish an independent Bedouin party in the Naqab. This local grassroots initiative led to the establishment of a political party called Nida al-Wifaq on August 5, 1995, in the village of Lakiya. The local activist Saed al-Zabarqa was its head, and its general secretary was Hassan Abu Saad. Its main agenda was to improve the situation in the Naqab and represent the Bedouin community (Nida al-Wifaq, 1995).[7] *Davar* reported that 200 people from the Naqab had attended the launch of the party. In an impressive initial move, Nida al-Wifaq declared that one of the party's aims was to put the Bedouin on the political map of the Arabs in Israel (*Davar*, August 27, 1995).

Nida al-Wifaq represented a new form of indigenous politics that struggled against the traditional politics of the shaikhs. According to Mohamad al-Sayed, a local journalist writing in 1995, the Naqab saw growing nationalism following the Oslo Accords. This was directly linked to the prevailing political situation. Clashes occurred between police and the local youth in Rahat, where Mohammad Abu Jammaʾ had been killed after the Haram al-Ibrahimi massacre (*Panorama*, August 18, 1995). Hassan Abu Saad observed that the several days of *intifada* in the Naqab following the al-Ibrahimi massacre contributed to increasing nationalism among the Bedouin during the mid-1990s (interview with Hassan Abu Saad, Lakiya, April 20, 2014).

Meetings took place between PLO representatives and local leaders in Nazareth and in the Naqab. In the villages of Lakiya, PLO representatives were hosted by MK Talab al-Sanne to celebrate the peace process (interview with Abu Ahmad, Lakiya, April 2014). Former MK ʿAbd al-Wahab Darawsha discussed in an interview how a number of Palestinian leaders, including Jibril al-Rjob and Saeb Erikat, visited the Naqab to find out more about the situation there. He noted that such visits to the minority were an active part of the peace process. He regarded the visits as the Naqab's backing the Oslo Accords. It also signaled a strengthening of the relationship among the

Palestinians in Israel, the West Bank, and Gaza (interview with ʿAbd al-Wahab Darawsha, October 25 2014, Iksal).

Talal al-Kirnawi, the mayor of Rahat in 1995, described in another interview how Yitzhak Rabin was welcomed to Rahat. Rabin was praised as a hero of the peace process by thousands thronging the streets of the town. This was one of the most memorable moments of the peace celebrations in Rahat (interview with Talal al-Kirnawi, March 2015). Rabin sold the peace process to the Palestinians in Israel, but not to the Israeli Jewish population.

Bedouin delegations, including leading Bedouin shaikhs, visited Yasser Arafat and congratulated him on signing the peace accords. Shaikh Sulaiman Mustafa al-Nasasrah delivered a speech in 1994 in front of the Palestinian leadership in Ramallah about the situation of the Bedouin and their struggle for recognition (Shaikh Sulaiman Mustafa al-Nasasrah, private collection, Rahat). The Arab Democratic Party sent their greetings to Arafat during their third general party conference in Nazareth. The party stressed the importance of continuing the peace process and establishing a Palestinian state (The Arab Democratic Party Conference, Nazareth, December 1994).[8]

Arab leaders and politicians in Israel criticized the exclusion of the Arab minority from the peace process because they feared their continued marginalization. At a public event organized in Nazareth in 1994, Ramez Jaraysi, the former mayor, stated, "I fear that as a minority we will be the first to pay the price of the peace process with the Palestinians through further discriminatory policies and continued land discrimination" (*al-Ittihad*, September 11, 1994).

The Oslo Accords focused attention on the situation in the Naqab. They also encouraged the Palestinian leadership to visit the Naqab and support the Bedouin cause. Those acts of solidarity continue partly because of their shared struggle.

## The Goldberg/Prawer Initiative

The government initiated the Goldberg/Prawer plan in 2007. The aim of the plan was to deal with the issue of land claims and unrecognized Bedouin villages. The Goldberg/Prawer committee is one more in the long list of committees that deal with Bedouin land claims. Many mainstream Israeli politicians regard it as the most likely committee so far to force a solution to the conflict with the Bedouin. Ehud Olmert, a former prime minister, established the Goldberg Commission in December 2007.[9] He tasked the commission with finalizing the status of Bedouin land claims in the Naqab (Nasasra 2012).

The Bedouin sought to confirm that 800,000 *dunams* of land (a small portion of their historical lands) were recognized and recorded in the state registry. A report submitted in 2008 recommended that the government formally recognize some of the Bedouin land. The registry offices would list around 200,000 *dunams* (50,000 acres) as Bedouin territory. This was less than half of Bedouin land claims submitted since the 1970s.

The Goldberg Commission also recommended recognition of a limited number of the unrecognized villages.[10] The government formed a panel in January 2009 headed by Ehud Prawer, chief of the Policy Planning Department within the prime minister's office. The Prawer panel worked to implement the Goldberg recommendations by offering to settle less than 27 percent of the Bedouin claims. The Bedouin, represented by the Regional Council of Unrecognized Villages and other local grassroots organizations, refused the offer. The Bedouin community could see that the Goldberg and Prawer recommendations would mean another catastrophe (*nakba*) for them (interview with Huda, March 2013).

Yisrael Beiteinu, the political party led by Foreign Minister Avigdor Lieberman, urged the government to cancel the offer later in 2011 in response to the possible implementation of the Goldberg recommendations. The party recommended reducing the amount of land to be recognized (Nasasra 2012). Right-wing members of the Knesset and local Israeli council leaders in the Naqab also came out against the plan. This pressure from right-wing Israeli politicians paid off. The commission made modifications to the official recommendations of their report that included a reduction of the amount of land available to Bedouin communities. They also made a reduced offer of compensation to the Bedouin in order to persuade them to leave their land.

## The Peaceful Movement

In 2010, it became apparent that public action would be vital in preventing this discriminatory bill from passing into law.[11] It was essential to appeal to the media in order to influence public opinion by dismantling misconceptions about the Bedouin community. Such public actions caught the attention of both national and international media outlets. The rights of the indigenous people of the Naqab became a much discussed and contested issue.

The controversial Prawer plan received extensive national and international media coverage throughout 2013. In an unprecedented show of solidarity, Palestinians in Israel, the West Bank, Gaza, and the diaspora rallied alongside those marching in the Naqab. As the Bedouin MK Talab Abu ʿArar explained, it was Bedouin awareness of their rights as a minority that prompted massive demonstrations against the Prawer plan. He argued that the bill had been contested by international as well as local organizations since its aim was to confiscate "what remained of Bedouin land, which [was] done under the cover of Israeli law" (interview with MK Talab Abu ʿArar, Jerusalem, February 2014). Similarly, ʿAbed al-Wahab Darawsha, a former MK from the Arab Democratic Party, pointed out that the Naqab today had undergone an intensive change. He said that the emergence of young leadership contributed immensely to the Naqab cause. The best example was the way in which the Naqab unified against the Prawer plan: "We have seen motivated youth who are seeking recognition and their rights" (interview with MK ʿAbd al-Wahab Darawsha, Iksal, February 2014).

The UN issued several statements that called directly for the withdrawal of the Prawer plan. It demanded immediate steps to connect unrecognized villages to the electricity and water grids while improving their infrastructure. Speaking in Geneva on July 25, 2013, Navi Pillay stated that "if this bill becomes law, it will accelerate the demolition of entire Bedouin communities, forcing them to give up their homes, denying them their rights to land ownership, and decimating their traditional cultural and social life in the name of development."[12] Other local organizations such as ACRI (the Association of Civil Rights in Israel) and Bimkom (planners for planning rights) campaigned for cancellation of the Prawer plan and urged people to boycott the bill.[13]

The bill edged through its first Knesset vote in June 2013, forty-three votes to forty. It was thought that the bill would become law before the end of the year. This emphasized the urgent need for public mobilization. Bedouin initiatives arose that included boycotting the government's plans at different levels and organizing protests in Arab villages across the country.

Protesters held demonstrations outside the Knesset in November 2013 while the bill was debated. There were also protests outside the Supreme Court during the hearings concerning the planned demolition of the unrecognized village of Um al-Hiran.[14]

Yitzhak Aharonovitch, the minister for public security, warned of the deteriorating situation and escalating demonstrations in the Naqab. He warned that "problems, fire in the south and the blocking of roads, [were] in response to efforts to regularize the Bedouin communities." He stressed the need for another 400 police officers in the southern region based on worst-case scenarios and increasing protests (*Haaretz*, July 18, 2013).

Public action against the Prawer plan gained momentum in the summer of 2013 with the organizing of national Day of Rage protests under the banner of "Prawer Won't Pass." On July 15, 2013, the High Follow-Up Committee for Arab Citizens of Israel declared a public strike concurrent with demonstrations held in Biʾr al-Sabaʿ, Gaza City, Ramallah, Jerusalem, Jaffa, Bethlehem, and the Galilee. The largest protest took place in Biʾr al-Sabaʿ. The authorities declared this protest when the protestors staged a peaceful sit-in intended to block the main street by Ben Gurion University.[15] Protestors held further demonstrations on August 1 in Biʾr al-Sabaʿ, Wadi ʿArra, the Triangle area of central Israel, the West Bank, and in many cities around the world. Ten demonstrators were arrested in the northern Arab village of ʿAraʾra. The Haifa District Court released them under house arrest the following day. On August 31, around 1,000 demonstrators took to the streets in the center of Tel Aviv. Bedouin from al-ʿAraqib and other unrecognized villages led the protests.[16]

The Day of Rage protests reached a high point on November 30, 2013, the eve of the Knesset's second vote on the Prawer plan. Protesters organized in Israel, in the Occupied Territories, and in two dozen other locations worldwide. According to *Haaretz*, thousands protested the plan in the Naqab (in Hura), Jerusalem, and Haifa. At least twenty-eight people were arrested, and police officers were wounded. Avigdor Lieberman responded to the Day of Rage by claiming, "The fight is over Jewish land."[17]

The police continued to arrest activists in the Naqab and the north after the Day of Rage. The astonishing brutality displayed by the riot police was highly controversial for the Israeli public. Some right-wing groups criticized this violence, stating that the response of the riot police had been entirely disproportionate to the peaceful nature of the demonstrations. The image that most encapsulated the arbitrary nature of the arrests was the troubling footage of a young teenager violently arrested in Hura.[18] Other international actions to denounce and oppose Israel's Prawer plan occurred alongside these protests. One was a letter signed by fifty high-profile British actors, writers, and musicians urging Israel to cancel the plan. This helped to raise awareness of the issue in Britain and beyond.[19]

The Israeli General Security Service threatened political activists involved in the movement against the Prawer plan, particularly those organizing the demonstrations. It sent letters informing the activists that it had identified them and that they would be arrested if they attended the protests. The police even called in activists for interrogation. Such open intimidation intended to deter activists from political activity conflicts with the basic duty of the police to protect freedom of expression in the public sphere. The police threatened bus companies hired to take protestors from various towns and villages around Israel to Day of Rage demonstrations. They claimed that they would treat the transport companies as accomplices in "an illegal activity."[20]

The Joint List led the most recent organized struggle against the Prawer plan after its election to the Knesset in March 2015.[21] The Joint List is active in pursuing the preservation of Bedouin culture. It opposes the Prawer plan's forced relocation of up to 30,000 Naqab Bedouin. On March 26, 2015, the Joint List led the four-day March for Recognition protest for Palestinian Bedouin rights. According to the organizers, the aim of the protest was to raise awareness of the terrible living conditions in unrecognized Bedouin villages and to present a plan to President Reuven Rivlin for formal recognition of the villages.[22] Ayman Odeh, an adamant opponent of the Prawer plan, seeks the termination of all ongoing demolition and relocation projects in the Naqab. On the first day of the march, Odeh stated, "We are indulging in a popular democratic civilian movement to recognize these villages. I am confident at the end of the journey, the villages will be recognized, and everyone will benefit from this achievement" (Deger 2015).[23]

The main goal of this protest was for the Israeli government to give formal recognition to the unrecognized Bedouin villages. This would allow building permits that would enable the Bedouin people to preserve their way of life. After the election of the Joint List, a number of MKs visited the Naqab and prioritized their struggle according to the agenda of the Joint List's campaign for the Naqab cause. As MK Yousef Jabareen stated, "the Naqab context and the struggle against Prawer helps to unify us as a joint list. The urgent need to deal with the situation in the Naqab is more important than our internal disagreement on various issues" (MK Yousef Jabareen, interview in Hura, June 25, 2015).

## Organized Community and the Emergence of Youth Leadership

The Bedouin formed the Bedouin High Committee (*lajnat al-tawjeh al-ʾulya la ʿarab al-naqab*) to stop the Prawer plan from going any further. The committee included representatives from the community, political parties, NGOs, local institutions such as Shatil, women's organizations, activists, the Islamic movement, Bedouin lawyers, and members of the Knesset. Other Arab political and legal bodies, such Balad, Adalah, and the Islamic Movement, were accused of radicalizing the struggle and pushing the Bedouin to protest.[24]

The northern and southern branches of the Islamic movement both took part in recruiting people for demonstrations. The Islamic movement played a crucial role in encouraging people to demonstrate by using its media sources and its mosques as bases for activities (interview with Yousef Abu Jammaʾ, Rahat, April 2014). The Islamic movement was the most organized group in the campaign against the Prawer plan. It is hard to imagine that any vital decisions could have been made in the Naqab without its views being taken into account. Using mosques as recruiting points for demonstrations is still the movement's strongest form of organization.

The young leaders, *al-hirak al shababi*, directed the other powerful form of organization against the Prawer plan. This motivated leadership emerged because of internal struggles among the old guard and as more young people became involved in protest marches. Though not formally declaring themselves as new leaders, they used their own initiative and led the struggle against the Prawer plan and were arrested by the police at the protests. Their activity not only signaled the loss of control over the youth but also challenged the old leadership. Huda Abu Obeid, a leading organizer of the *hirak*, remarked, "The state treats us like an object that can be moved from place to place . . . they are denying us the basic right to decide our own fate, to decide where we will live, what we will do with our property and our basic right to a home."[25] Suddenly, key Israeli and international newspapers were interviewing young Bedouin leaders about their rejection of the Prawer plan. They stated clearly that they would continue to protest peacefully to stop it.

Although political organization emerged among the Bedouin during the Prawer contestation, there was evidence of leadership fragmentation at the institutional level. Two heads were elected to the Regional Council for the Unrecognized Villages (RCUV) in the crisis period—ʿAtiya al-ʿAssam and Ibrahim al-Wagili. The community perceived al-Wagili, RCUV's former leader, as linked to the Arab Democratic Party. Thus, the level of trust in his ability to lead the villages in their struggle against the Prawer plan was minimal. Al-Wagili was also accused of promoting the Prawer plan during some of his visits to the villages. He was seen as leading the pragmatic line for resolving Prawer issues and making further concessions. Because of these factors, ʿAtiya al-ʿAssam—regarded as affiliated with the Islamic Movement—was elected as the new head of the RCUV. This led to an ongoing leadership crisis and a representational conflict because al-Wagili refused to recognize his leadership (interview with Sami, Beersheba, March 2014). The fragmentation of traditional leadership resulted in the emergence of the young organizers who directed the demonstrations on the ground.

Arab and Jewish political parties began to pay more attention to the Bedouin situation. They tried to talk about the struggle of the Arabs and the Jews in the Naqab as a unified front. This timing enabled the Arab parties and the Joint List to speak out about the marginalization of the Naqab alongside the Bedouin who were trying to promote the Naqab cause.

One of the positive effects of the Prawer plan was that the Israeli Jewish community began to hear about the Naqab and the Bedouin communities. Suddenly, senior Israeli politicians were talking about how the government had marginalized the Bedouin for years. Meanwhile, the Israeli public was also learning more about the Bedouin and the need for recognition of their rights, even though decades of profound neglect were evident in the Israeli media reports. Following the demonstrations in Hura, the Israeli government suddenly recognized the presence and the reality of Bedouin communities and Israeli citizens that did not exist on the maps.

The Bedouin High Committee continues to organize community meetings to raise awareness of the need for recognition of Bedouin villages and to continue the struggle against Prawer. Bedouin mayors often host the committee meetings. The committee held two of its meetings in 2016 in Hura, where the mayor, Dr. Mohammad al-Nabari, played an important role. The support of Bedouin mayors strengthens and encourages the community to continue the struggle against the Prawer plan.

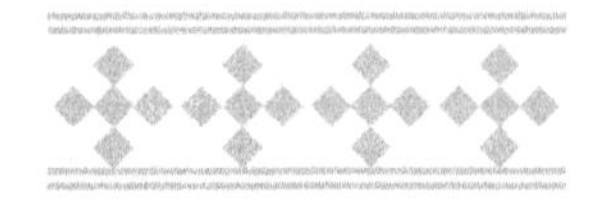

ELEVEN

# The Ongoing Denial of Bedouin Rights and Their Nonviolent Resistance

IN THIS BOOK I HAVE argued that we should rethink the relationship between the state and the indigenous minorities within its boundaries. Despite conventional wisdom I found that the Arab indigenous Bedouin of the Naqab and Biʾr al-Sabaʿ had succeeded in modifying the policies of the Ottoman rulers, the British Mandate, and Israeli military rule by employing creative forms of nonviolent and everyday resistance. The success of Bedouin indigenous resistance teaches us much about power and resistance. Bedouin actions must be framed in more complex ways. In particular, it is essential to start looking at nonviolent and everyday indigenous resistance. Power must be viewed differently, not as a thing or a capability. Doing so leads only to the crude assumption that the Bedouin were always passive and had no power. Instead, power must be understood as a relationship. This view offers a more nuanced and complex understanding of the dynamics of the Israeli state and its indigenous Bedouin citizens.

Indigenous and native people pose a challenge to settler states. Long after the establishment of the state, indigenous peoples continue to live on their land and refuse to relinquish their historical claims. This challenge leads settler states to impose tight controls on indigenous communities and to try to extinguish their way of life. The settler state aims to secure more land for its citizens and so must reject the demands of indigenous national communities by attempting to control, deny, or oppress them.

A number of different conclusions can be drawn from examining how the Ottoman rulers, the British Mandate, Israeli military rule, and modern Israel each dealt with Bedouin tribes in the Naqab. Conventional wisdom says that there was no Bedouin resistance to any of these authorities. While conventional wisdom may acknowledge a few incoherent and ineffective actions, it does not consider consistent and creative nonviolent resistance. The book's findings, however, suggest otherwise. Like other indigenous and national communities in the Middle East and elsewhere, the Naqab Bedouin used multiple forms of resistance to protect their historical land and identity. Their relationships with Ottoman, British, and Israeli military rule were more complex than it first appears. Bedouin actions and resistance were followed by state action.

In the final analysis, the Ottoman era was a period of greater freedom and autonomy for the Bedouin in southern Palestine. The Naqab Bedouin of the Ottoman era exercised their power, clashed with the government over land and resources, and dominated the main trade routes across the desert. Ottoman policies in southern Palestine were aimed at limiting tribal domination over the desert. A long-term goal was the Ottomanization policies of the Bedouin by Istanbul through investment in education and other public services, such as the railways and rebuilding the old city of Biʾr al-Sabaʿ as an administrative and economic center. As the Ottomans began to invest more in this part of the country, Gaza, Hebron, and Beersheba played a significant administrative and economic role in Bedouin life.

The British Mandate adopted a different approach toward the Bedouin in southern Palestine. The indigenous Bedouin system was maintained and strengthened by the colonial power. Incorporating the Bedouin into the colonial administrative structure proved to be more successful than in the Ottoman era. The town of Beersheba was run by Bedouin mayors who gained support from the colonial authorities. The colonial authorities also set about enhancing the education system. At the same time, the British avoided clashing with the indigenous system of conflict resolution and with the land system. They even strengthened these systems by enhancing tribunal relations with the Bedouin tribes in Transjordan and Sinai. There was also cooperation between the British and French colonial powers in relation to Bedouin tribes in Palestine, Syria, and Lebanon.

Bedouin played a significant role in Palestinian institutions in Jerusalem and Gaza during the British colonial era. They were an important element in events in Palestine during the Great Revolt. A review of the political role of the Bedouin in the 1930s shows that Bedouin leaders boycotted the White Paper, joined Palestinian delegations, sent official letters to London, and joined in the Great Revolt in 1936. They played a significant role by using their power to secure their territory and space. Though the Mandatory authorities perceived the Bedouin as a separate community, the Bedouin were an organic part of official Palestinian institutions in Jerusalem.

The situation of the Bedouin was more complex under Israeli military rule since 1948. Like other Palestinian communities, most of the Bedouin educated elite had fled or been forcibly expelled from their land. After the war, the Bedouin faced the trauma of the Nakba. Some found themselves trapped between the borders. Others became internally displaced persons. Many tried to return home over the new borders but were regarded by the military rule as infiltrators (*muhajareen*). Some were pushed to leave the western Naqab to live in the enclosed zone of the *siyaj*. Others were pushed into positions of uncertain citizenship, especially the ʿAzazma.

The Bedouin of the Naqab and Biʾr al-Sabaʿ managed to survive under harsh military regulations by cooperating with the system when it served their purposes and resisting when it did not. New findings by Ahmad Saʾdi (2015) list a significant number of acts of protest and demonstrations against the military rule in the north and the Galilee. This represents a significant development in our understanding of the situation of the Palestinian minority and their resistance to military rule. The Bedouin resisted the system on a variety of levels. This was not a situation unique to the north and the Galilee.

I found that the Bedouin, resisted military rule through political actions and nonviolent, cultural, and everyday economic resistance. The Bedouin continue to act against the Prawer plan by involving significant components of the community in their protests.

I found a range of tactics and methods that targeted military regulations, although some of them were neither political nor particularly influential. Noncooperation methods were among the strongest acts directed against the military rule system. Methods of noncooperation are both social and political. Noncooperation that focused on ignoring the military government's orders and regulations proved to be a successful method for the Bedouin.

Noncooperation was political. Bedouin refused to supply military rule officials with details about tribes and internal issues. This included the refusal of Bedouin shaikhs to follow instructions given by military officials. The Bedouin boycotted censuses and registration exercises conducted by the military government for the purpose of control. Bedouin women played a significant part by not cooperating with military rule. Bedouin shaikhs and leaders maintained their relationships with their families and relatives across the borders despite strict regulations.

Remnant Bedouin gathered more agency against the regulations imposed on them. They cooperated with their relatives across borders for economic purposes and hosted *muhajareen*. This phenomenon continued until military rule came to an end. Military rule was unable to restrict the movement of goods that maintained the cross-border economy. Bedouin cross-border relations represented a significant form of survival and challenged the modern state borders. These noncooperation tactics led to harsh retaliation. The authorities invited shaikhs to meetings where they were ordered to tighten their control over their tribes or face dire consequences. The Bedouin ignored these warnings and broke the military regulations every day.

My research suggests that the last decade of military rule saw greater awareness and knowledge among the Bedouin of their land rights as a national and indigenous minority. Bedouin actions became more politically organized. They escalated their campaign for legal recognition and the right to return to their historical lands. Israeli archival records reveal that after 1956, Bedouin started to claim their land through tribal conferences and petitions to the Israeli authorities. They reacted to the exploitation of their land by resisting the military rule system in an organized way. They also campaigned for their right to education. The continued marginalization of Bedouin education led the shaikhs to appeal to the government to improve their education system. At the same time, they also found avenues for better education by sending their boys away to Arab schools in the north.

In the closing years of the military rule, Bedouin reactions to Israeli urbanization and sedentarization plans gave rise to organized Bedouin movements. During this time, Bedouin resistance to the prospect of urbanization increased. Bedouin leaders became better organized in the struggle to gain their land rights. They warned military officials publicly that their land rights needed to be dealt with before there could be any implementation of urbanization plans. Slowly, Bedouin started to revisit their indigenous land. They put forward memory claims, relived their past, and symbolically claimed their right of return.

Despite intense scrutiny of this particular period, most existing scholarship has overlooked the phenomenon of Bedouin nonviolent action. Regarding the Bedouin as passive and weak does not help us to understand how they resisted military rule. A new discourse is needed, and it is essential to start by looking at nonviolent actions. Under military rule Bedouin nonviolent resistance was consistent, complex, and successful enough to provoke harsh reprisals. Our understanding of the initial years of the Bedouin-Israeli dynamic from 1948 to 1967 should help us to understand more clearly the modern relationship between the Naqab Bedouin and the state of Israel.

After 1948, the Naqab Bedouin faced two decades of discriminatory policies. From its inception, the new state attempted to demolish Bedouin culture and identity. The state perceived the Bedouin as both a security risk and a demographic threat. But the Naqab Bedouin have maintained their identity through traditional practices such as songs, poetry, and wedding festivals.

## The Court Denial of Bedouin Land Rights and the Internationalization of Their Struggle

Decades after the end of military rule, Israeli authorities continue to deny Bedouin their rights. At the same time, the Bedouin struggle for recognition is taking new forms. An examination of how the Bedouin cause in the Naqab has developed over the last few years will show that their struggle has taken three forms: internationalization of the Bedouin case through conferences and forums; international and local organizations producing new research on the Bedouin situation; and local grassroots movements. The Bedouin are also lodging appeals in the Israeli courts in an attempt to secure their indigenous land rights, as in the cases of ʿAtir Um al-Hiran and al-Oqbi.

In recent years, the Bedouin have campaigned locally and internationally for a rejection of the Prawer plan. They have presented their cause to the United Nations, the UK Parliament's House of Commons, the European Parliament, Amnesty International, and the Minority Rights Group in London. Several international workshops addressing the Bedouin cause from a variety of perspectives have been organized overseas, including at the University of Exeter in the UK and at Columbia University in New York. This has produced an influx of new research on the Bedouin community, mostly within European and American institutions.[1] International organizations such as the Norwegian Refugee Council and the Minority Rights Group have produced new scholarship in this field that links the Bedouin cause to other Palestinian Bedouin communities in the West Bank and Area C (Amara and Nasasra 2015).

Israeli authorities still reject the notion of granting the Bedouin land rights. I have argued that both the Ottomans and the British authorities in Palestine recognized the indigenous systems and land rights of the Bedouin. This is supported by Ottoman and British archival records that acknowledge that the Bedouin are the native communities in southern Palestine.

Although a number of local and international scholars have taken historical archival records from Istanbul, Ankara, and London to be used in legal and court discussions in Israel, this has not helped in granting the Bedouin any historical and indigenous rights. The cases of al-ʿAraqib and ʿAtir Um al-Hiran have been debated within the Israeli court system for years, but no recognition of Bedouin rights has yet been achieved.

A prolonged struggle in the Israeli court system over the case of the village of al-ʿAraqib (al-Oqbi) did not lead to the court recognizing Bedouin land and indigenous rights. No progress has so far been made on the specific case of al-Oqbi, even though the village's case is supported by Ottoman and British records. However, the case did spark an intellectual debate between scholars who supported the official position and those who supported the Bedouin.

The Supreme Court of Israel concluded in its summary that the al-Oqbi tribe did not have any rights to the land that they were claiming and were not entitled to a remedy (*Al-Oqbi v State of Israel* judgment of May 14, 2015). Bedouin land claims that were based on Bedouin customary law were rejected by the state despite Ottoman and British recognition of the Bedouin tribes in southern Palestine.

The al-Oqbi tribe had also tried to have their land rights recognized according to the UN Declaration on the Rights of Indigenous Peoples, hoping that the declaration would be considered by the Israeli courts. The case was rejected based on the argument that Israel had not voted in favor of the declaration and that it was therefore not part of the Israeli legal system. Given the court's conclusion that the declaration did not confer land rights, the question of Bedouin indigeneity was not addressed there (Margalit 2010, 3).

Visiting the unrecognized village of Um al-Hiran, I listened to an account by the local village representative:

> We were moved by the military rule officials in 1956, and were promised that we could settle here permanently. Now we face being expelled and relocated from our land again. The government's plans to remove us from our village, even though we have been living here since the 1950s, in order to build a Jewish settlement called Hiran on the remains of our village, is not realistic. Relocating us for settling others on our land is something that we will never accept, even if we remain as refugees for ever.
> (INTERVIEW IN ʿATIR UM AL-HIRAN, JUNE 10, 2015)

A second judgment dealt with the forced eviction of members of the Abu al-Kiyaʾan Bedouin tribe from the unrecognized village of Um al-Hiran (*Adalah Newsletter* 2015).[2] The Israeli government is planning to build a new Jewish settlement called Hiran at that location (Abu al-Kiyaʿan v State of Israel judgment of May 5, 2015). The Abu al-Kiyaʿan families had been moved in 1956 on the basis of a military order by the Israeli authorities from the area near today's Kibbutz Shoval (whose Arabic name is Wadi Suballa) to their current location in ʿAtir Um al-Hiran. Though the Abu al-Kiyaʿan families lived in this area for six decades, the authorities have refused to recognize their right to stay in their current villages. These actions show that the government is still treating its citizens as trespassers on their own land. This leads the Bedouin to distrust the government.

These two examples are the most recent court judgments for such claims. Both judgments were against the Bedouin.[3] The Israeli court system continues to reject Bedouin land claims despite significant archival data showing evidence of historic land ownership. The ongoing denial of Bedouin indigenous rights by the Israeli authorities speaks clearly of the injustice toward the community, and this injustice is likely to continue for years to come.

Marginalizing international law and the norms of indigenous and native people's rights will only escalate the struggle between the state and its local unrecognized citizens. Indigenous and national minorities have staying power. By using *sumud* and nonviolent resistance, the Bedouin can achieve significant success in protecting their communities, identities, and histories.

# Notes

## Introduction

1. The Bedouin use the historical terms "Biʾr al-Sabaʿ" and the "Naqab" to refer to the southern part of Palestine. The Naqab region, which extends from Biʾr al-Sabaʿ (Beersheba) to ʿAqaba and covers some 12,577 square kilometers, accounts for half of historic Palestine (Dabbagh 1965, 116–122). As mentioned in *Muʾjam al-buldan* (Dictionary of Countries), during the Islamic Empire Biʾr al-Sabaʿ was the base of operations for ʿAmr ibn al ʿAss, a Muslim commander and the governor of Egypt from 658 to 664 (Hamawi 1957, 185).

   British archival documents use the name "Beersheba" (see the discussion in chapter 1); in Arabic the place is known as "Biʾr al-Sabaʿ [بئر السبع]." Throughout the book, I will use "Biʾr al-Sabaʿ," "Beersheba," and the "Naqab" interchangeably to refer to area that the Bedouin have populated since the Ottoman era and before.

## 1. Understanding the State Project: Power, Resistance, and Indigeneity

1. For discussion on the emergence of the state debate, see Mitchell (1991, 77); also Skocpol (1985, 3).
2. On the question of whether states can achieve their goals see Skocpol (1985).
3. Useful cases providing more information on indigenous peoples' resistance, especially resistance to urbanization, include: Native Americans in the United States, First Nations Peoples in Canada, Aboriginal People in Australia, and the Palestinian Indigenous Peoples in Israel (see Abu Saad 2008).

4. For other cases of subaltern, poor, women, and peasant resistance see Bayat (2010); see also a wide literature by the "subaltern studies group" on peasant resistance in postcolonial India: especially Guha (1997) and Spivak (1988).
5. In defining the term, Scott points out that "*infrapolitics* . . . seems an appropriate shorthand to convey the idea that we are dealing with an unobtrusive realm of political struggle" (1990, 183).

## 2. Ruling the Desert: Ottoman Policies Toward the Frontiers

1. Historically, Biʾr al-Sabaʿ was the basis for ʿAmr ibn al ʿAss, a Muslim commander and the governor of Egypt from 658–664.
2. Hamad al-Sufi was a leading shaikh of the Tarabin and mayor of Biʾr al-Sabaʿ in 1913. The Ottoman authorities gave him the title of "pasha" and he served as the Amir of southern Palestine.
3. TL = Turkish lira

## 3. British Colonial Policies for the Southern Palestine and Transjordan Bedouin, 1917–1948

1. LP (or £P) = Palestine pounds (*livres*).

## 4. Envisioning the Jewish State Project

1. Zeʾev (Vladimir) Jabotinsky was born on October 18, 1880, in the city of Odessa, Russia.
2. Ben Gurion was born in Poland in 1886 and received a degree in law at the University of Constantinople. While in Poland, he founded a left-wing socialist party (Paole Zion). In 1915, he was exiled by the Turkish government and spent a few years in the United States. Later, he was one of the founders of the Palestine Labor Party (Mapai) (PRO, CO, 733/446/17).
3. Interview with Dr. Weizmann, March 8, 1945, conducted by Brigadier Clayton. Copies were sent by Anthony Eden to the minister resident in the Middle East, the high commissioner for Palestine, and His Majesty's representatives at Baghdad, Beirut, and Jedda (March 15, 1945).
4. The term *kasret al-Sabaʿ*, meaning the Nakba of Beersheba, was used by Bedouin elders about the fall of Beersheba, which the Bedouin remembered as the most crucial incident during the 1948 war. The fall of the Bedouin capital city marked the end of their economic, cultural and administrative center, as well as of their freedom. In narrating their stories to their sons—and to me when I interviewed

some of them—they used the term *kasret al-Saba*ʿ and not Nakba. This Bedouin dialect term is embedded in the minds of the older generation, and they did not even use the term "1948 war." In their minds, *kasret al-Saba*ʿ also means the Nakba of all Palestine, to which they referred using their own memory and words.

5. According to Moshe Dayan, some Bedouin were not welcome to stay because they were regarded as a "grave security risk"; he was referring to the ʿAzazma Bedouin in particular. The ʿAzazma were categorized by Dayan as a hostile tribe who did not give up their right to live on their land or to cross the borders freely between Egypt and Jordan. As Dayan noted, the ʿAzazma "wanted to settle accounts with us" as a result of the Israelis having periodically expelled them (Dayan 1976, 154).

## 5. The Emergence of Military Rule, 1949–1950

1. Sarah Lazar (2002), Habib Qahawaji (1972), Sabri Jiryis (1973; 1976), Yair Bauml (2002), Ahmad Saʿdi (2001), Shira Robinson (2013), and Alina Korn (1996; 2000) have all written in detail about military rule in Israel.
2. A committee was appointed by the defense minister in 1955, chaired by Justice Ratner, to study the problems of the military administration: it reported in 1956. The report, summarizing the system of military government and its goals and the options for reducing it, was sent by the Press Department to Prime Minister David Ben Gurion on February 24, 1956. Its final conclusion was that the military administration of the Arab minority should be maintained (Lazar 2002).
3. The Bedouin used this term to refer to the closed zone, which they were not allowed to enter. If they did, the military police punished them, and they risked being arrested. Israel employed this policy to prevent the Bedouin from returning to their land, which had been categorized as a closed zone. Sometimes this meant that a Jewish settlement could be built there.
4. Even under Israeli control, Biʾr al-Sabaʿ remained a central city in the Naqab. After 1948, the Bedouin who came to the city found themselves in a weak position, which had not been the case before the war. Neither the Ottomans nor the British had ever restricted entrance to the city for the Bedouin.

## 6. Reshaping the Tribes' Historical Order, 1950–1952: Border Issues, Land Rights, IDPs, and UN Intervention

1. *ʿAshira/ʿashair* refers to tribes as a social unit. The term *qabail* (singular *qabila*) refers to Bedouin confederations/clans existing in Palestine before 1948, and partly thereafter. I use the following tribal structure in my discussion: The *qabail* are divided into tribes (*ʿashair*); tribes are divided into *rubaʾs* and *rubaʾs* into clans. Each clan is made up of individual households or families.

2. Regarding the expulsion of the main *qabail* from the Naqab, Abu Sitta (2008) records that the majority of the Jabarat ended up in Jordan; of the Tarabin, most ended up in Gaza as refugees, a considerable number went to Jordan, and 100 families remained in Israel. Half the Tayaha were expelled to Gaza and Jordan, and half remained in Israel. The majority of al-ʿHanajreh left for Gaza; and the ʿAzazma were expelled into Sinai, Egypt, and Jordan (Abu Sitta 2008).
3. Ghazi Falah's (1989b) publication (in Arabic) provides a detailed list of the Bedouin tribes that left for, or were exiled to, Egypt, and Jordan during and after the war.
4. All the tribes ended up in the *siyaj*, and some were moved from their original land (western Naqab). Reports from the ISA slightly contradict what Falah (1989) found: eleven tribes that had lived in western Naqab before 1948 were evicted and transferred into the *siyaj* area. These tribes found themselves living within the state of Israel, while the majority of the other tribes fled. All the tribes who ended up concentrated in the *siyaj/sayeg* region were the remnants of the ninety-five tribes that had existed in Palestine during the latter years of the British Mandate (ISA GL 17003/1). This means that the other eight tribes (out of the recognized nineteen tribes) had remained on their land and were included in the geographic region of the enclosed zone. Later these tribes, like the others, lost their land.
5. The Hebrew word *blagim* (singular *belig*) in Hebrew refers to tribes or parts of tribes, i.e., the sections of tribes that remained in Israel after the Nakba.
6. As Tully notes, the political structure of indigenous peoples is important as part of their "self-conscious traditionalism" (2000, 58–59). This example shows clearly that the remaining Bedouins resisted Israeli policies of fragmenting and breaking up their historical order and structure.
7. The case of the ʿAzazma refusing to swear loyalty to the new state can be considered as self-determination (Falk 1988, 18; Tully 2000), as counter ideology, or as the indigenous claims of the ʿAzazma (Champagne 2003; Yiftachel 2003, 2008).
8. The United Nations defines IDPs as: "Persons or groups of persons who have been forced or obliged to flee or to leave their homes or places of habitual residence, in particular as a result of or in order to avoid the effects of armed conflict, situations of generalized violence, violations of human rights or natural or human-made disasters, and who have not crossed an internationally recognized State border" (Farber and Chen 2006, 154). According to this definition, the majority of the Bedouin became IDPs since most of them had left or been expelled from their native land and were forced to live on other areas of land that belonged to exiled tribes. Enacting the Absentees' Property Law in 1950 enabled Israel to control land belonging to Palestinian refugees as well as to IDPs. This law affected the Bedouin who, having been exiled from western Naqab into the enclosed zone, were categorized as IDPs. They had also lost their properties, which were controlled by the Custodian of Absentees' Properties (Abu Hussein and McKay 2003).

9. *Diyarna*, "our homeland," is the term for their place of existence. From this example, it is obvious that the Bedouin also used this concept in referring to *watan*—their land and the village from which they were expelled.
10. Report sent to the minister of justice, October 20, 1952, from Yousef Weitz, Benjamin Fishman, and Yihosua Palmon, in Ministry of Justice documents in the Israel State Archives (ISA G 5742/10). Yosef Weitz played a crucial role in establishing the Israel Land Authority (ILA). As one of the most important agencies dealing with the Bedouin, the ILA disrupted Bedouin who were continuing to live on their land by raiding them to try and impose land utilization on them. The ILA paradigm for such raids was that the Bedouin had built illegally on state land without permission (Jakubowska 1992, 90).
11. Al-Jahalin, a Bedouin tribe that had lived on their land in Tal ʿArad before the creation of Israel but, like other Bedouin tribes in the Naqab, were exiled in 1948. Some then settled in the eastern parts of the West Bank, but the majority moved into Jordan where they still live. Since the 1970s, around fifty families of al-Jahalin have lived on land at Abu Dis east of Jerusalem Today they still face expulsions and have refused Israeli plans to settle them (*Akhbar Al Naqab*, May 15, 2009). The culture, traditions, and historical tribal areas of the Jahalin Bedouin are discussed by Aref al-Aref (1999) who points out that the Jahalin Bedouin are one of the main tribal confederations that populated Tal ʿArad. Today, the Jahalin Bedouin are the group most affected by Israeli policies amongst the Palestinians within Area C, having lost their original lands after being displaced from Tel ʿArad (within present day Israel) and most of land they occupied more recently since their displacement to settlements and military use. The *Guardian* reported that al-Jahalin were refugees from the Negev desert whose grazing lands had been squeezed by expanding Palestinian towns, the rapid emergence of large Jewish settlements, and the vast concrete and steel barrier in the West Bank. Approximately 3,000 Bedouin, most from the Jahalin tribe, lived next to land taken by one of the largest Jewish settlements, Maʾale Adumim (which is illegal under international law), where they faced constant house demolitions and attempts to exile them (Rory McCarthy, "Negev Desert Nomads on the Move Again to Make Way for Israel's Barrier," *Guardian*, February 28, 2007, http://www.guardian.co.uk/world/2007/feb/28/israel).

## 7. Traditional Leadership, Border Economy, Resistance, and Survival, 1952–1956

1. According to Scott (1977, 124–125), the patron-client relationship is "an exchange relationship between roles—[it] may be defined as a special case of dyadic (two-person) ties involving a largely instrumental friendship in which an individual of higher socioeconomic status (patron) uses his own influence and resources to

provide protection or benefits, or both, for a person of lower status (client) who, for his part, reciprocates by offering general support and assistance, including personal services, to the patron." For more on the patron-client relationship and the role of quasi groups, see Schmidt et al. (1977).

2. There was a meeting of the military governor of the Negev with seventeen Bedouin shaikhs in Beersheba, June 2, 1955. Participating were the military governor Yihoshua Verbin, Sasson Ben Zvi, Emanuel Shababo, Yoav Katan, Benjamin Gur-Arieh. The seventeen Bedouin shaikhs included Musa al-ʿAtawna, Hassan Abu ʿAbdon, ʿAwadd Abu Rqaiq, Suliman al-Sanne, Suliman al-Oqbi, Mansor al-Sanne, Hlayel Abu ʿAmrah, Hammad Abu Rabiaʿ, Muhammad al-Afenish, Muhammad Abu Jweyaʾd, Jabir Abu Srihan, al-Assad, Muhammad al-ʾAssam, Oda Abu Maʿamar, ʿAli Abu Qrinat, ʿAmmer al-Talalqa, and Salman al-Huzayil.
3. The Tarabin, who lived to the south of Beersheba, had a long history of enmity against governments. A report dated March 14, 1913 by Sir G. Lowther, GCMG, CB, at Constantinople describes them as having an old grievance against the Ottoman government and its officials (see chapter 2).
4. Although not formally educated, this woman knew the words of all the songs by heart.

## 8. The Second Phase of Military Rule, 1956–1963

1. The letter was sent to Minister of Justice Rosen on April 21, 1958, by the following shaikhs: Musa al-ʿAtawna, Saqr al-Huzayil, Hajj ʿAbdallah ʿEid al-Sanne, Salim al-Oqbi, Jaber Abu Srihan, ʿAwadd Abu Rqaiq, Mansor al-Sanne, Jadoaʾ al-Huzayil, Salman Abu Bilal, Hassan Abu ʿAbdon, and Khalil Abu ʿAmrah.
2. According to a report by Verbin (the military governor of the Naqab), dated September 9, 1954, nine Bedouin students were issued with permits to live in the Nazareth area in 1954 and 1955. The list included Muhammad Ali Abu Qrinat, Salman Ali Abu Qrinat, Ali Salim Abu Qrinat, Muhammad Salman Abu Rabiaʾ, Younes Ibrahim Abu Rabiaʾ, Yousef Ibrahim Abu Rabiaʾ, ʿEid ʿAwda Abu Rabia, Mosa Saleh Abu ʿAjaj, and Suliman Salim Abu ʿAjaj (IDFA 490 /1956–33).
3. Mapai was the dominant political party in Israel until its merger with the modern day Israeli Labor Party in 1968. It was natural that Mapai and the military government would work together to persuade the Bedouin to join Mapai. Mapam was another Jewish party that sought Bedouin votes. Mapam was founded in 1948 through the merging of Hashomer Hatzaʾir Workers Party and Ahdut Ha-ʿAvoda Poale Zion Movement. Today it is the Meretz party. Mapam was the second biggest political force in Israel after the ruling party, Mapai.
4. The participants included Shaikhs ʿAli Abu Qrinat, Hammad Abu Rabia, Abu Jweya'd, Musa al-ʿAtawna, Muhammed al-Afenish, Mansor al-Sanne, Salim al-Oqbi, ʿOda Abu Maʿamar, Muhammad Abu Shiban, Hlayel Abu ʿAmrah, and Jaber Abu Srihan.

## 9. The End of Military Rule and Resistance to Urbanization Plans, 1962–1967

1. The letter was signed by eighteen Bedouin shaikhs on behalf of their tribes: Shaikh Salman al-Huzayil, Shaikh Hammad Abu Rabiaʾ, Shaikh Kayid al-ʿAtawna, Shaikh ʿAwadd Abu Rqaiq, Shaikh Ali Abu Qrinat, Shaikh Muhammad Abu Jweyaʾd, Shaikh Mansor al-Sanne, Shaikh Salman al-Oqbi, Shaikh Salman al-Assam, Shaikh Muhammad Abu Shiban, Shaikh Jaber Abu Srihan, Shaikh Muhammed al-Afenish, Shaikh Faraj al-Assad, Shaikh Oda Abu Maʿamar, Shaikh Hlayel Abu ʿAmrah, Shaikh Yousef Abu Bilal, Shaikh Slamma Abu al-Kiya'an, Shaikh Hassan Abu ʿAbdon.
2. In the case of al-ʿAraqib, despite the success of Bedouin *sumud* resistance, the village was demolished more than one hundred times ("Israel Police Raze 'Illegal' Bedouin Village in Negev," *BBC News*, July 27, 2010, http://www.bbc.co.uk/news/world-middle-east-10777040).

## 10. Postmilitary Rule, the Oslo Era, and the Contemporary Prawer Debate

1. *Ynet* (Israel News) reported on al-Talalqa Bedouin (near the village of Laqiya) who had fought for years to live on their land. They accused the Bedouin of attacking JNF and Green Patrol workers: "According to witnesses, the detainees embarked on a sabotage campaign against JNF and Green Patrol workers over their claim to lands near the Lakiya region." (Curiel 2010).
2. After the state realized that the Bedouin had gone back to living on their land and would not submit their land claims, it turned to expulsion activities. Al-ʿAraqib village, one of the symbols of Bedouin *sumud*, was virtually obliterated by the Israeli authorities. Neve Gordon describes the appearance of the village of al-ʿAraqib after it had been bulldozed: "The signs of destruction were immediately evident. I first noticed the chickens and geese running loose near a bulldozed house, and then saw another house and then another one, all of them in rubble. A few children were trying to find a shaded spot to hide from the scorching desert sun, while behind them a stream of black smoke rose from the burning hay. The sheep, goats and the cattle were nowhere to be seen—perhaps because the police had confiscated them" (Gordon 2010).
3. See Ilana Curiel, "Police Arrest Bedouins Suspected of Attacking JNF Workers," *Ynet News*, June 10, 2010, www.ynetnews.com/articles/0,7340,L-3907862,00.html.
4. There are many other cases of Bedouin going to live on their original land. For example, families of Abu Gardud (ʿAzazma) went to live on their land near Kibbutz Revivim. The clan of 500 members decided to return to their land and reclaim it in an attempt to escape from the chemical waste area of Ramat Hovav. The government claimed that the Bedouin were taking over state land, even though the land belongs to the Bedouin, not the state.

5. The land claims of families from al-ʿAraqib are still in the Beersheba district court, with no final decision from the government. See Tom Segev, "The Making of History: Who Owns This Country?" *Haaretz*, July 9, 2010, http://www.haaretz.com/magazine/week-s-end/the-making-of-history-who-owns-this-country-1.300956.
6. Moshe Arens, "A Bedouin Tragedy, an Israeli Tragedy," *Haaretz*, May 29, 2013, http://www.haaretz.com/opinion/a-bedouin-tragedy-an-israeli-tragedy.premium-1.526440.
7. Private collection, August 7, 1995 (Nida al Wifaq by Hassan Abu Saad, Lakiya).
8. Private papers of the Arab Democratic Party, reports about the third annual conference of the party, December 15–16, 1995, Nazareth.
9. Eliezer Goldberg is a former Israeli high court judge.
10. Mansour Nasasra, "Before You Expel the Bedouin . . . ," *Haaretz*, September 23, 2011, http://www.haaretz.com/opinion/before-you-expel-the-bedouin-1.386384.
11. For more details on the Prawer Bill, please see "The Prawer-Begin Bill and the Forced Displacement of the Bedouin." *Adalah and the Negev Coexistence Forum for Civil Equality*, May 2013, 1–8. https://www.adalah.org/uploads/oldfiles/Public/files/English/Publications/Articles/2013/Prawer-Begin-Plan-Background-Adalah.pdf.
12. "Pillay Urges Israel to Reconsider Proposed Bill That Will Displace Tens of Thousands of Bedouin," United Nations Office of the High Commissioner for Human Rights. July 25, 2013, http://www.ohchr.org/EN/NewsEvents/Pages/DisplayNews.aspx?NewsID=13577.
13. Rawia Aburabia, Debbie Gild-Hayo, and Nili Baruch. "Joint Position Paper: Bill on the Arrangement of Bedouin Settlement in the Negev," *The Association for Civil Rights in Israel (ACRI) and Bimkom—Planners for Planning Rights*, May 2013, http://www.acri.org.il/en/wp-content/uploads/2013/05/Bimkom-ACRI-Position-Paper-Prawer.pdf.
14. Haggai Matar, "Al-Araqib Demolished for Sixty-Second Time as Residents Attend Knesset Protest on Prawer Plan," *+972 Magazine*, November 30, 2013, http://972mag.com/nstt_feeditem/62nd-demolition-of-al-araqib-takes-place-as-residents-go-to-demonstrate-in-knesset/.
15. Shamus Slaunwhite, "Protests in the Negev, the West Bank, and Gaza Against the Begin-Prawer Plan," *IMEMC News*, July 15, 2013, http://www.imemc.org/article/65820; Yanir Yagna, "Israeli Arabs Protest Against Bedouin Relocation Plan; at Least Fourteen Arrested," *Haaretz*, July 15, 2013, http://www.haaretz.com/news/national/1.535858.
16. Haggai Matar, "Demonstrators March in Tel Aviv Against Plan to Uproot Bedouins," *+972 Magazine*, September 1, 2013, http://972mag.com/1000-march-against-plan-to-uproot-bedouins-in-tel-aviv/78285/.
17. Shirly Seidler, Jack Khoury, and Yaniv Kubovich. "Thirty-Four Arrested, Fifteen Police Wounded: Police, Protesters Clash Across Israel at Rallies Against Bedouin Relocation," *Haaretz*, November 30, 2013, http://www.haaretz.com/news/national/1.560995.
18. Mairav Zonszein, "Police Drag, Arrest, and Allegedly Beat Bedouin Child at Anti-Prawer Protest," *+972 Magazine*, December 1, 2013, http://972mag.com/police-drag-arrest-and-allegedly-beat-bedouin-child-at-anti-prawer-protest/82770/.

19. Harriet Sherwood, "Britons Protest Over Israel Plan to Remove up to 70,000 Palestinian Bedouins," *Guardian*, November 29, 2013, http://www.theguardian.com/world/2013/nov/29/britons-protest-israel-plan-remove-palestinian-bedouin.
20. Haggai Matar, "Police Threaten Activists, Bus Companies as Anti-Prawer Protest Intensifies," *+972 Magazine*, November 29, 2013, http://972mag.com/police-threaten-activists-bus-companies-as-anti-prawer-protest-intensifies/82677/.
21. The Arab political parties in Israel—Balad, Hadash, Taʿal, and the Islamic Movement—agreed to join forces as the Joint List on January 22, 2015, to increase their strength in the March 2015 election. The four Arab political parties hold different ideologies and political platforms but joined together for fear of being undermined and weakened in the Knesset. As MK Yousef Jabareen pointed out, the list unified and combined the Islamists, the Jabhawi (communists), and the Qawmi (nationalists) for the first time in history (MK Yousef Jabareen, interview in Hura, June 25, 2015).
22. Berman, Lazar. "Joint Arab List Sets out on Protest March for Bedouin Rights," *Times of Israel*, March 26, 2015, http://www.timesofisrael.com/joint-arab-list-sets-out-on-protest-march-for-bedouin-rights/#ixzz3XGM.
23. Allison Deger, "Joint List Leads March to Jerusalem Demanding Recognition and Equal Rights for Bedouin," *Mondoweiss*, April 1, 2015, http://mondoweiss.net/2015/04/jerusalem-demanding-recognition#sthash.JTneYAUx.dpuf.
24. Seidler, Khoury, and Kubovich. "Thirty-Four Arrested, Fifteen Police Wounded."
25. Moshe Arens, "A Bedouin Tragedy, an Israeli Tragedy," *Haaretz*, May 29, 2013, http://www.haaretz.com/opinion/a-bedouin-tragedy-an-israeli-tragedy.premium-1.526440.

## 11. The Ongoing Denial of Bedouin Rights and Their Nonviolent Resistance

1. See, for example, Sophie Richter-Devroe, "Gender and Settler Colonialism: Women's Oral Histories in the Naqab," University of Exeter Institute of Arab and Islamic Studies, February 1, 2014, http://socialsciences.exeter.ac.uk/iais/research/projects/details/index.php?id=328, presented at the Minority Rights Group Event, London, October 2015, http://minorityrights.org/2015/09/30/the-naqab-bedouin-new-perspectives/.
2. See the Adalah report and the appeal against the government decision to transfer the residence of ʿAtir Um al- Hiran. Adalah: The Legal Center for Arab Minority Rights in Israel, "Israeli Supreme Court Refuses to Reconsider Decision to Demolish Bedouin Village of Atir-Umm Al-Hiran and Evict All Residents," news release, January 17, 2016, https://www.adalah.org/en/content/view/8729.
3. Even though Adalah appealed to the Israeli Supreme Court in 2015 to change its decision, the court rejected the appeal in January 17, 2016, and it is likely that a

new settlement called Hiran will be built on the ruins of ʿAtir Um al Hiran. "Civil Further Hearing 3959/15 Ibrahim Farhoud Abu al-Kiyaʿan and others, Atawa Isa Abu al-Qiʾan and others Versus The State of Israel—Israel Lands Authority Request for Further Hearing of the Supreme Court following the Supreme Court's judgment on Permission for Civil Appeal 3094/11 that was delivered on 5.5.2015," Supreme Court of Israel, January 17, 2016, archived at https://www.adalah.org/uploads/SCT-Decision-Rejection-2nd-Hearing-Umm-alHiran-17-Jan-2016.pdf.

# References

Abu Hussein, H., and F. McKay. 2003. *Access Denied: Palestinian Land Rights in Israel.* London: Zed Books.

Abu Jaber, Kamel, Fawzi Gharaibeh, and Alan Hill. 1987. *The Badiya of Jordan: The Process of Change.* Amman: University of Jordan.

Abu-Lughod, Lila. 1986. *Veiled Sentiments: Honor and Poetry in a Bedouin Society.* Berkeley: University of California Press.

—. 1990. "The Romance of Resistance: Tracing Transformations of Power Through Bedouin Women." *American Ethnologist* 17 (1): 41–55.

—. 1993. *Writing Women's Worlds: Bedouin Stories.* Berkeley: University of California Press.

Abu Rabia, Aref. 1994. *The Negev Bedouin and Livestock Rearing: Social, Economic, and Political Aspects.* Oxford: Berg Publishers.

—. 2001. *A Bedouin Century: Education and Development Among the Negev Tribes in the Twentieth Century.* New York: Berghahn Books.

—. 2002. "Negev Bedouin: Displacement, Forced Settlement, and Conservation." In *Conservation and Mobile Indigenous Peoples: Displacement, Forced Settlement and Sustainable Development*, ed. Dawn Chatty and Marcus Colchester. New York: Berghahn Books.

—. 2006. "A Century of Education: Bedouin Contestation with Formal Education in Israel." In *Nomadic Societies in the Middle East and North Africa: Entering the Twenty-First Century*, ed. Dawn Chatty. Leiden: Brill.

Aburabia, Rawia, Debbie Gild-Hayo, and Nili Baruch. "Joint Position Paper: Bill on the Arrangement of Bedouin Settlement in the Negev." *The Association for Civil Rights in Israel (ACRI) and Bimkom—Planners for Planning Rights.* May 2013. http://www.acri.org.il/en/wp-content/uploads/2013/05/Bimkom-ACRI-Position-Paper-Prawer.pdf.

Aburabia, Safa. 2014. "Land, Identity, and History: New Discourse on the Nakba of Bedouin Arabs in the Naqab." In *The Naqab Bedouin and Colonialism: New Perspectives*, ed. M. Nasasra, et al., 90–120. London: Routledge.

Abu Saad, Ismael. 2004. "Education as a Tool of Expulsion from the Unrecognised Villages." *Adalah Newsletter* 8 (December): 1–5. http://www.adalah.org/newsletter/eng/dec04/ar4.pdf.

——. 2005. "Forced Sedentarization, Land Rights, and Indigenous Resistance: The Palestinian Bedouin in the Negev." In *Catastrophe Remembered: Palestine, Israel, and the Internal Refugees: Essays in Memory of Edward W. Said*, ed. Nur Masalha. London: Zed Books.

——. 2006. "Palestinian Education in Israel: The Legacy of the Military Government." *Holy Land Studies: A Multidisciplinary Journal* 5 (1): 21–56.

——. 2008. "Spatial Transformation and Indigenous Resistance: The Urbanization of the Palestinian Bedouin in Southern Israel." *American Behavioral Scientist* 51 (12): 1,713–54.

——. 2008. "State Rule and Indigenous Resistance Among Al Naqab Bedouin Arabs." *Hagar: Studies in Culture, Polity and Identities* 8 (2): 3–24.

——. 2010, *Arabs of the Naqab: Past, Present and Future Challenges* [in Arabic]. Beer-Sheva: Negev Centre for Regional Development, Ben Gurion University of the Negev.

Abu Saad, Ismael, and C. Creamer. 2012, "Socio-Political Upheaval and Current Conditions of the Naqab Bedouin Arabs." In *Indigenous (In)Justice*, ed. A. Amara, I. Abu-Saad, and O. Yiftachel. Cambridge, MA: Harvard University Press.

Abu Saad, Ismael, H. Lithwick, and K. Abu-Saad. 2004. *A Preliminary Evaluation of the Negev Bedouin Experience of Urbanisation: Findings of the Urban Household Survey*. Beer Sheva: Negev Center for Regional Development, Center for Bedouin Studies and Development.

Abu Saad, Ismael, T. R. Horowitz, and K. Abu-Saad. 2007. *Weaving Tradition and Modernity: Bedouin Women in higher Education*. Beer-Sheba: Ben-Gurion University of the Negev.

Abu Saad, Ismael, Y. Yonah, and A. Kaplan. 2004. "De-Arabisation of the Bedouin: A Study of Inevitable Failure." *Interchange* 35 (4): 387–406.

Abu-Sitta, Salman. 1995. "Al-ʿArab al-mansyon, badu beir al-sabaʿ" [The forgotten Arabs: Beersheba Bedouin]. *Al Hayat*, no. 11907, Wednesday September 28.

——. 2008. "The Forgotten Half of Palestine: Beersheba District, where the Naqba Continues" [in Arabic]. *The Palestinian Studies Magazine* (73): 1–15.

Adalah and the Negev Coexistence Forum for Civil Equality. "The Prawer-Begin Bill and the Forced Displacement of the Bedouin." May 2013. https://www.adalah.org/uploads/oldfiles/Public/files/English/Publications/Articles/2013/Prawer-Begin-Plan-Background-Adalah.pdf.

Al-Hamawi, Yakut al-Rumi. 1957. *Mu'ajam al-Buldan*. Vol. 3. Beirut: Dar Sader.

Alon, Yoav. 2005. "The Tribal System in the Face of the State-Formation Process: Mandatory Jordan, 1921–1946." *International Journal of Middle Eastern Studies* 37:213–40.

——. 2009. *The Making of Jordan: Tribes, Colonialism, and the Modern State*. London: I. B. Tauris.

Amara, Ahmad, I. Abu Saad, O. Yiftachel, eds. 2012. *Indigenous (In)Justice*. Cambridge, MA: Harvard University Press.

Amara, A., and Z. Miller. 2012. "Unsettling Settlements: Law, Land, and Planning in the Naqab." In *Indigenous (In)Justice*, ed. A. Amara, I. Abu Saad, and O. Yiftachel, 68–126. Cambridge, MA: Harvard University Press.

Amara, A., and M. Nasasra. 2015. "Bedouin Rights Under Occupation: International Humanitarian Law and Indigenous Rights for the Palestinian Bedouin in the West Bank." Norwegian Refugees Council, East Jerusalem.

Anaya, S. J. 2004. *Indigenous Peoples in International Law*. 2nd ed. New York: Oxford University Press.

Anderson, Benedict. 2006. *Imagined Communities: Reflections on the Origin and Spread of Nationalism*. London: Verso.

Anderson, L. 1987. "The State in the Middle East and North Africa." *Comparative Politics* 20 (1): 1–18.

Anonymous. 1963. "How the Military Administration Was Saved: A Report." *New Outlook* (Israel).

Aref, Aref al-. 1956. *Al-Nakbah: nakbat bayt al-maqdis wa-al-firdaws al-mafqud, 1947–1952* [Catastrophe of the Holy Land and the loss of paradise]. Sayda: Al-Maktabah al-Aṣriyah.

——. 1962. *The Tragedy of Palestine in Pictures*. Sidon, Lebanon: The Modern Library.

——. 1974. *Bedouin Love, Law, and Legend: Dealing Exclusively with the Badu of Beersheba*. New York: AMS Press.

——. 1999. *Tarikh' Biʾr al-Sabaʿ wa qabailuha* [The history of Beersheba and its tribes]. Cairo: Maktabat Madbouli.

Arens, Moshe. 2013. "A Bedouin Tragedy, an Israeli Tragedy." *Haaretz*, May 29.

Armstrong, J. 2010. "Nats Give In to Maori Over Rights Declaration." *New Zealand Herald*, April 20. http://www.nzherald.co.nz/politics/news/article.cfm?c_id=280&objectid=10639516.

Asia, I. 1994. *Focus of the Conflict: The Struggle for the Negev 1947–1956* [in Hebrew]. Jerusalem: Yad Yitzhak Ben Zvi.

Avci, Yasmin. 2009. "The Application of Tanzimat in the Desert: the Bedouins and the Creation of a New Town in Southern Palestine (1860–1914)." *Middle Eastern Studies* 45 (6): 969–83.

Axtmann, R. 2004. "The State of the State: The Model of the Modern State and Its Contemporary Transformation." *International Political Science Review* 25 (3): 259–79.

Ayubi, Nazih. 1995. *Over-Stating the Arab State: Politics and Society in the Middle East*. London: I. B. Tauris.

Bailey, Clinton. 1980. "The Negev in the Nineteenth Century: Reconstructing History from Bedouin Oral Traditions." *Asian and African Studies* 14:35–80.

——. 1990. "The Ottomans and the Bedouin Tribes of the Negev." In *Ottoman Palestine 1800–1914: Studies in Economic and Social History*, ed. G. G. Gilbar. Leiden: Brill.

——. 1991. *Bedouin Poetry from Sinai and the Negev: Mirror of a Culture*. Oxford: Clarendon Press.

Baldwin, David A. 1989. *Paradox of Power*. Oxford: Basil Blackwell.

Barbalet, J. M. 1985. "Power and Resistance." *The British Journal of Sociology* 36 (4): 531–48.

Barkey, K., and S. Parikh. 1991. "Comparative Perspectives on the State." *Annual Review of Sociology* 17:532–49.

Bar Zvi, Sasson. 1973. *Controlling the Bedouin Tribes* [in Hebrew]. Vol. 4. http://snunit.k12.il/bedouin/arti/0462.html.

Bauml, Yair. 2002. "Ha-Mimshal ha-Tsvai ve-Tahalikh Bitulo, 1958–1968" [The military government and the process of its revocation]. *Ha-Mizrah he-Hadash*, 133–56.

Bayat, Asef. 2000. "From 'Dangerous Classes' to 'Quiet Rebels': Politics of Urban Subalterns in the Global South." *International Sociology* 15 (3): 533–57.

—. 2010. *Life as Politics: How Ordinary People Change the Middle East*. Stanford, CA: Stanford University Press.

Belge, C. 2009. "From Expert Rule to Bureaucratic Authority: Governing the Bedouin." *Israel Studies Forum* (Association for Israel Studies) 24 (1): 82–108.

Bell, Gawain. 1983. *Shadows on the Sand: The Memoirs of Sir Gawain Bell*. London: Hurst.

Bitzan, John. 2006. "When Lawrence of Arabia Met David Ben-Gurion: A History of Israeli 'Arabist' Expertise in the Negev, 1943–1966." Master's diss., Department of Middle Eastern Studies, Ben Gurion University of the Negev, Beer Sheva, Israel.

Brown, M. F. 1996. "On Resisting Resistance." *American Anthropologist*, n.s., 98 (4): 729–35.

Brownlie, Ian. 1988. "The Rights of People in Modern International Law." In *The Rights of Peoples*, ed. J. Crawford. Oxford: Clarendon Press.

—. 1992. *Treaties and Indigenous Peoples*. Oxford: Clarendon Press.

Bunton, Martin. 2007. *Colonial Land Policies in Palestine, 1917–1936*. Oxford: Oxford University Press.

Burns, E. L. M. 1962. *Between Arab and Israeli*, London: Harrap.

Champagne, Duane. 2003. "The Crisis for Native Government in the Twenty-First Century." In *The Future of Indigenous Peoples: Strategies for Survival and Development*, ed. D. Champagne and I. Abu Saad, 205–19. Los Angeles: University of California Los Angeles, American Indian Studies Center.

Champagne, Duane, and I. Abu Saad, eds. 2003. *The Future of Indigenous Peoples*. Los Angeles: University of California Los Angeles, American Indian Studies Center.

Chatty, Dawn. 1986. *From Camel to Truck: the Bedouin in the Modern World*. New York: Vantage Press.

—. 1996. *Mobile Pastoralists: Development Planning and Social Change in Oman*. New York: Columbia University Press.

—. 1998. "Enclosures and Exclusions: Conserving Wildlife in Pastoral Areas of the Middle East." *Anthropology Today* 14 (4): 2–7.

—, ed. 2006. *Nomadic Societies in the Middle East and North Africa: Entering the Twenty-First Century*. Leiden: Brill.

—. 2010. "The Bedouin in Contemporary Syria: The Persistence of Tribal Authority and Control." *The Middle East Journal* 64 (1): 29–49.

—. 2014. "The Persistence of Bedouin Identity and Increasing Political Self-Representation in Lebanon and Syria." *Nomadic People* 18 (2): 16–33.

Cobo, J. M. 1986. "Study of the Problem of Discrimination against Indigenous Populations." UN Doc. E/CN.4/Sub.2/1986/7/Add.4, paras. 378–80.

Cohen, H. 2006. *Good Arabs: The Israeli Security Services and the Israeli Arabs* [in Hebrew]. Ivrit: Hebrew Publishing House.

—. 2008. *Army of Shadows: Palestinian Collaboration with Zionism, 1917-1948*. Trans. Haim Watzman, Berkeley: University of California Press.

——. 2010. *Good Arabs: The Israeli Security Agencies and the Israeli Arabs, 1948–1967*. Berkeley: University of California Press.

Curiel, Ilana. 2010. "Police Arrest Bedouins Suspected of Attacking JNF Workers." *Ynet News*, June 10. www.ynetnews.com/articles/0,7340,L-3907862,00.html.

Dabbagh, M. 1965. *Biladna Falastin* [Palestine our homeland]. Beirut: Dar al-Taliʿa.

Davenport, C. 1995. "Multi-Dimensional Threat Perception and State Repression: An Inquiry Into Why States Apply Negative Sanctions." *American Journal of Political Science* 39 (3): 683–713.

Dayan, Moshe. 1976. *The Story of My Life*. London: Weidenfeld and Nicolson.

Deger, Allison. 2015. "Joint List Leads March to Jerusalem Demanding Recognition and Equal Rights for Bedouin." *Mondoweiss*, April 1. http://mondoweiss.net/2015/04/jerusalem-demanding-recognition/.

Deringil, Selim. 2003. "They Live in a State of Nomadism and Savagery: The Late Ottoman Empire and the Post-Colonial Debate." *Comparative Studies in Society and History* 45 (2): 311–42.

Dickson, H. R. P. 1983. *The Arab of the Desert*. London: Allen and Unwin.

Edross, Ali El-. 1980. *The Hashemite Arab Army, 1908–1979: An Appreciation and Analysis of Military Operations*. Amman, Jordan: The Publishing Committee.

Eickelman, Dale F. 1989. *The Middle East: An Anthropological Approach*. New York: Prentice-Hall.

Eini, Rosa El-. 2006. *Mandated Landscape: British Imperial Rule in Palestine, 1929–1948*. London: Routledge.

Esco Foundation for Palestine. 1947. *Palestine, a Study of Jewish, Arab, and British Policies*. Oxford: Oxford University Press, and New Haven, CT: Yale University Press.

Essaid, Aida. 2013. *Zionism and Land Tenure in Mandate Palestine*. Routledge Studies on the Arab-Israeli Conflict. London: Routledge.

Fabietti, U. 2000. "State Policies and Bedouin Adaptations in Saudi Arabia, 1900–1980." In *The Transformation of Nomadic Society in the Arab East*, ed. Martha Mundy and Basim Musallam. Cambridge: Cambridge University Press.

Falah, Ghazi. 1985. "How Israel Controls the Bedouin in Israel." *Journal of Palestine Studies* 14 (2): 35–51.

——. 1989a. "Israeli State Policy Toward Bedouin Sedentarization in the Negev." *Journal of Palestine Studies* 18 (2): 71–91.

——. 1989b. *Al-filastinyun al-mansyon: ʿarab al-naqab* [The forgotten Palestinians: the Nagab Arabs, 1906–1987]. Taiybe: Arab Heritage Centre.

——. 2005, "The Geopolitics of 'Enclavisation' and the Demise of a Two-State Solution to the Israeli–Palestinian Conflict." *Third World Quarterly* 26 (8): 1,341–72.

Falk, Richard. 1988. "The Rights of People (in Particular Indigenous Peoples)." In *The Rights of Peoples*, ed. J. Crawford. Oxford: Clarendon Press.

Fanon, Frantz. 1963. *The Wretched of the Earth*. London: Penguin Books.

——. 2008. *Black Skin White Masks*. London: Pluto Press.

Farber, D. A., and J. Chen. 2006. *Disasters and the Law: Katrina and Beyond*. New York: Giroux.

Finkelstein, Norman G. 2001. *Image and Reality of the Israel-Palestine Conflict*. London: Verso.

Firro, K. M. 1999. *The Druzes in the Jewish State: A Brief History*. Leiden: Brill.

Flapan, S. 1987. "The Palestinian Exodus of 1948." *Palestine Studies* 16 (4): 3–26.
Foucault, Michel. 1977. *Discipline and Punish: The Birth of the Prison*. London: Penguin.
——. 1990. *The History of Sexuality*. Vol. 1: *The Will to Knowledge*. London: Penguin.
Frantzman, S. J., H. Yahel, and R. Kark. 2012. "Contested Indigeneity: The Development of an Indigenous Discourse on the Bedouin of the Negev." *Israel Studies* 17 (1): 78–104.
Frey, Frederick W. 1971. "On Issues and Non-issues in the Study of Power." *The American Political Science Review* 65 (4): 1,081–101.
——. 1989. *The Location and Measurement of Power: A Critical Analysis*. Philadelphia: University of Pennsylvania.
Gandhi, M. K. 1951. *Satyagraha: Non-Violent Resistance*. Ahmedabad: Navajivan.
Gerber, H. 1986. "A New Look at the Tanzimat: The Case of the Province of Jerusalem." In *Palestine in the Late Ottoman Period*, ed. David Kushner. Leiden: Brill.
Ghanem, A. 2001. *The Palestinian Arab Minority in Israel, 1948–2000: A Political Study*, Albany: State University of New York Press.
Ghuri, A. 1972. *Palestine in Sixty Years* [in Arabic]. Beirut: Dar al Nahar.
Glubb, John Bagot. 1976. *The Story of the Arab Legion*. New York: Da Capo Press.
Gordon, Neve. 2010. "Ethnic Cleansing in the Israeli Negev." *Guardian*, July 28. http://www.guardian.co.uk/commentisfree/2010/jul/28/ethnic-cleansing-israeli-negev.
Gorny, Y. 1987. *Zionism and the Arabs, 1882–1948: A Study of Ideology*. Oxford: Clarendon Press.
Gottheil, F. M. 1986. "Money and Product Flows in Mid-Nineteenth-Century Palestine: The Physiocratic Model Applied." In *Palestine in the Late Ottoman Period*, ed. D. Kushner. Jerusalem: Yad Izhak Ben-Zvi and Leiden: Brill.
Government of Israel. CA 4220/12. *Al-Oqabi v State of Israel*. Judgment of May 14.
Government of Israel. CA 3094/11. *Al-Kiya'an v State of Israel*. Judgment of May 5.
Greenspan, Itay. 2005. "Mediating Bedouin Futures: the Role of Advocacy NGOs in Land and Planning Conflicts between the State of Israel and the Negev Bedouins." Master's thesis, York University, Toronto, Canada.
Guha, R., ed. 1997. *A Subaltern Studies Reader, 1986–1995*. Minneapolis: University of Minnesota Press.
Gurr, Ted R. 1970. *Why Men Rebel*, Princeton, NJ: Princeton University Press.
——. 1993. *Minorities at Risk: A Global View of Ethno-political Conflict*. Washington, DC: United States Institute of Peace Press.
Gurr, Ted R., and Barbara Harff. 2004. *Ethnic Conflict in World Politics: Dilemmas in World Politics*. 2nd ed. Boulder, CO: Westview Press.
Gutmann, Matthew C. 1993. "Rituals of Resistance: A Critique of the Theory of Everyday Forms of Resistance." *Latin American Perspectives* 20 (2): 74–92.
Hadawi, S. 1989. *Bitter Harvest: A Modern History of Palestine*. London: Scorpion Publishing.
Hall, Bogumila. 2014. "Bedouins' Politics of Place and Memory: A Case of Unrecognized Villages in the Negev." *Nomadic People* 18 (2): 147–64.
Hanan, O. al-. 1986. "The Settlements in the Negev: Battles During the Independence War" [in Hebrew]. In *The Negev Settlements, 1900–1960*, ed. M. Naoor. Jerusalem: Yad Yitzhak Ben Zvi.
Havemann, P., ed. 1999. *Indigenous Peoples' Rights in Australia, Canada, and New Zealand*. Auckland, NZ: Oxford University Press.

Herb, Michael. 2009. "A Nation of Bureaucrats: Political Participation and Economic Diversification in Kuwait and the United Arab Emirats." *IJMES* 41 (3): 375–95.
Herzl, Theodor. 1946. *The Jewish State: An Attempt at a Modern Solution of the Jewish Question*, ed. Jacob M. Alkow. New York: American Zionist Emergency Council.
—. 1958. *The Diaries of Theodor Herzl.* London: Gollancz.
Hind, Robert J. 1984. "The Internal Colonial Concept." *Comparative Studies in Society and History* 26 (3): 543–68.
Hindess, Barry. 1996. *Discourse of Power from Hobbes to Foucault.* Oxford: Blackwell.
Hobbs, J. Joseph. 2014. "Bedouin Place Names in the Eastern Desert of Egypt." *Nomadic People* 18 (12): 123–46.
Hollander, Jocelyn, and Rachel Einwohner. 2004. "Conceptualizing Resistance." *Sociological Forum* 19 (4): 533–54.
Hood, Kathleen, and Mohammad al-Oun. 2014. "Changing Perfomance Traditions and Bedouin Identity in the North Arabiya, Jordan." *Nomadic People* 18 (2): 78–99.
Horne, Edward. 1982. *A Job Well Done (Being a History of the Palestine Police Force, 1920–1948).* Essex: Palestine Police Old Comrades Benevolent Association.
Hourani, Albert. 1991. *A History of the Arab Peoples*, London: Faber and Faber.
Human Rights Watch. 2008. "Off the Map: Land and Housing Rights Violations in Israel's Unrecognized Bedouin Villages." *HRW Report*, March 20. http://www.hrw.org/reports/2008/iopt0308/.
Husri, S. Abu Khaldun al-. 1951. *Araʾ wa-ahadith fi al-qawmiyya al-ʿarabiyya.* Cairo: Matbaʾat al-ʾItimad.
Hussein, A. 1949. *The Episode of El Faluje: What the Egyptian Army Proved in Palestine.* Trans. Labib Saad. Pamphlet Number 6. London.
Hutchison, E. H. 1956. *Violent Truce: A Military Observer Looks at the Arab-Israeli Conflict, 1951–1955.* London: John Calder.
Ibn Khaldun, A. 1969. *The Muqaddimah: An Introduction to History.* Translated from the Arabic by Franz Rosenthal. Bollingen Series. Princeton, NJ: Princeton University Press.
Imray, Colin. 1995. *Policeman in Palestine: Memories of the Early Years.* Devon: Edward Gaskell.
Jakubowska, L. 1992. "Resisting 'Ethnicity': The Israeli State and Bedouin Identity." In *The Path to Domination, Resistance and Terror*, ed. C. Nordstrom and J. Martin, 85–106. Berkeley: University of California Press.
Jiryis, Sabri. 1973. *Al-ʿArab fi Israel* [The Arabs in Israel]. Beirut: Muassasat al-Dirasat al-Filasṭiniya.
—. 1976. *The Arabs in Israel.* Foreword by Noam Chomsky. New York: Monthly Review Press.
Kanaaneh, Rhoda A. 2002. *Birthing the Nation: Strategies of Palestinian Women in Israel.* Berkeley: University of California Press.
—. 2009. *Surrounded: Palestinian Soldiers in the Israeli Army.* Stanford, CA: Stanford University Press.
Kark, Ruth. 1981. "Jewish Frontier Settlement in the Negev, 1880–1948: Perception and Realization." *Middle Eastern Studies* 17 (3): 334–56.
—. 2002. *Pioneering Jewish Settlement in the Negev, 1880–1948* [in Hebrew]. Jerusalem: Ariel Press.

Kark, Ruth, and Seth Frantzman. 2012. "The Negev: Land, Settlement, the Bedouin, and the Ottoman and the British Policy, 1871–1948." *British Journal of Middle Eastern Studies* 39 (1): 66.

Karmi, Ghada. 2007. *Married to Another Man: Israel's Dilemma in Palestine*. London: Pluto Press.

Karsh, E. 1997. *Fabricating Israeli History: The New Historians*. London: Frank Cass.

Kayam, M. al-. 1994. *Forty Years of Settling Gaza Jews: Beer Sheva and the Establishment of Rohama* [in Hebrew]. Nitsarim: Atarot Print.

Kedar, Alexander. 2004. "Land Settlements in the Negev in an International Law Perspective." *Adalah* newsletter, no. 8 (September): 1–7.

Kellerman, A. 1993. *Society and Settlement: Jewish Land of Israel in the Twentieth Century*. Albany: State University of New York Press.

Khoury Philip, and Joseph Kostiner, eds. 1991. *Tribes and State Formation in the Middle East*. London: I. B. Tauris.

Kingsbury, Benedict. 1998. "Indigenous People in International Law: A Constructivist Approach to the Asian Controversy." *The American Journal of International Law* 92 (3): 414–57.

——. 2001. "Reconciling Five Competing Conceptual Structures of Indigenous Peoples' Claims in International and Comparative Law." In *People's Rights*, ed. P. Alson, 69–250. Oxford: Oxford University Press.

KKL-JNF (Jewish National Fund). "Realizing Visions in the Negev, JNF America-Missions visit—Interview with Russell Robinson." *Jerusalem Post*, January 12. http://www.jpost.com/GreenIsrael/KKLJNFSOLIDARITYWITHTHESOUTH/Article.aspx?id=165783.

Kolinsky, Martin. 1993. *Law, Order, and Riots in Mandatory Palestine, 1928-35*. London: Macmillan.

——. 2000. "Military Government, Political Control, and Crime: The Case of Israeli Arabs." *Crime, Law, and Social Change* 34:159–82.

Korn, Alina. 1996. "Crime and Its Control in the Israeli Arab Population During the Military Government, 1948–1966" [in Hebrew]. Ph.D. diss., Tel Aviv University, Israel.

Kostiner, Joseph. 1991. "Transforming Dualities: Tribe and State Formation in Saudi Arabia." In *Tribes and State Formation in the Middle East*, ed. Philip Khoury and Joseph Kostiner. London: I. B. Tauris.

——, ed. 2000. *Middle East Monarchies: The Challenge of Modernity*. Boulder, CO: Lynne Rienner.

Kram, Noa. 2012. "The Naqab Bedouins: Legal Struggle for Land Ownership Rights in Israel." In *Indigenous (In)Justice*, ed. Ahmad Amara, Ismael Abu Saad, Oren Yiftachel. Cambridge, MA: Harvard University Press.

Krasner, S. D., et al. 1984. "Approaches to the State: Alternative Conceptions and Historical Dynamics." *Comparative Politics* 16 (2): 223–46.

Landau, J. M. 1969. *The Arabs in Israel: A Political Study*. Oxford: Oxford University Press.

Lange, Katharina. 2014. "Producing Tribal History: Gendered Representations of Genealogy and Warfare in Northern Syria." *Nomadic People* 18 (8): 34–52.

Lavie, S. 1990. *The Poetics of Military Occupation: Mzeina Allegories of Bedouin Identity Under Israeli and Egyptian Rule*. Berkeley: University of California Press.

Lawrence, T. E. [1926] 1997. *Seven Pillars of Wisdom*. Hertfordshire: Wordsworth Editions.

Law-Yone, Hubert. 2003. "From Sedentarization to Urbanization: State Policy Towards Bedouin Society in Israel." In *The Future of Indigenous Peoples: Strategies for Survival and Development*, ed. D. Champagne and I. Abu Saad, 175–184. UCLA American Indian Studies Center. Los Angeles: University of California Press.

Lazar, Sarah O. 2002. "The Military Government as Mechanism of Controlling the Arab Citizens: the First Decade (1948–1958)" [in Hebrew]. *Ha-Mizrah he-Hadash, Kirakh* 43:103–31.

Levin, Noam, Ruth Kark, and Emir Galilee. 2010. "Maps and the Settlement of Southern Palestine, 1799–1948: An Historical/GIS Analysis." *Journal of Historical Geography* 36:1–18.

Lewallen, Ann- Elise. 2003. "Strategic 'Indigeneity' and the Possibility of a Global Women's Movement." *Michigan Feminist Studies* 17. http://hdl.handle.net/2027/spo.ark5583.0017.005.

Lewando-Hundt, J. 1979. "Tel-Sheva: A Planned Bedouin Village." In *The Land of the Negev* [in Hebrew], ed. A. Shmueli and Y. Gradus. Jerusalem: Defence Ministry Press.

Likhovski, Assaf. 2006. *Law and Identity in Mandate Palestine*. Chapel Hill: University of North Carolina Press.

Lithwick, H. 2003. "Urbanization Policy for Indigenous Peoples: A Case Study of Israel's Negev Bedouin." In *The Future of Indigenous Peoples: Strategies for Survival and Development*, ed. D. Champagne and I. Abu Saad, 184–205. UCLA American Indian Studies Center. Los Angeles: University of California Press.

Lustick, Ian. 1980. *Arabs in the Jewish State: Israel's Control of A National Minority*. Austin: Texas University Press.

Lyne, Linda. 1989. "The Dialogics of Tribal Self-Representation in Jordan." *American Ethnologist* 16 (1): 24–39.

Maddrell, P. 1990. *The Bedouin of the Negev*. London: Minority Rights Group.

Mann, Michael. 1984. "The Autonomous Power of the State: Its Origins, Mechanisms, and Results." In *States in History*, ed. J. Hall, 109-136. Oxford: Blackwell.

Maʾoz, Moshe, ed. 1968. *Ottoman Reform in Syria and Palestine, 1840–1861: The Impact of the Tanzimat on Politics and Society*. Oxford: Clarendon Press.

Margalit, Alon. 2015. "ʿAl-Oqbi (Al-Araqib) and Abu al-Kiyaʾan (Um Al-Hiran) Cases: Analysis of the Supreme Court Decisions and Their Implications." Norwegian Refugees Council, Jerusalem.

Martin, Robin H. 2007. *Palestine Betrayed: A British Palestine Policeman's Memories*. Ringwood, UK: Seglawi Press.

Marx, Emanuel. 1967. *Bedouin of the Negev*. Manchester: Manchester University Press.

——. 1974. *Hahevra Habeduit Banegev* [The Bedouin of the Negev]. Tel Aviv: Reshafim.

Marx, Emanuel, and A. Meir. 2005. "Land, Towns, and Planning: The Negev Bedouin and the State of Israel." *Geography Research Forum*, no. 25:43–61.

Marx, Emanuel, et al. 2007. *Land of the Negev Bedouin: A Local Anthropology*. Detroit: Wayne State University Press.

Masalha, Nur. 1992. *Expulsion of the Palestinians: The Concept of 'Transfer' in Zionist Political Thought, 1882–1948*. Washington, DC: Institute of Palestine Studies.

McKernan, L. 1993. "The Supreme Moment of the War: General Allenby's Entry Into Jerusalem." *Historical Journal of Film, Radio and Television* 13 (2).
Meir, Avinoam. 1997. *As Nomadism Ends: The Israeli Bedouin of the Negev*. Boulder, CO: Westview Press.
——. 2009. "Contemporary State Discourse and Historical Pastoral Spatiality: Contradictions in the Land Conflict Between the Israeli Bedouin and the State." *Ethnic and Racial Studies* 32 (5) 823–43.
Migdal, Joel. 1988. *Strong Societies and Weak States: State Society Relations and State Capabilities in the Third World*. Princeton, NJ: Princeton University Press.
Mitchell, Timothy. 1990. "Everyday Metaphors of Power." *Theory and Society* 19 (5): 545–77.
——. 1991. "The Limits of the State: Beyond Statist Approaches and Their Critics." *American Political Science Review* 85 (1): 77.
Morris, Benny. *Israel's Border Wars, 1949–1956: Arab Infiltration, Israeli Retaliation, and the Countdown to the Suez War*. Oxford: Clarendon Press.
——. 2002. *The Road to Jerusalem: Glubb Pasha and the Jews*. London: I. B. Tauris.
——. 2004. *The Birth of the Palestinian Refugee Problem Revisited*. Cambridge: Cambridge University Press.
——. 2005. *The Birth of the Palestinian Refugee Problem, 1947–1949* [in Hebrew]. Tel Aviv: Am Oved.
Musil, A. 1928. *The Manners and Customs of the Rwala Bedouins*. Vol. 6. New York: American Geographical Society.
Nasasra, M. 2009. "Bedouin Resistance to the Imperial State: Memories from the Naqab During the British Mandate, 1917–1948." *ISA E-Bulletin*, 12.
——. 2011a, "Before You Expel the Bedouin . . ." *Haaretz*, September 23. http://www.haaretz.com/opinion/before-you-expel-the-bedouin-1.386384.
——. 2011b. "The Southern Palestine Bedouin Tribes and British Mandate Relations, 1917–48: Resistance to Colonialism." *The Arab World Geographer* 14 (4): 305–35.
——. 2012. "The Ongoing Judaisation of the Naqab and the Struggle for Recognising the Indigenous Rights of the Arab Bedouin People." *Settler Colonial Studies* 2 (1): 81–107.
——. 2013. "Muktatafat mn Tarikh al-Naqab wa Biʾr al-Sabaʿ." *Mada al-Carmel: Arab Centre for Applied Social Research* 1 (1): 1–15.
Nasasra, M., et al., eds. 2014. *The Naqab Bedouin and Colonialism: New Perspectives*. London: Routledge.
Neep, Daniel. 2012. *Occupying Syria Under the French Mandate: Insurgency, Space, and State Formation*. Cambridge: Cambridge University Press.
Nimr, Sonya F. El-. 1990. "The Arab Revolt of 1936–1939 in Palestine: A Study Based on Oral Sources." Ph.D. diss., Institute of Arab and Islamic Studies, University of Exeter, UK.
Palmer, E. H. 1871. *The Desert of the Exodus: Journey on Foot in the Wilderness of the Forty Years Wandering: Undertaken with the Ordinance Survey of Sinai and the Palestinian Exploration Fund*. Vols. 1–2. Cambridge: Deighton and Bell.
Pappe, Ilan. 1992. *The Making of the Arab Israeli Conflict, 1947–1951*. London: I. B. Tauris.
——. 2004. *A History of Modern Palestine: One Land, Two Peoples*. Cambridge: Cambridge University Press.

—. 2005. *The Modern Middle East.* London: Routledge.
—. 2006. *The Making of the Arab-Israeli Conflict, 1947–1951.* 2nd ed. London: I. B. Tauris.
—. 2008. *The Ethnic Cleansing of Palestine*. Oxford: Oneworld.
Parizot, Cedric. 2004. “Crossing and Constructing Borders Within Daily Contacts: Social and Economic Relations Between the Bedouin in the Negev and Their Networks in Gaza, the West Bank, and Jordan.” *Notes de Recherche*, no. 287. Centre d'Economie Régionale, Université Paul Cézanne, Aix-Marseille III, Aix-en-Provence, France.
—. 2006. “Counting Votes That Do Not Count: Negev Bedouin and the Knesset Elections of May 17, 1999, Rahat, Israel.” In *Nomadic Societies in the Middle East and North Africa: Entering the Twenty-First Century*, ed. D. Chatty. London: Brill.
—. 2006. *Entrepreneurs Without Borders: Policies of Closure and Border Economy Between the Southern West Bank and the Northern Negev, 2000–2005*. Oxford: Centre for European Studies.
Polet, F., ed. 2007. *The State of Resistance*, London: Zed.
Porat, Chanina. 1996. *From Wasteland to Inhabited Land: Purchasing Land and Settling in the Negev, 1930–1947* [in Hebrew]. Sde Boker: Yad Yitshak Ben Zvi.
—. 1998. “Development Policy and the Question of the Bedouin in the Negev in the First Years of the State, 1948–1953” [in Hebrew]. *Eioneem Be- Tkomat Yisrael* 7:360–88.
—. 2007. “The Bedouin in the Negev: Confrontation and Disagreements on Questions of Land Ownership and the Establishment of Permanent Townships, 1960–1973” [in Hebrew]. *Katidra*, 129–156.
—. 2015. *Jewish Mukhtars in the Negev: The Story of Jewish Settlements: Their Relationship with the British Mandatory Government and Their Bedouin Neighbors, 1908–1948.* Yehuda Dekel Library.
Porter, P. 2013. *Military Orientalism: Eastern War Through Western Eyes.* Oxford University Press.
Qahawaji, H. 1972. *The Arabs Under Israeli Occupation Since 1948* [in Arabic]. Beirut: Palestine Liberation Organisation Research Centre.
Rae, J. 2000. “The Days of Agreement: Tribal Division of the Syrian Steppe.” Paper delivered at the annual meeting of the Middle East Studies Association of North America (MESA), Orlando, FL.
Robinson, S. N. 2005. “Occupied Citizens in a Liberal State: Palestinians Under Military Rule and the Colonial Formation of Israel Society, 1948–1966.” Ph.D. diss., Stanford University, Stanford, CA.
—. 2013. *Citizen Strangers: Palestinians and the Birth of Israel's Liberal Settler State* Stanford, CA: Stanford University Press.
Rogan, Eugene L. 1996, “Asiret Mektebi: Abdulhamid II's School for Tribes (1892–1907).” *International Journal of Middle East Studies* 28 (1): 83–107.
—. 1999. *Frontiers of the Late Ottoman Empire: Transjordan, 1850–1921.* Cambridge: Cambridge University Press.
Rogan, Eugene L., and Avi Shlaim, eds. 2007. *The War for Palestine*. Cambridge: Cambridge University Press.
Rubin, Jeffrey W. 1996. “Defining Resistance.” *Studies in Law, Politics, and Society* 15:237–60.

Saʿdi, A. H. 1996. "Minority Resistance to State Control: Towards a Re-analysis of Palestinian Political Activity in Israel." *Social Identities* 2 (3): 395–412.

——. 2000. "Israel as Ethnic Democracy: What Are the Implications for the Palestinian Minority?" *Arab Studies Quarterly* 22 (1): 25–37.

——. 2001. "Control and Resistance at Local-Level Institutions: A Study of Kafr Yassif's Local Council Under the Military Government." *Arab Studies Quarterly* 23 (3): 31–47.

——. 2003. "The Koenig Report and Israeli Policy Towards the Palestinian Minority, 1965–1976: Old Wine in New Bottles." *Arab Studies Quarterly* 25 (3): 51–61.

——. 2014. *Thorough Surveillance: The Genesis of Israeli Policies of Population Management, Surveillance, and Political Control Towards the Palestinian Minority*, Manchester: Manchester University Press.

——. 2015. "Social Protest Under Authoritarianism: A Critique of Regime Type and Instrumental Rationality-Based Explanation." *Sociology* 49 (3): 455–70.

Saʿdi, A. H., and L. Abu-Lughod, eds. 2007. *Nakba: Palestine, 1948, and the Claims of Memory*. New York: Columbia University Press.

Sadik, Walid. 1978. "The Goal: Peace with the Israeli Arab." *New Outlook: Middle East Monthly* 21 (5/184): 53–55.

Said, Edward W. 2003a. *Culture and Resistance: Conversations with Edward W. Said*. Cambridge, MA: South End Press.

——. 2003b. *Orientalism*, Harmondsworth, UK: Penguin.

Said, Edward, and H. Christopher, eds. 1988. *Blaming the Victims: Spurious Scholarships and the Palestinian Question*. London: Verso.

Sayigh, Rosemary. 1979. *Palestinians: From Peasants to Revolutionaries*, London: Zed Press.

Schaap, Andrew. 2009. "The Absurd Proposition of Aboriginal Sovereignty." In *Law and Agonistic Politics*, ed. A. Schaap, 209–23. Farnham, UK: Ashgate.

Schmidt, S. W., et al., eds. 1977. *Friends, Followers, and Factions: A Reader in Political Clientelism*. Berkeley: University of California Press.

Scott, James C. 1977. "Patron-Client Politics and Political Change in Southeast Asia." In *Friends, Followers, and Factions: A Reader in Political Clientelism*, ed. S. W. Schmidt et al. Berkeley: University of California Press.

——. 1985. *Weapons of the Weak: Everyday Forms of Peasant Resistance*. New Haven, CT: Yale University Press.

——. 1987. "Resistance Without Protest and Without Organization: Peasant Opposition to the Islamic Zakat and the Christian Tithe." *Comparative Studies in Society and History* 29 (3): 417–52.

——. 1990. *Domination and the Arts of Resistance: Hidden Transcripts*. New Haven, CT: Yale University Press.

——. 1992. "Domination, Acting, and Fantasy." In *The Paths to Domination Resistance and Terror*, ed. C. Nordstrom and J. Martin. Berkeley: University of California Press.

——. 1998. *Seeing Like a State: How Certain Schemes to Improve the Human Condition Have Failed*. New Haven, CT: Yale University Press.

Segev, Tom. 2010a. "Are Israeli Arabs the New African Americans." *Haaretz*, April 5. http://haaretz.com/hasen/spages/1160941.html.
—. 2010b. "The Making of History/Who Owns This Country?" *Haaretz*, July 9. http://www.haaretz.com/magazine/week-s-end/the-making-of-history-who-owns-this-country-1.300956.
Shalhoub-Kovorkian, Nadera. 2015. *Security Theology, Surveillance, and the Politics of Fear*. Cambridge Studies in Law and Society. Cambridge: Cambridge University Press.
Shamir, R. 1996. "Suspended in Space: Bedouin Under the Law of Israel." *Law and Society Review* 30 (2): 231–58.
Shapira, Anita. 1992. *Land and Power: The Zionist Resort to Force, 1881-1948*. Oxford: Oxford University Press.
Sharp, Gene. 1973. *The Politics of Nonviolent Action*. Boston: Porter Sargent.
—. 1990. "The Role of Power in Nonviolent Struggle." In *Nonviolent Political Struggle*. Amman, Jordan: Arab Thought Forum; Boston: Albert Einstein Institute.
Shepherd, Naomi. 1999. *Ploughing Sand: British Rule in Palestine, 1917–1948*. London: John Murray.
Shlaim, Avi. 2000. *The Iron Wall: Israel and the Arab World*. London: Penguin Books.
Shuqayr, N. 1991. *History of Ancient and Modern Sinai and Its Geography* [in Arabic]. Beirut: Dar Al-Geel.
Sinclair, Georgina. 2006. *Colonial Policing and the Imperial Endgame, 1945–1980: 'At the End of the Line.'* Manchester: Manchester University Press.
Skocpol, Theda. 1985. "Bringing the State Back In: Strategies of Analysis in Current Research." In *Bringing the Sate Back In*, ed. P. Evans, D. Rueschemeyer, and T. Skocpol, 1–35. Cambridge: Cambridge University Press.
Smith, Linda T. 1999. *Decolonizing Methodologies: Research and Indigenous Peoples*. London: Zed.
Smooha, Sammy. 1980. "Existing and Alternative Policy Towards Arabs in Israel" [in Hebrew]. *Magamot* 26 (1): 16–27.
—. 1999. "The Advances and Limits of the Israelization of Israel's Palestinian Citizens." In *Israeli and Palestinian Identities in History and Literature*, ed. Kamal Abdel-Malek and David Jacobson. New York: St. Martin's Press.
Soen, D., and A. Shmuel. 1987. "The Israeli Bedouin: Political Organisation at the National Level." *Middle Eastern Studies* 23 (3): 329–47.
Spivak, Gayatri. 1988. "Can the Subaltern Speak?" In *Marxism and the Interpretation of Culture*, ed. C. Nelson and L. Greenberg, 271–313. Chicago: University of Illinois Press.
Stanley, B. 2007. "Aqaba/Eilat." In *Cities of the Middle East and North Africa: A Historical Encyclopedia*, ed. M. Dumper and B. Stanley. Santa Barbara, CA: ABC Clio.
Swirski, S., and Y. Hasson. 2006. *Invisible Citizens: Israeli Government Policy Toward the Negev Bedouin*. Tel Aviv: Adva Centre.
Teveth, S. 1987. *Ben Gurion: The Burning Ground*. London: Hale.
Tilly, Charles. 1985. "War Making and State Making as Organized Crime." In *Bringing the State Back In*, ed. P. B. Evans, D. Rueschemeyer, and T. Skocpol, 169–92. Cambridge: Cambridge University Press.

Tully, James. 2000. "The Struggle of Indigenous Peoples for and of Freedom." In *Political Theory and the Rights of Indigenous Peoples*, ed. D. Ivison, P. Patton, and W. Sanders, 36–60. Cambridge: Cambridge University Press.

United Nations Committee on Economic, Social, and Cultural Rights. 2003. "The Unrecognized Villages in the Negev." New York: UN Committee on Economic, Social and Cultural Rights, 30th Session–Israel.

Vashitz, J. 1971. "Coexistence and Confrontation." *New Outlook: Middle East Monthly* 14 (4/123): 40–45.

Wasserstein, B. 1991. *The British in Palestine: The Mandatory Government and the Arab-Jewish Conflict, 1917–1929*. 2nd ed. Oxford: Basil Blackwell.

Weber, Max. 1947. *The Theory of Social and Economic Organization*. New York: The Free Press.

Weingrod, Alex. 1977. "Patrons, Patronage, and Political Parties." In *Friends, Followers, and Factions: A Reader in Political Clientelism*, ed. S. W. Schmidt et al. Berkeley: University of California Press.

Weitz, Joseph. 1947. *Our Settlement Activities in a Period of Storm and Stress 1936–1947* [in Hebrew]. Palestine: Sifriat Poʾalimʾ.

——. 1965. *My Diary and Letters to the Children: Watching the Walls (1945–1948)*. Vol. 3. Ramat Gan: BEC.

Weitz, Rose. 2001. "Women and Their Hair: Seeking Power Through Resistance and Accommodation." *Gender and Society* 15 (5): 667–86.

Willacy, Mark. 2005. *Evicting the Bedouin*. Television broadcast. Directed by Mark Willacy. Produced by ABC Australia. Performed by Mark Willacy (reporter). Australia: ABC Australia. Posted to YouTube December 17, 2007. https://www.youtube.com/watch?v=eQoWJt5wfJ8.

Williams, S. 1977. "Internal Colonialism, Core-Periphery Contrasts, and Devolution: An Integrative Comment." *Area* (Royal Geographical Society, with Institute of British Geographers) 9 (4): 272–78.

Wolfe, P. 2006. "Settler Colonialism and the Elimination of the Native." *Journal of Genocide Research* 8:387–409.

Worden, S. 1998. "Global News-stand." *American Journal of International Law* 113 (July): 121–23.

Yagna, Yanor. 2010. "Bedouin Damage to State Infrastructure Soars . . ." *Haaretz*, July 9. http://www.haaretz.com/print-edition/news/bedouin-damage-to-state-infrastructure-soars-by-87-percent-in-2010-ministry-says-1.300843.

Yahel H., R. Kark, and S. J. Frantzman. 2012. "Are the Negev Bedouin an Indigenous People? Fabricating Palestinian History." *Middle East Quarterly* 19 (3): 3–14.

Yiftachel, Oren. 1998. "Democracy or Ethnocracy? Territory and Settler Politics in Israel/Palestine." *Middle East Report*, no. 207:8–13.

——. 2003. "Bedouin Arabs and the Israeli Settler State: Land Policies and Indigenous Resistance." In *The Future of Indigenous People*, ed. D. Champagne and I. Abu Saad, 21–48. UCLA Center for American Indian Studies. Los Angeles: University of California Press.

——. 2008. "Epilogue: Studying Naqab/Negev Bedouins: Toward a Colonial Paradigm?" *Hagar: Studies in Culture, Polity, and Identities* 8 (2): 173–91.
——. 2012. "Naqab Bedouins and the (Internal) Colonial Paradigm." *Indigenous (In) Justice: Law and Human Rights Among the Bedouins in the Naqab/Negev*, ed. A. Amara, I. Abu-Saad, and O. Yiftachel, 281–310. Cambridge, MA: Harvard Human Rights Press.
Yuval-Davis, N. 1989. "National Reproduction and 'the Demographic Race' in Israel." In *Women-Nation-State*, ed. N. Yuval-Davis and F. Anthias. Basingstoke, UK: Macmillan.
Zureik, Elia. 1979. *The Palestinians in Israel: A Study in Internal Colonialism*. London: Routledge and Kegan Paul.

## Archival Collections

### *United Kingdom*

#### KEW GARDENS, LONDON, ENGLAND, PUBLIC RECORDS OFFICE (PRO), INCLUDING:

CO—Colonial Office Papers.
FO—Foreign Office Papers.
WO—War Office Papers.

#### ST ANTONY'S COLLEGE, OXFORD UNIVERSITY, MIDDLE EAST CENTRE ARCHIVE (MECA), INCLUDING:

Aref al-Aref Papers.
Glubb Pasha Papers.

#### KING'S COLLEGE LONDON ARCHIVES (KCLMA), LIDDELL HART CENTRE FOR MILITARY ARCHIVES (LHCMA), INCLUDING:

Allenby Papers.
Bartholomew Papers.
Ismay Papers.
O'Connor Papers.

## *Israel*

Archive of Israel Defence Forces (IDFA), Givatayim.
Central Zionist Archive (CZA), Jerusalem.
Israel State Archive (ISA), Jerusalem.
Kibbutz Lahav Archive (KLA), Lahav.
The Moshe Dayan Centre at Tel Aviv University, Tel Aviv.
The Palmach Museum, Tel Aviv.
Toviaho Archive at Ben Gurion University, Beer-Sheva.

## *Personal Archives and Papers*

Assistant District Commissioner of Beersheba (southern Palestine) in 1943–45: Julian Edward George KCMG (1964), 2nd Earl of Oxford and Asquith (Lord Oxford), Somerset, UK.

Private collection, Hassan Abu Saad, August 7, 1995 (Nida al Wifaq private collection, Lakiya).

The Arab Democratic Party, reports about the third annual conference of the party, December 15–16, 1995, Nazareth.

## Interviews

Between 2007 and 2016, 120 in-depth interviews were conducted with Naqab Bedouin from Biʾr al-Sabaʿ region (southern Israel), with Bedouin in Jordan, and with former Israeli and British officials (UK).

## Newspapers, Magazines, and Periodicals

*Adalah Newsletter*
*Akhbar Al-Naqab*
*Al-ʿArab*
*Al-Difaʾ*
*Al-Hamishmar*
*Al-Yawm*
*Daily Telegraph*
*Davar*
*Egyptian Gazette*
*Falastin (Palestine Daily)*
*Haʿolam Hazeh*
*Haaretz*

*Ha-boker*
*Hatsofeh*
*Huna al-Quds*
*Jerusalem Post*
*Jewish Chronicle*
*Jewish Observer*
*Kol Haʿam*
*Kul al-ʻArab*
*La-merhav*
*Maʾariv*
*New Outlook*
*New York Times*
*Palestine Post*
*Panorama*
*Sawt al-Bilad*
*Sidreh* newsletter
*The Guardian*
*Times* (London)
*Yedioth Aharonot (ynet news)*

# Index

Page numbers in italics indicate figures.